D1421252

German Wine Atlas

and Vineyard Register

with an Introduction by Edmund Penning-Rowsell

English Edition Translated by Nadia Fowler

MITCHELL
ARTISTS
HOUSE
BEAZLEY

Contents

This edition published by
Mitchell Beazley London Limited
Mitchell Beazley Artists House
14/15 Manette Street, London, W1V 5LB

Fourth revised edition 1980
Copyright 1976 by Stabilisierungsfonds für Wein, Gutenbergplatz 3–5
D 6500 Mainz 1. P. O. Box 3860
Copyright English Introduction 1977 by Edmund Penning-Rowsell
Designed by J. W. Thompson, Frankfurt/Main, West Germany
Maps, Vineyard Register and Printing by Georg Westermann,
Braunschweig, West Germany
Printed in West Germany
ISBN 0 86134 018 3

In search of Wine

How to make use of this book

Two sample questions illustrate how to use this Wine Atlas and Register: Where do the Mandelpfad and the Schwarze Katz come from? The bottle label shows that the first is grown in the Rheinpfalz and the second in the Mosel. The Register in the appendix of this book lists in alphabetical order under the appropriate specified region, the community, district, and general site. The birthplace of the wine can then be traced on the map that goes with the site indicated in the Register. Individual sites are not alphabetically listed because various places often have sites which carry the same name. There are many Sonnen-, Schloss- and Nonnenberge.

This process can be reversed, of course, and the appropriate label discovered by starting with the wine's vineyard. Visitors to Germany locating a particularly sunny cultivated hill, or drinking wine from the local vineyard which gives special enjoyment, can find the relevant individual site on the appropriate map in this book. All the many places – districts, general sites and individual sites – which have been entered in the register – can be traced on these maps, from the north to the south.

General sites are set against a green, individual sites against an ochre-coloured background. Numbering indicates simply order of sequence – certainly not order of merit – of vineyards and their wine.

The order of sequence of the eleven specified wine-growing regions is from north to south. Brief notes on data and facts relevant to each area are given. The editorial text amplifies the history of the wine and describes the habitat and other items of interest to the traveller. This Wine Atlas attempts only to be explicit about the birthplace of wine. The motoring map will help to reach destinations more easily. The delight in drinking the wine will come independently when the traveller has reached the spot where it grows.

References

Register: Specified regions, places, districts and general sites are entered in alphabetical order. Individual sites can be found under names of wine-growing towns/villages.

Sequences in describing specified region: from north to south.

Picture credits: last page of book.

Key to signs: signs used in texts with maps:

+ Site situated outside the cartographically shown specified region.

T Often only a section of a site belongs to a certain parish. Whenever this is so, the site will reappear within the same general site at one or several other place-names, under the same number.

△ Name or boundary of this site not yet determined.

Reference to site maps: The areas shown give the current extent of sites, but do not extend into built-up areas.

INTRODUCTION

It is necessary only to open a page or two of this *German Wine Atlas* to realize how exceptionally attractive the German wine districts are. It is often thought by those unfamiliar with any great wine-growing region that the countryside must be unfailingly beautiful and peopled by smiling vineyard workers, male and female, everready to break into song and dance. Perhaps this view of the inhabitants owes something to the world of advertising and publicity, though it is certainly true that those engaged in the arduous business of producing wine are usually exceptionally agreeable. But more often than not vineyards exist in dull, commonplace country.

In Germany, on the other hand, the eleven main wine districts are nearly all attractively sited from a landscape point of view. More often than not the vineyards lie on mountain slopes or hillsides, and they are frequently bounded by rivers. The towns and villages that give their names to the local wines are commonly very agreeable, with fine churches, noble buildings and ancient houses that lean out over narrow lanes. This calls to my mind such places I have visited, as Bernkastel on the Mosel, Bad Kreuznach on the Nahe, the string of riverside towns on the Rheingau and the Rhine Front towns of Rheinhessen. Also I remember perhaps less well-known places as Durbach in Baden and Iphofen in Franconia. I could add many more to my personal visiting list, but I do not claim to have been everywhere in these eleven German wine districts that cover less than one per cent of the country's total area.

Superb Palaces

Then there are the magisterial wine cities and towns, such as Würzburg, Mainz and Trier, with their superb palaces, cathedrals and churches, as well as other features of great archaeological and architectural interest. The Cistercian abbey of Kloster Eberbach, much of it dating from the 12th century and lying just above the famous Steinberg vineyard formerly owned by the immensely rich monastery, is among the most perfect mediaeval abbey complexes in existence. Then, at the other end of the scale there is the splendid Residenz in Würzburg, built by the great baroque architect Balthasar Neumann for the powerful prince-bishops of Würzburg. Below this architectural gem, and running the full length of its façade are the finest old cellars that I have seen anywhere. Lofty enough to drive a coach and horses through them, this Hofkellerei is now the property of the Bavarian state Wine Domaine.

Moreover, museums with wine departments or associations with wine are all over the place, headed by the celebrated one at Speyer, which includes the famous 4th century Roman glass amphora still containing wine; and Trier, with its fine historical collection.

Altogether, one need not visit the German wine districts just for the wines, as is sometimes the case elsewhere; although it would be a thousand pities to neglect them, and those intent on wine will find well-marked "wine-roads" in every district, skilfully plotted to lead the visitor through villages that hitherto have just been names on a wine list. Personally, everywhere in the wine world I always find these associations particularly exciting, as they bring the wine list to life, and afterwards, whenever one drinks a bottle from a place that one has visited, the wine acquires an extra significance and reality.

The German "wine-roads" are unusually extensive. One of the more agreeable is in the Palatinate, leading through such "names" as Wachenheim, Forst and Deidesheim. This is parallelled by the Rhine Front road in Rheinhessen from Worms to Bingen, the Rheingauer Riesling route from Lorchhausen to Hochheim, the Nahe Weinstrasse, and the similar Baden road that winds for most of its length along the foothills of the Black Forest. Even the very small Ahr Valley has its "red wine path".

Breathtaking

Above all, from a scenic-plus-wine point of view, are the lovely river valleys, whose sides are clothed with vines; particularly the Ahr, Mosel, Middle Rhine and the Neckar. My vote goes particularly to the winding, exceptionally steep-sided Mosel (who was it that said that it could take from two hours to two weeks to follow its course in Germany?), and the Middle Rhine. The railway journey from Bonn to Bingen is one of the most breathtaking in the world.

A highly agreeable feature of the German wine districts are the annual wine festivals. There are about 25 of them, taking place from June to October, and a list will be found on page 90.

However, this is not an introduction to a travel book, but to one devoted to wine, and very special wines at that. For German wines possess qualities unmatched elsewhere in the world. Although some of the grape varieties that have made them famous have been exported to other countries, elsewhere they have not met with anything like the same success; much less so than with some French grapes, such as the Merlot and the Chardonnay. And, of course, much of the wines from other countries labelled "Riesling" are not derived at all from the German or Rhine Riesling, but from an inferior if acceptable variety sometimes known as the Italian or Welsch Riesling.

One reason for the comparative lack of success of the German grape varieties in most other countries – perhaps they do best in Alsace in the Rhine Valley itself – is that the finer wines are nearly always made in situations and circumstances unfavourable to other crops. For the grape vine, though quantitatively so fecund if untrammelled and naturally a plant that can climb to great heights, produces best when heavily pruned. Extraordinarily tenacious of life and able to penetrate the most unfavourable, rocky terrain to surprising depths, the varieties offering the finest wines do so in adversity; when they have to struggle. Nowhere is this more evident than in Germany which contains the most northerly vineyards in Europe. The northernmost limit of the wine-producing vine is generally reckoned to be the 50th parallel of latitude. The Ahr and the most northerly stretches of the Mosel are just above that line. It is no co-incidence that Germany is the home of Eiswein, made from grapes frozen by late autumn or even early winter frosts (wine made from grapes picked on Twelfth Night is familiarly if not officially known as Drei Königs Wein). The grapes are picked early on cold, dark mornings and quickly crushed while the liquid inside the shrivelled skins remains congealed by the low temperature.

Owing a great deal to the geographical situation of many of Germany's vineyards, the system of wine production is rather different from that employed in other wine-producing lands; and it cannot be denied that to those unfamiliar with the German system – and that includes most of us wine drinkers outside Germany – this presents problems. These are readily recognized by the German viticulturists, wine merchants and those responsible for the regulation of wine production within the country. What often seem like complications and a mass of words, not least on the otherwise often very attractive wine labels, is in fact accurately defined clarification and information as to what the drinker may expect to find within the bottle once he or she has drawn the cork.

EEC Regulations

For the German wine grower faces problems more or less unknown in the other major wine-producing regions of the world. The most obvious of these is the difficulty of securing sufficiently high alcoholic strength to make and maintain the wine. Under the European Economic Community regulations, the minimum alcoholic strength, as expressed in terms of percentage of volume, is 8.5. Less than that officially it is not wine, although in the past some fine German wines were produced at considerably lower strengths, though these were very special, particularly luscious varieties.

It should be said at once that there is no special virtue in high alcoholic strength. No one wants wine without a reasonable amount of alcohol in it, but if it is alcohol rather than aroma and flavour that is looked for, then there are other drinks that can satisfy that demand more easily and quickly. Few German wines are strong alcoholically, and to me this is one of their most agreeable features. One can drink and enjoy so much more of them without feeling any ill-effects afterwards than is possible with more powerful wines. Ten degrees is a perfectly adequate strength for

most German wines, compared with twelve, thirteen and even more degrees for some wines of other countries; and a degree or so either way may make quite a difference as to how one feels next morning!

Partly owing to Germany's geographical situation, but also because its wine industry is both highly responsible and sophisticated, production is more rigorously controlled here than in any other important wine-producing country. The first German wine law was passed as long ago as 1879 – many years before the French wine laws, which essentially derive from the inter-world wars period, though territorial demarcation began before the First World War. Germany's initial legislation was followed by further wine laws in 1901, 1909 and 1930. This last-named, very comprehensive law, held, with minor amendments, until 1969, but that law was almost immediately superseded by the 1971 wine law, described later in this book. It fell into line with EEC legislation and regulations on wine.

"Good Old Days"

There are those who react against such strict control of wine as practised in Germany, and suggest that wines were as good, if not better, "in the good old days". This is certainly not true. For one thing, as several notorious cases even in recent years have shown, wine fraud is particularly easy to achieve and often hard to detect. The historical records of all the older wine-drinking countries are full of cases of fraud. Secondly, wine is by no means so easy to produce as some may think, especially white wine, predominant in Germany, but science has made enormous contributions to the improvement of production, not least in Germany. Whether the finest wines of today are as good as or better than those of the past may be a matter of lively discussion that can never be conclusively decided. Once I drank a perfectly sound German wine of the 1540 vintage that had long lain in the Bavarian royal cellars, and in 1975 I sampled in London a 1727 Rüdesheim Apostelwein from the famous Bremen Ratskeller. No doubt refreshed from time to time, it tasted like a fine old madeira. And at a dinner in London in 1976 I drank in succession a Schloss Johannisberg 1870, a Marcobrunn 1870 and a Marcobrunn 1868. All were in good condition, and the 1868 had some of the lusciousness of an old sauternes.

It is improbable that German wines of today would last as long as those ancient vintages, often kept for many years in cask, but it is certain that the general level of German wine-making is much higher than it was, a difficult result to achieve in a geographical situation that makes success more uncertain than in warmer, more southerly regions.

This does, however, call for careful control, which is most evident to the consumer in the system of grading, essentially exclusive to Germany. As in France and

elsewhere, wine can only be produced on land authorized for viticulture, but in Germany how it will be described on the bottle chiefly depends on the quality. If of moderate quality it will be called Deutscher Tafelwein (German Table Wine) and may be sold under a brand name. (If it is labelled just Tafelwein, it may be a blend of wines from other EEC wine producers, but not from outside the Community.) A Deutscher Tafelwein may have sugar added in order to raise its natural alcoholic strength from a minimum usually of 5% of alcohol by volume, usually described in terms of degrees. In Baden, the southernmost German wine region this minimum natural strength must be 6%, but for all German Table Wine the minimum strength when sold must be 8.5%, as the result of sugar being added as legally permitted.

It should be mentioned, by the way, that the method of sugaring the grape-must before fermentation to receive higher alcohol strength for certain wines is not confined to Germany, but is found in all northern wine-growing regions like Burgundy and Alsace, Austria, parts of Italy and such. Preconditions and degrees of sugaring are regulated by Common Law for all member countries of the European Community. In Germany sugaring is legally binding only for the quality gradings Tafelwein and Quality Wine of specified regions.

From this point in quality upwards the German system diverges from French and the practice elsewhere. For a French *appellation contrôlée* covers a defined area, large or small. There may be enclaves of superior *appellation* within broader districts: for example, Médoc within Bordeaux Rouge, and Pauillac within Médoc, but all the wine from a single vineyard, say, Château Lafite, bears the same appellation, subject, of course, to control of the varieties of grapes that may be planted and to the wine reaching a certain level of quality. Similarly the whole 50 hectares of Clos de Vougeot in Burgundy carries the *appellation* Clos Vougeot, irrespective of where in the vineyard the wine derives, when the grapes are picked by the various owners and whether sugar has been added or not. In Italy too the *Denominazione di Origine Controllata* (DOC) system for superior wines covers whole districts without vineyard distinctions.

Three Categories

In Germany this is entirely different. There are three categories: Deutscher Tafelwein, Qualitätswein bestimmter Anbaugebiete (Quality wine of specified regions) and Qualitätswein mit Prädikat (Quality wine with distinction). It is not necessary here to go into technical details, but above the Deutscher Tafelwein level there are two other main categories, based essentially on the amount of natural sugar in the grapes when picked. This is known as the "must weight" and means the specific gravity of the grape must. It is measured on an Oechsle scale, named after the German physicist who devised it.

The first of these two superior categories is known as Qualitätswein. It must have a minimum strength of 6% or 7% according to district, but may have sugar added to increase this to a maximum of 9% depending on region and type of wine. This applies to red as well as to white wine. It can be blended with wine within a designated area, and the most celebrated "Quality wine" is Liebfraumilch.

This ascription is not, however, purely a geographical one, and depends very much on the rating of each particular vintage. In very fine years, such as 1971, 1975 and 1976, there may be very little Qualitätswein, as defined, for, though coming from the same vines in the identical vineyard, the wine will, as the result of good weather conditions, have a much higher proportion of natural sugar, a higher Oechsle rating. The wine then becomes a Qualitätswein mit Prädikat. This last word, originating from the 1971 wine law, is very hard to translate, but it broadly means that the wine so labelled is a quality wine "with honours", or "with distinction". Once recognized it need not detain us consumers.

Natural Sugar

This highest category of German wines is divided into five sub-classes: Kabinett, Spätlese, Auslese, Beerenauslese and Trockenbeerenauslese. The rather rare Eiswein is usually in the Auslese class. Once a wine arrives, as it were, in the "honours" category its final classification depends on the amount of natural sugar in the wine, the Oechsle-scale must-weight; and no wines in this category may have sugar added. The exact minimum to classify a wine will vary not only from district to district, with, broadly, a higher Oechsle rating being required in the more southerly districts, but also according to the grape variety employed. For example a wine made from the Riesling grape will often qualify with a lower must-weight than other varieties, such as the Müller-Thurgau; and a higher must-weight may be required of a red wine than a white. But it all depends on the district, and need not concern us here. I mention this mostly in order to demonstrate the careful regulation of the making of superior quality German wines.

The lowest class of "honours" wines, Kabinett, corresponds more or less to the previous class of Naturwein or Naturrein, as may be found on old labels. These terms passed out of use with the 1971 wine law. A Kabinett wine must derive purely from one district (Bereich) and normally comes from a single vineyard, as do all the other four types of "Prädikat" wine.

At this point it may well be asked why, if Kabinett and upwards wines may not be sugared, most German white wines have some degree of sweetness. Not all do, for some wines are so fermented out that

they are very dry indeed, but most are permitted to retain some residual sugar. Also before the wines are bottled, it is permitted to add a certain amount of unfermented grape juice (Süssreserve) derived from the same district or vineyard and prevented from fermenting. Then, the richer types, such as Spätlese and above all Beerenauslese and Trockenbeerenauslese contain so much natural sugar that the yeasts working to convert sugar into alcohol are vanquished and the wines remain naturally sweet; but they will not be very strong alcoholically.

The higher classes of Spätlese (late-picked) and Auslese (selected – by bunch of grapes) are determined by their natural Oechsle must-rating, and can only be made in fine vintages. This applies much more so to Beerenauslese (selected – grape by grape) and Trockenbeerenauslese (selected grape by grape dried up by a type of mould called *botrytis cinerea*). Only a combination of very fine weather and some humidity in the pre-vintage period will produce this "noble rot" – *Edelfäule* in German, *pourriture noble* in French. As a result the grapes shrivel up and become raisiny, resulting in those wonderful, luscious bottles that are the crown of German wines, unmatched anywhere else in the world. An Auslese wine will also contain a certain amount of grapes affected by this noble rot.

It need hardly be said that German red wines do not normally go beyond the Spätlese class, though Auslesen are possible.

Bottling

It is unnecessary here to go into the bottling regulations, but one item to be found on the label of all German wines above the Tafelwein level deserves mention: The A.P. No. (Amtliche Prüfnummer). For all such quality wines must be sent for official testing by State Authorities after bottling, and if and when approved will be given a number; and a new one for each bottling batch of the same wine. The number on the label, therefore, is a form of guarantee that the wine in the bottle has attained a certain specified standard.

I hope that, armed with the above information, necessarily abbreviated in this introduction, amateurs of German wines will appreciate that the labels are not to be regarded with apprehension, but are highly sophisticated aids to understanding what lies in the bottle; and more such information is provided on German wine labels than on those anywhere else.

Fine Whites

But all this is mere preparation to enjoyment. So, finally, how best to drink German wines. The red wines, of course, normally accompany food in the same way that red wines do the world over. It is with the fine whites that German wines have a special place. Here I do not intend

to provide one of those lists of what wines go with various foods. Personally, when I am in Germany I find I can enjoy with savoury dishes wines sweeter than I would probably choose at home. Perhaps one is influenced by the surroundings, more often than not agreeable, especially in the wine districts themselves.

What, however, is clear is that the finer, more luscious wines are best drunk with no other accompaniment than a dry biscuit. Certainly a great Rhine or Mosel wine can be accompanied by certain food, but I believe that they stand best on their own, with the biscuit, or a piece of bread to freshen the palate. This, undoubtedly, is a problem in countries where wine is closely associated with meals, but should not be allowed to stand in the way of the enjoyment of the best that the German wine grower, after great efforts in difficult conditions, can offer. Those wines with marked but not excessive acidity make admirable aperitifs, for their crispness stimulates the appetite. Otherwise, rules as to what wines are supposed to go with differing kinds of food are to be avoided rather than obeyed. Obviously strongly flavoured dishes, such as smoked dishes, inhibit the flavour of many wines. My choice here would be a Gewürztraminer, whose insistent flavour can compete with the strong taste. Similarly a very sweet white is likely to taste cloying with savoury food, but not at all so with something more neutral. For the normal main course of a family meal one might well choose a Qualitätswein or a Kabinett, while the higher levels of Spätlese and Auslese may be reserved for special occasions. But, it must again be emphasised, there are no rules, no social conventions or obligations. It can only be said that within Germany the most luscious wines, from a great Auslese to a rare Trockenbeerenauslese will usually be drunk on their own, with nothing but a piece of bread or biscuit to distract from the essential flavour. For a party of friends to sit round a bottle of fine German wine from one of its many distinctive regions, districts and even villages and individual vineyards, is one of the most agreeably social, and surely most innocent of pleasures; and this can be done with German wines as with very few other. For their natural acidity, derived principally from their northern origin, stops them from being sickly or cloying.

The subject of wine is often considered difficult and abstruse. In itself this is not so. The problem is that there are so many wines with different characteristics. It helps enormously if a particular wine can be related to its source, whether or not we have the opportunity to visit it. Accordingly, this excellently planned, designed and produced Wine Atlas provides a wealth of information for the greater enjoyment of German wines.

Edmund Penning-Rowsell
London, 1977

3

Foreword

The label on a German wine bottle describes the pleasure wine-lovers expect when they come to drink the wine. This goes for "everyday" German Table Wine as well as for officially certified Quality Wine (QbA) from one of the eleven German specified regions for Quality Wine, and particularly for top-class Quality Wine with one of the five special titles (Prädikat), Kabinett, Spätlese, Auslese, Beerenauslese or Trockenbeerenauslese. Details referring to the "birthplace" of a wine – specified region of origin (Anbaugebiet), district (Bereich), town or village and/or site (Lage) – of Quality Wines are important guides to the expert in search of his favourite type of wine.

But why is it not enough simply to state the region of origin? For other wine growing countries this might well suffice; but the taste of a German wine is determined by the individual conditions of growth (soil, climatic influences) even of a single vineyard. This fact, once appreciated, will make clear how helpful such detailed information really is, and the wine enthusiast will come to make a habit of seeking it out so that it becomes increasingly easy to understand and value, as experience grows.

Nobody becomes a true wine-lover without a sound knowledge of his subject. To start with, he must know the fundamental differences between the natural conditions and various methods of cultivation, and the differences between laws prevailing in German wine growing regions and those in force in other wine producing countries.

Why are details of origin so important for German wine?

German viticulture (approximately at 50 degrees latitude) is intensely diverse and varied.
* As the world's most northerly major wine-growing country, conditions are entirely different for German viticulture compared with other wine-growing countries. For over a 1000 years, German viticulture has flourished in regions most favourable to the vine – the river valleys of the Rhine and its tributaries where a variable but favourable climate and widely differing geological conditions influence the character and quality of German wine. There are as many types of wine as variations in the landscape and soil of the German wine-growing regions. Geographical detail on a wine label, therefore, is of supreme importance: it is each German wine's "birth certificate".

The natural factors determining a German wine's character and quality are the soil and climate of its "birthplace". The deep German river valleys twist and turn through mountainous, mainly wooded regions, forming wide, basin-shaped land areas whose variations in soil structure stem directly from the earth's history. On steep inclines, the soil is frequently slatey; where the incline gently slopes down to its base, there is fertile, alluvial land; other areas show lime deposits or volcanic rocks; all of which naturally influences the taste of the wine.

The micro-climate of a vineyard depends on several factors: whether it faces south or west; the gradient of its incline; the intensity of the sun's reflection from the surface of the river; the proximity of sheltering forest or mountain peak; altitude; and soil humidity. It is a fact that, separated by a distance of only a few hundred metres, wine of world fame may grow – or nothing more than gorse bushes.

The great variety of climatic conditions in the eleven German specified regions accounts for the great number of German vineyards.

Additionally, the wide variety of German wine is reflected in the many different grape varieties of quality vines – Riesling, Silvaner, Müller-Thurgau and Ruländer, among the white wine range; blauer Spätburgunder, Lemberger, Trollinger and Portugieser among the red. A combination of experience and scientific research have, in the course of time, established exactly which growing regions are best for each individual type of vine: for example, the Trollinger vine in the Fellbacher Lämmler has for centuries been as typical as the Riesling in the Bernkasteler Doktor, or the Portugieser in Dürkheimer Feuerberg. Characteristics of the many birthplaces of German wine, fashioned by nature and developed by growers with the help of science and the authorities, have combined to produce and name over 25,000 individual vineyard sites (Einzellagen), and successfully map out the foundations of German wine-geography.

How the authorities help the wine enthusiast

A minimum size of 5 ha (hectar) for sites was laid down in 1969, along with new guide-lines for describing a wine's place of origin.

The new Federal German wine law confirmed 31 districts, approximately 130 general sites and roughly 2,600 individual sites.

In the course of a general European harmonization of wine-law, clarity and easy comprehension of terms used to describe wine – particularly in giving information about its place of origin – have been introduced to help the consumer.

The German Wine Law confirmed the following geographical designations:

1: Anbaugebiete (specified regions); 2: Bereiche (districts); 3: names of wine-growing communities or towns/ villages; 4: names of Lagen (sites) entered into the register of vineyards.

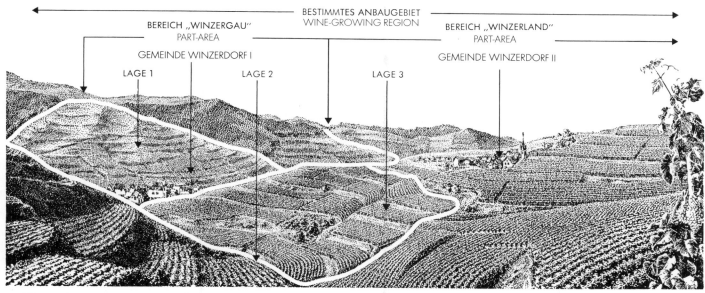

BESTIMMTES ANBAUGEBIET
WINE-GROWING REGION

BEREICH „WINZERGAU"
PART-AREA

BEREICH „WINZERLAND"
PART-AREA

GEMEINDE WINZERDORF I

GEMEINDE WINZERDORF II

LAGE 1   LAGE 2   LAGE 3

(Gemeinde = community or parish) ·   The 11 German wine-growing regions: some 130 general sites and around 2,600 individual sites

1: Each specified area for growing quality wine covers a coherent, wine-producing countryside, offering relatively equal natural conditions to individual sites throughout its area.

2: Bereiche are part-areas within the Anbaugebiete, where conditions of growth are largely similar, so that wines growing there show similar aspects of quality. For this reason wines of highest quality, bearing the titles Kabinett, Spätlese, Auslese, and so on, must by law originate from a single Bereich. A Bereich embraces a fairly large number of wine-growing communities.

3: The "Community" is identical with the political community.

4: The smallest geographical unit is the vineyard site (Weinbergslage).

A Lage is a specific cultivated hill, slope, valley, or any similar natural surface where, because of similar soil-structure and local climatic conditions, wines of equal quality and taste characteristics are known to grow. All such sites have been given exactly fixed boundaries and their names have been entered into the official Weinbergsrolle (register of vineyards). The minimum size of a site is five hectars according to the law, but if equal conditions of growth exist, a site can span a hundred or more hectars (1 ha = nearly 2½ acres). In practice, however, the need arose to find a term for situations where several communities, say occupying an extended ridge of hills, or rising upwards on slopes from a specific valley, experienced the same production conditions throughout their areas. This is how the distinction between Einzellage and Grosslage came about. Einzellage means a vineyard within narrowly fixed boundaries. Grosslage combines several Einzellagen of similar character into a larger unit. Einzellagen represent the highest degree of individuality. Grosslagen are no more than large scale Einzellagen, showing similar climatic and geological characteristics.

The New German Wine Atlas – an absorbing study

The special significance of geographical detail in the specification of a wine's origin, and the new regulations governing it, gave rise to the publication of this *German Wine Atlas and Vineyard Register*. Although a comprehensive reference book, it cannot, however, be taken as the final word on the subject, as future EEC wine-market regulations may effect the present system of determining origins; also, modifications are still possible within German wine-producing states, particularly affecting administrative reform.

This Wine Atlas therefore contains *a complete compilation of all the names of sites at present recorded by the wine-producing areas.* We should like to thank the relevant authorities in the name of all wine enthusiasts for their help in compiling and checking the register.

This new publication now enables the expert as well as the novice to trace the birthplace of his favourite wine on a map of the relevant specified region, or to find it in the register, and further opens up the opportunity for fascinating study by all who love good wine.

So that the reader may be able to put his interest to more practical use by travelling to the wine-growing regions, maps of individual and general sites are preceded by general maps of the region, showing relevant roads and routes.

The wines of the eleven German specified regions for Quality Wines may be compared to large families whose histories also make a unique geographical chronicle involving some 20,000 producers who today use the 2,600 individual sites and 130 general sites for the names of their wines.

These "families" are not only proud of the origin, but also the character and properties of their wine – down to the last drop. That is why year by year thousands of vintagers and cellar-masters labour to achieve originality and quality in their local wine. For wine producers – like wine consumers – enjoy being individualists. They love, above all, the specially-developed traits in their wine. And to ensure that striving after perfection remains a permanent process, authority also decrees that every German wine of quality must pass a strict examination, executed in three stages. It is only after it has proved itself to be faultless, that an official examination number is granted and the wine may be called Qualitätswein.

Origin is the commencement of this, the finest accolade in the long history – and geography – of German wine.

C. M. Baumann
F. W. Michel

Mainz, July 1976

Specified Regions for Quality Wines

Each specified region forms a separate natural unit. Wine from a certain specified region will confirm its origin through specific characteristics of taste, created by similar climatic and geographical conditions. The 11 specified regions are: Ahr, Hessische Bergstrasse, Mittelrhein (Middle Rhine), Mosel-Saar-Ruwer, Nahe, Rheingau, Rheinhessen (Rhenish Hesse), Rheinpfalz (Rhenish Palatinate), Franconia, Württemberg and Baden.

Areas where Table Wine is grown are divided into much larger regional sections: named by the great rivers Rhine and Mosel for the provinces of Rheinland-Pfalz (Palatinate) and Hessen (Hesse), the river Main for Bayern (Bavaria), the Neckar for Württemberg, and the upper reaches of the Rhine for Baden.

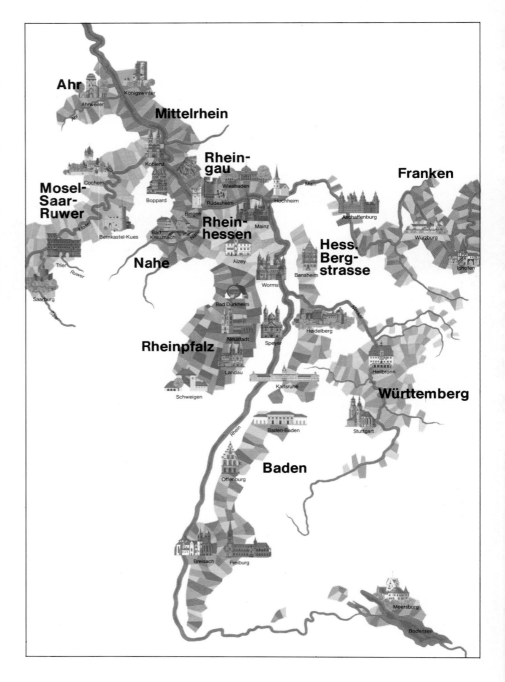

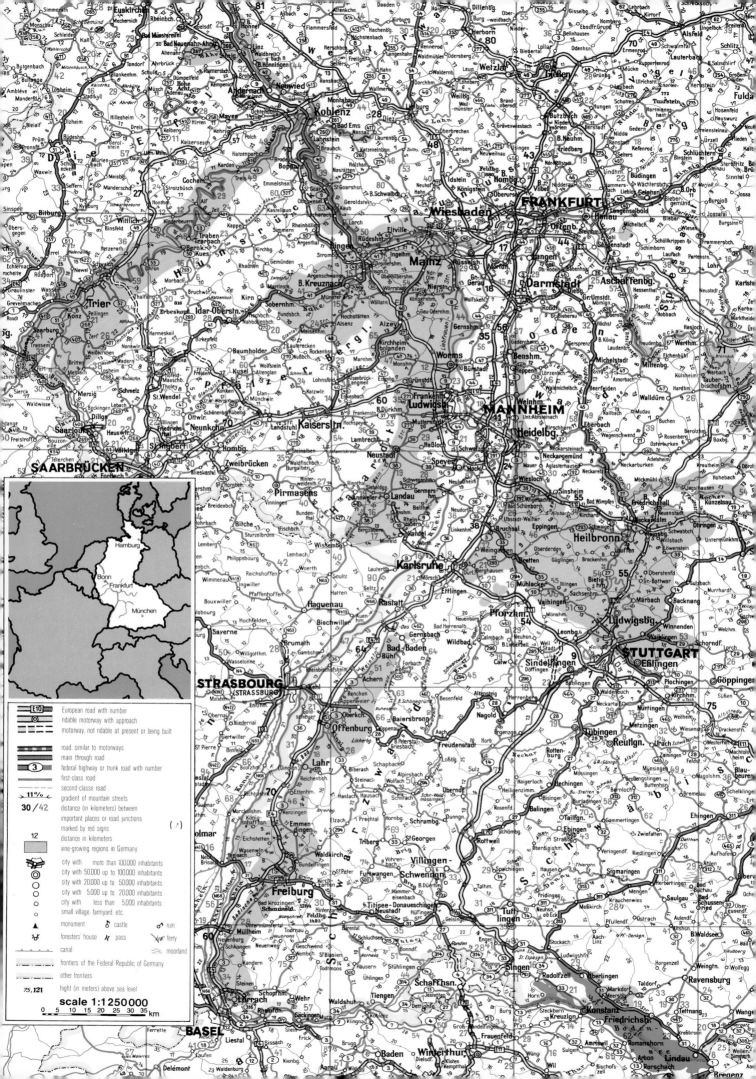

Legend

E10	European road with number
	ridable motorway with approach
	motorway, not ridable at present or being built
	road, similar to motorways
	main through road
3	federal highway or trunk road with number
	first-class road
	second-class road
11%	gradient of mountain streets
30 / 42	distance (in kilometers) between important places or road junctions marked by red signs
12	distance in kilometers
	vine-growing regions in Germany
	city with more than 100.000 inhabitants
	city with 50.000 up to 100.000 inhabitants
	city with 20.000 up to 50.000 inhabitants
	city with 5.000 up to 20.000 inhabitants
	city with less than 5.000 inhabitants
	small village, farmyard, etc.
	monument • castle • ruin
	foresters' house • pass • ferry
	canal • moorland
	frontiers of the Federal Republic of Germany
	other frontiers
75, 121	hight (in meters) above sea level

scale 1:1 250 000

0 5 10 15 20 25 30 35 km

Climate and Wine

The uniquely special character of the German wine-growing regions is determined by their geographical location between the moist, maritime climate of the Gulf Stream region of the west and the dry, continental climate of the east. Thanks to the influence of the western Gulf Stream climate, temperatures do not drop too low in winter or rise too high in summer. When the continental climate's autumn weather with its high atmospheric pressures spreads across Middle Europe, its warm, dry late autumn days can often add weeks to the viticultural growing season. Weather conditions in the wine-growing regions of the Rhine basin and its tributaries depend from year to year mainly on whether the cooler and moister maritime climate of the west, or the drier and, in summer, warmer climate of the continental east, has the predominant influence. Usually the influences of the western maritime climate with its rainfalls will be felt in Middle Europe even during summer, so that in the wine-growing regions the grapes benefit from generous and repeated rainfall during the growing season. This means that in the Rhine basin, on the boundary line between two fundamentally different climatic zones, weather conditions for wine-growing are ideal: temperate in summer and winter, with a long, warm autumn and sufficient rainfall; all of which contributes to

the freshness and harmony of German wine. It is thanks to these natural assets that the grapes can grow apace during the summer months without the danger of ripening too early. The must-weight tends to rise gradually to its peak during August, September and October, whereby the acid content – an important quality factor – is preserved. This is the reason why German wines, in comparison with those of neighbouring climatic zones, are marked by particular elegance, freshness and a fruity aroma.

The freshness and delicacy of the wines are also furthered by comparatively cooler temperatures at vintage times in October and early November, because the grapes gathered cannot oxidize so rapidly and taste-substances remain unimpaired; fermentation too takes place at comparatively lower degrees of temperature and this protects the delicate bouquet-substances. It is therefore no coincidence that German wines are stimulating, light, refreshing and distinguished by a delicate bouquet.

In the more northerly parts of the German wine-growing lands, in the "battle zone" between two opposing climates, ideal conditions for viticulture exist only in the sheltered river valleys of the Rhine basin and its tributaries. As the "climate map" (top left), showing the beginning of spring, indicates, apple-blossom-time starts, in the Rhine basin, for instance, on average four weeks earlier than in

the higher altitudes of neighbouring regions, and just as early as in the Alpine regions of the Po valley. The German growing regions along the Rhine and its tributaries, therefore, already have a decisive advantage at springtime. It is true that apple-blossom-time starts equally early in Hungary's low-lying plains, but in summer the plains are dominated by a hot continental climate, which means that the all-important rainfalls are missing. The early beginning of springtime as an indication of sheltered climatic conditions, is, therefore, important to the development of the wine, but it is not the only decisive factor. As is also indicated by the map, the most sheltered wine-growing climate in any part of Middle Europe exists on the 50th degree of latitude, which passes through the town of Mainz. Consequently, it was historically quite logical that viticulture, which in the Middle Ages extended as far as Pommerania and East Prussia, should have contracted and concentrated on the ideally-suited growing regions of the Rhine basin. It is not surprising, therefore, that practically no wine is grown in other parts of Germany. To compensate, viticulture finds the best possible conditions for growing wines of the highest quality in the Rhine basin.

Ahr

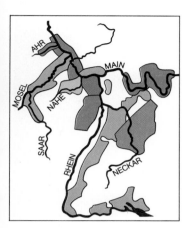

The Ahr flows into the Rhine not far from Bonn, where the "little paradise of red wine" begins – a particularly precious jewel among the wine-growing regions. The vineyards stretch a bare 25 km – planted as if in a garden – from the lower to the middle reaches of the Ahr, where the valleys become narrow and twist around steeply rising rocks.

The Ahr has the second smallest specified wine region of origin in Germany; only two to three per cent of German red wine is grown here, but it includes delicious Spätburgunder, an astonishingly velvety, noble wine.

Gottfried Kinkel, the 19th-century German poet, describes this region intimately: "Rocks, crowding narrowly together, intensify the heat of the sun by reflecting it; black, mottled slate-stone,

Walking through red wine country

intentionally covering the ground in the vineyards, soaks up the heat of the day and lets it act upon the grapes through the cool of the night. And the river, too, gives the wine-growers encouragement: from its lukewarm waters the gentle mists rise up into the night air during summer, when they can be seen – wonderfully still and brooding – hanging over the valley on a summer's morning; they drench the parched rocky soil and soften the grapes' skins for the hot, ripening rays of the sun".

Ahr-wine and the past

Most probably it was the ubiquitous Romans who planted the first vines along the banks of the river Ahr. Near Bad Neuenahr, an old vineyard was excavated at a depth of four metres and is thought to date from roughly 260 AD and the time of the "Wine Emperor" Probus, who did so much for viticulture north of the Alps.

Documents from the year 770 prove the existence of viticulture in the Ahr valleys. In the succeeding eight centuries it grew apace, for in 1602 the Councillor of Ahrweiler recorded that wine-growing was "right noble nourishment in these parts and should be kept going without ceasing".

Even earlier – with the arrival of Christianity – the Abbey of Prüm registers a number of estates – among them Ahrweiler, Walporzheim, Dernau and

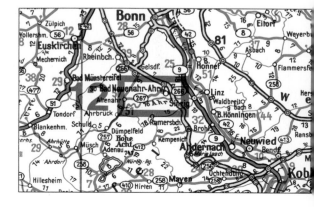

Blauer Spätburgunder

Main types of vine on the Ahr:

Spät- and Frühburgunder	28.7%
Portugieser	24.9%
Riesling	21.5%
Müller-Thurgau	19.5%

Altenahr – which paid a tribute in wine to the Abbey. Today, 600 years later, they are still famous for their wines.

Red vines were not planted until after The 30 Years War, in 1680, but then became so popular that only a century later, very few white vines were to be found along the Ahr. (In those days, Burgunder grapes were pressed without their skins, so the wine produced was pale red, and that is the reason why it is sometimes still called by its old name Ahrbleichert [bleichen = to bleach]).

Rotweinwanderweg: footpath through red wine country

The small valley of the Ahr provides exactly the right preparation for more ambitious wine journeys. A car trip through the valley on the B266 near Sinzig, or on B267 near Neuenahr, gives access from each of the 11 villages en route to the Rotweinwanderweg, where leisurely walks of up to 30 km can be made, starting at Lohrsdorf along the wine path clearly marked by signposts featuring a red grape.

The charming old villages dotted along the way from Sinzig and Altenahr are ideal for unhurried wine sampling, before reaching Bad Neuenahr, with its alkaline thermal springs, via Heimersheim. The springs testify to the volcanic origin of the region and the excellent growth conditions for the Ahrburgunder.

From Walporzheim the river valley narrows along a high cliff called Bunte Kuh where the Ahr winds through blue shimmering rock in a multitude of twists and narrow bends past vineyards and

Mayschoss – Ahr

castles. In wild, romantic scenery lies Altenahr – last stop on the journey through the Ahr wine country.

Local dishes that go ideally with the noble Spätburgunder, the fresh Portugieser, or the light, lively white wine of the area include: Neuenahrer Rauchfleisch (smoked meat) Neuenahrer Champignons, Ardennenschinken (ham from the Eifel region), and trout from the Ahr.

Information and literature about the wine-growing region of the Ahr – including wine-festivals – from:

Gebietsweinwerbung Ahr e.V.
Elligstr. 14
5483 Bad Neuenahr-Ahrweiler
Western Germany.

Visitors' Gazetteer

Altenahr: *Romanesque church, ruins of Are castle; Kreuzburg castle with archway and town-wall.*
Bad Neuenahr-Ahrweiler: *The town quarter of Walporzheim: romantic rock formations Bunte Kuh; old town wall of Ahrweiler, church of St. Laurentius; Kloster Kalvarienberg (monastery).*
Dernau: *Church (1775).*
Marienthal: *Ruins of monastery.*
Rech: *Church (1730), oldest bridge across Ahr, ancient wine-cellars (wine-tasting).*

AHR
Individual
sites

0 1 2 3 km

Ahrweiler   Neuenahr   Heppingen
29 25 27
28 26 23 21
30
Dernau 37
Mayschoß 42 31 32
Altenahr 40 38 36 35 34
43 41 39 33
Marienthal 22
Walporzheim
Rech
Bad Neuenahr-Ahrweiler
Bachem
Heimersheim
Ahr

The marked on this map form individual sites the general site of Klosterberg and the district of Walporzheim/Ahrtal

**Bereich
Walporzheim/
Ahrtal**

GROSSLAGE
KLOSTERBERG

Heimersheim
Ortsteil von Bad
Neuenahr-Ahrweiler
Kapellenberg 1
Landskrone 2
Burggarten 3

Heppingen
Ortsteil von Bad
Neuenahr-Ahrweiler
Berg 4

Neuenahr
Ortsteil von Bad
Neuenahr-Ahrweiler
Sonnenberg 5
Schieferlay 6
Kirchtürmchen 7

Bachem
Ortsteil von Bad
Neuenahr-Ahrweiler
Karlskopf 8
Sonnenschein 9
Steinkaul 10

Ahrweiler
Ortsteil von Bad
Neuenahr-Ahrweiler
Daubhaus 11
Forstberg 12
Rosenthal 13
Silberberg 14
Riegelfeld 15
Ursulinengarten 16

Walporzheim
Ortsteil von Bad
Neuenahr-Ahrweiler
Himmelchen 17
Kräuterberg 18
Gärkammer 19
Alte Lay 20
Pfaffenberg 21
Domlay 22

Marienthal
Ortsteil von Bad
Neuenahr-Ahrweiler
Rosenberg 23
Jesuitengarten 24
Trotzenberg 25
Klostergarten 26
Stiftsberg 27

Dernau
Hardtberg 28
Pfarrwingert 29
Schieferlay 30
Burggarten 31
Goldkaul 32

Rech
Hardtberg 33
Blume 34
Herrenberg 35

Mayschoß
Mönchberg 36
Schieferley 37
Burgberg 38
Silberberg 39
Laacherberg 40
Lochmühlerley 41

Altenahr
Eck 42
Übigberg 43

Mosel-Saar-Ruwer

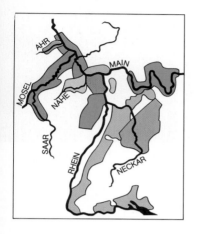

The Mosel engineers its way through a deeply cut valley with more bends and loops than any other German river, revealing fascinating scenery after each turn of the way.

Nearly 130 villages cluster from Koblenz to the Luxembourg border surrounded by large and small vineyards. On every sunny patch of ground, however small, the vine flourishes.

It started with the Celts

Whatever it was that attracted the Celts to the Mosel – climate, landscape, or the river teaming with fish – they were the first settlers along its banks. Aspects of the Mosel's history have come down to us since Roman times: Caesar, on his victorious campaign against Gaul, marched through the Mosel valley; a few decades later Augusta Treverorum (Trier today) was built and in 7 to 8 BC the Romans

The Neumagener "wine ship",
Landesmuseum, Trier

installed the great military camp of Confluentes – Koblenz. After the Romans came the Celts and Teutons, followed by the Franconians, who were the first to sack Trier on their drive upstream along the banks of the Mosel.

In the meantime the vine had begun to flourish along the Mosel. The Romans had introduced it from Marseilles. In 317 AD they already sang to "fragrant Bacchus"; Emperor Probus decreed the first wine laws, and thanks to the Romans importing their culture, the "Neumagener Weinschiff" can still be admired today in the Trier museum. This tomb of a Roman wine merchant, featuring a typical wine ship of the period, was found at Neumagen (Novionagus), one of the oldest German wine-growing communities.

From the 12th century onwards ecclesiastical princes with secular powers encouraged cultural advance and supported viticulture with the help of the monasteries. But with the beginning of The 30 Years' War, and after French troops

Riesling

Main types of vine in the Mosel-Saar-Ruwer

Riesling	62.1
Müller-Thurgau	20.7
Elbling	9.5

had stormed castles, palaces and monasteries in 1687/89, there was hardly any respite from battle for 50 years – and the inhabitants of the Mosel Valley sought peaceful refuge in their wine.

"... how the vine thrives on accidental, natural terraces"

Goethe admired this phenomenon in his account of an adventurous flight from France during a boat-trip on the Mosel.

The same natural vineyards, climbing in terraces up the mountain slopes, still commence at the start of a journey through the Mosel country at Koblenz.

Each vine is reared on a vine-prop, because slaty soil and steep sites make the use of frames impossible.

On this the left river bank, is one of the largest, unbroken wine-growing areas of the Mosel country. In Winningen, Kobern-Gondorf, Löf, and Kattenes with the "valley of 13 mills", just as in Alken and Brodenbach, there are villages whose

The Mosel near Wolf

The castle ruin at Landshut

names represent wines of quality. The elegant, often lively, wine from the Mosel's lower reaches grows on slaty soil. The drive upstream passes the impressive watch-tower of Hatzenport through Moselkern, Müden, Karden and Pommern.

There is an abundance of medieval buildings, timbered houses, old churches, towers and proud castles on high. On the Mosel's right bank alone, there are seven castles in close proximity. The name of Burgen – castles – has been given to a nearby village. At Treis the road along the right bank joins the left-bank route and follows the stream to Klotten, where truly dramatic scenery opens up and with it the full panorama of the Mosel country: the mountain ranges of the Eifel and the Hunsrück, from where the river can be seen disappearing onwards behind a rock. Near the beauty spot of Cochem, important wine-growing places cluster in profusion along both river banks: Ellenz, Bremm, Alf and opposite, Valwig, Beilstein and Bullay.

Names of villages and towns read like a wine-list: Zell, with its round tower and the famous Schwarze Katz (black cat) near the fountain; Pünderich with the old ferry-building, opposite the castle of Marienburg; the steep, fruitful southern mountain-slopes; Enkirch, whose origins go back to Keltic times, and the remnants of castle Starkenburg, renowned in the Middle Ages as the strongest fortification along the Mosel; and finally Traben-Trarbach, mentioned in 1143 as Travenderbach. Trarbach, on the right river bank, is the younger of the towns; Traben, the older, has a proud Celtic past. The "Mittel-moselmuseum" (museum of the Mosel's middle-region) contains historical aspects of wine; many cellars invite visitors to wine-sampling sessions while Mont Royal offers, after a short walk, an enchanting view of the panorama below.

In the mid-Mosel region, the Devon slate stores up strength, warmth, and minerals to give to the Riesling vine, which the vine returns in the style and spiciness of the resultant wine. This, the noblest representative of Mosel wine, has done most to bring fame to the names of towns and villages: Erden, Zeltingen, Rachtig, Ürzig, Graach, Wehlen, Bernkastel, names as precious as pearls to the lover of wine.

Bernkastel-Kues ranks as the heart of the Mosel's mid-region and enchants every visitor with its colourful, gabled and timbered houses on the market square, its late Renaissance guildhall, the beautiful Michaelsbrunnen (fountain), its church and the magnificent old wine taverns and Kurfürstliche Kellerei (wine cellars of the Electorate). The mountain-top with its castle ruins, although mentioned as far back as the 7th century, was given its name of Landshut only later. Many times destroyed and rebuilt, the castle is historically linked with the Merovingians, the two archbishops Poppo von Trier and Heinrich von Vinstingen, and with Franz von Sickingen and Bernhard von Weimar. Like Traben-Trarbach, Bernkastel-Kues is divided by the Mosel with the older part, Kues, also lying on the left river bank. In 1972 a village from the early stone-age – going back three to four thousand years BC – was excavated there. Kues became world-famous through the great theologian Nicolaus Cusanus (1401–1464), a thinker far ahead of his time. For half a millennium now, the St.-Nikolaus-Hospital, founded by Cusanus, has been in existence. An imposing complex of buildings, it houses treasures of outstanding historical importance, among them, handwritten documents and early prints as well as Cusanus's distinguished library.

Not only the "Bernkasteler Doctor", which reputedly cured Bishop Boemund of Trier of a serious illness in the 4th century, but many other good Mosel wines were said to have medicinal properties which can still be put to the test today in places like Brauneberg, Filzen, Wintrich, Minheim, Thörnich, Mehring, Drohn, Neumagen and Longuich.

Niederemmel, which grew out of the villages of Emmel, Reinsport and Müstert, has always stood somewhat in the shade of the better known Piesport. Lying on the left Mosel bank, its wealth of history includes ancient Roman temples and villas, and all manner of archaeological finds are displayed (Trier, regional museum). But the Piesporter, Trittenheimer, Leiwener and Klüsserather wines are better known than all these objects put together.

Before reaching Trier, there is an op-

View of the Doctorberg near Bernkastel (Aerial photo: Rhld-Pfalz No. 146605)

Visitors' Gazetteer

Alken: *Church; Michael's Chapel; timbered houses; Thurant castle.*

Beilstein: *Market place; town and guildhall; Zehnthaus; Hallenkirche (church); Fort Beilstein; close by, at Nehren: Roman tomb "Heidenkeller".*

Bernkastel-Kues: *Castle ruins, Landshut; stocks; old wine taverns; St. Michael's Church; St.-Nikolaus-Hospital.*

Cochem: *Baroque guildhall; Capuchin monastery; town fortifications; timbered houses; castle of Cochem; nearby: Winneburg, Marien-Wallfahrtskapelle (chapel); Cochemer Krampen; Ebernach monastery.*

Ediger-Eller: *Celtic round tower; timbered houses; late Gothic church; Kreuz-Kapellchen (chapel); St. Hilarius Church; old wine cellars.*

Enkirch: *Timbered buildings; wine-estates; Zehnthaus; museum; above the town: ruins of Starkenburg castle.*

Hatzenport: *Gothic church; nearby: Bischofstein castle; Eltz castle.*

Kobern-Gondorf: *Medieval market place; Dreikönigskapelle (chapel) Niederburg; Oberburg, the only Wasserburg (castle in the water) on the Mosel.*

Kröv: *St. Remigius Church; burial chapel of the Counts of Kesselstatt; Echternach monastery; wine-courtyard of Stablo Abbey; Mont Royal.*

Neumagen-Dhron: *Ancient sandstone bridges; Peterskapelle (chapel); church of Maria Himmelfahrt; Märtyrerkapelle (chapel); estate Sayn Wittgenstein.*

Pünderich: *Ferry building; Zehnthäuser (tithe-houses); wine-cellars; town hall; nearby: Marienburg (castle) Springiersbach Abbey.*

Saarburg: *Town-mill; church with west tower (Madonna of the Grapes); remnants of town fortifications; ruins of castle; nearby: in Beurig: pilgrims chapel and monastery of Franciscans.*

Traben-Trarbach: *Monasteries and wine-estates; Haus Kayser; Haus Böcking with museum; St. Peter Church; Nikolauskapelle (chapel).*

Treis-Karden: *St. Katharina (church); in Karden: St. Castor Cathedral; Zehnthaus; Probsteihaus; Stiftschule (school); nearby: Zillekapelle (chapel); castle ruins of Treis; Wildburg (castle); convent, Maria Engelport.*

Trier: *Porta Nigra; St. Peter (cathedral); Dreikönigshaus; market place with Cross; Wine-Tavern "Steipe" Palais Kesselstatt; Kurfürstliches Palais; Kaiserthermen; Amphitheatre; St. Matthias Abteikirche (abbey-church); Römerbrücke (bridge); Stift St. Irminen; Igeler Säule (pillar); county and town museum.*

portunity to compare wines and make an excursion to the Ruwer. The wine of this picturesque countryside with its old monasteries is of particular elegance.

Trier has rich historical interest commensurate with the town's great age. There are the Porta Nigra, the imperial thermal baths, and the Cathedral; a highlight must be the regional Museum, where most can be learned about the history of the Mosel.

Wine from the Saar – praised by connoisseurs

Just behind Konz, from Trier there is the 30 km-long Saar part of the specified region. Wines from the Saar as well as from the Ruwer, resemble the Mosel wines in character. They have the same freshness, piquant bouquet and fine, lively acidity.

Filzen, Wiltingen, Scharzhof, Kanzem, Ockfen or Ayl – all have excellent vineyards. History pervades from Konz to Serrig: baroque buildings in Konz; old wine-taverns in Wawern, Ayl, Wiltingen and Ockfen; churches; ancient castle ruins on hilltops as, for example at Saarburg.

Along the upper reaches of the Mosel

The "Porta Nigra" at Trier

the Elbling vine is still planted – just as it was in Roman times. Because of its delicate and piquant acid content, the grapes are particularly suitable for Sekt production.

For dates of wine-festivals and wine seminars contact:
Weinwerbung
Mosel-Saar-Ruwer
Neustrasse 86
5500 Trier
Western Germany

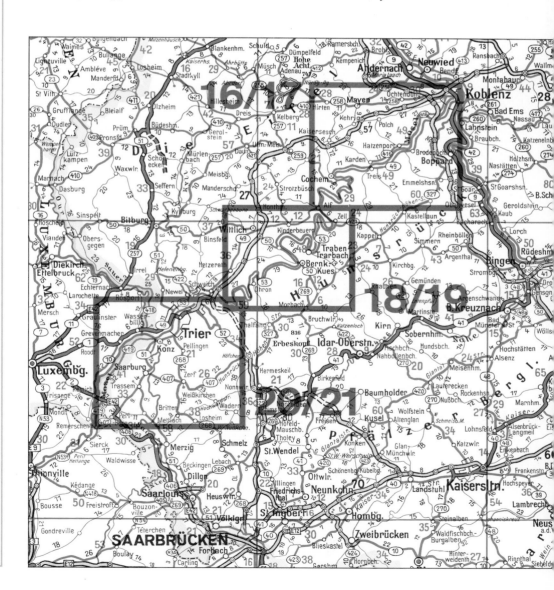

**Bereich Zell
(Untermosel)**

GROSSLAGE
WEINHEX

Güls
Ortsteil von Koblenz
Marienberg 1
Bienengarten 2
Königsfels 3
Im Röttgen 4 T

Moselweiß
Ortsteil von Koblenz
Hamm 5 T

Lay
Ortsteil von Koblenz
Hamm 5 T
Hubertusborn 6

Winningen
Im Röttgen 4 T
Brückstück 8
Domgarten 9
Hamm 10
Uhlen 11 T

Kobern-Gondorf
Uhlen 11 T
Fahrberg 12
Weißenberg 13
Schloßberg 14
Gäns 15
Fuchshöhle 16
Kehrberg 17

Dieblich
Heilgraben 18

Niederfell
Fächern 19
Kahllay 20
Goldlay 21

Lehmen
Lay 22
Klosterberg 23
Würzlay 24
Ausoniusstein 25

Oberfell
Goldlay 26
Brauneberg 27
Rosenberg 28

Moselsürsch
Fahrberg 29 T

Kattenes
Ortsteil von Löf
Fahrberg 29 T
Steinchen 30

Alken
Bleidenberg 31
Burgberg 32
Hunnenstein 33

Brodenbach
Neuwingert 34

Löf
Goldblume 35
Sonnenring 36

Hatzenport
Ortsteil von Löf
Stolzenberg 37
Kirchberg 38
Burg Bischof-
   stein 39

Burgen
Bischofstein 40

GROSSLAGE
GOLDBÄUMCHEN

Moselkern
Rosenberg 41
Kirchberg 42
Übereltzer 43

Müden
Funkenberg 44
Leckmauer 45
Sonnenring 46
St. Castorhöhle 47
Großlay 48

**Treis-Karden
Ortsteil Karden**
Dechantsberg 49
Münsterberg 50
Juffermauer 51

Pommern
Zeisel 52
Goldberg 53
Sonnenuhr 54
Rosenberg 55

Klotten
Rosenberg 55 a
Burg Coreidel-
   steiner 56
Sonnengold 57
Brauneberg 58

Cochem
Herrenberg 59
Pinnerkreuzberg 60
Schloßberg 61

**Cochem
Ortsteil Sehl**
Hochlay 62

**Cochem
Ortsteil Ebernach**
Klostergarten 63
Sonnenberg 64
Bischofstuhl 65

Ernst
Feuerberg 66
Kirchlay 67

**Bruttig-Fankel
Ortsteil Bruttig**
Götterlay 68

Ellenz-Poltersdorf
Kurfürst 69
Altarberg 70
Rüberberger Dom-
   herrenberg 71 T

Briedern
Rüberberger Dom-
   herrenberg 71 T

**Senheim
Ortsteil Senhals**
Rüberberger Dom-
   herrenberg 71 T
Römerberg 73

GROSSLAGE
ROSENHANG

**Treis-Karden
Ortsteil Treis**
Kapellenberg 74
Greth 75
Treppchen 76

**Cochem
Ortsteil Cond**
Arzlay 77
Rosenberg 78
Nikolausberg 79

Valwig
Schwarzenberg 80
Palmberg 81
Herrenberg 82

Bruttig-Fankel
Pfarrgarten 83
Rathausberg 84
Kapellenberg 85
Martinsborn 86
Layenberg 87
Rosenberg 88

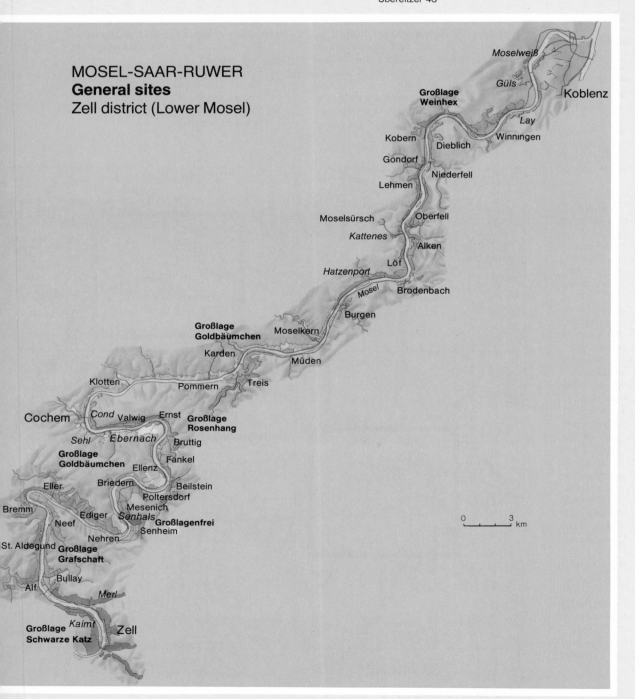

MOSEL-SAAR-RUWER
General sites
Zell district (Lower Mosel)

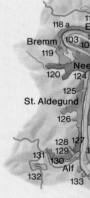

Ellenz-Poltersdorf
Woogberg 89
Silberberg 90

Beilstein
Schloßberg 91

Briedern
Herrenberg 92
Kapellenberg 93
Servatiusberg 94
Römergarten 95

Mesenich
Abteiberg 96
Goldgrübchen 97
Deuslay 98

Senheim
Wahrsager 99
Bienengarten 100
Vogteiberg 101
Rosenberg 102

Bremm
Abtei Kloster
Stuben 103

**Ediger-Eller
Ortsteil Eller**
Stubener
Klostersegen 104

GROSSLAGENFREI

Senheim
Lay 105

GROSSLAGE
GRAFSCHAFT

Nehren
Römerberg 106

**Ediger-Eller
Ortsteil Ediger**
Osterlämmchen
107
Hasensprung 108
Elzhofberg 109
Pfaffenberg 110
Feuerberg 111
Pfirsichgarten 112
Kapplay 113
Bienenlay 114

– Ortsteil Eller
Höll 115
Engelströpfchen
116
Schützenlay 117
Calmont 118

Bremm
Calmont 118 a
Schlemmertröpf-
chen 119
Laurentiusberg 120
Frauenberg 121 T

Neef
Frauenberg 121 T
Petersberg 122
Rosenberg 123

St. Aldegund
Himmelreich 124
Palmberg Terras-
sen 125
Klosterkammer 126

Alf
Kapellenberg 127
Katzenkopf 128
Herrenberg 129
Burggraf 130
Kronenberg 131
Arrasburg-
Schloßberg 132
Hölle 133

Beuren
Pelzerberger*

Bullay
Graf Beyssel-
Herrenberg 134
Brautrock 135
Kronenberg 136
Kirchweingarten
137
Sonneck 138

With vineyards in
Zell, Ortsteil Merl
sections not
included in the
individual sites

GROSSLAGE
SCHWARZE
KATZ

Zell, Ortsteil Merl
Sonneck 139
Adler 140
Königslay-
Terrassen 141
Stephansberg 142
Fettgarten 143
Klosterberg 144

Zell
Nußberg 145
Burglay-Felsen 146
Petersborn-
Kabertchen 147
Pommerell 148
Kreuzlay 149
Domherrenberg 150
Geisberg 151

**Zell
Ortsteil Kaimt**
Marienburger 153
Rosenborn 154
Römerquelle 155

MOSEL-SAAR-RUWER
Individual sites
Zell district (Lower Mosel)

Vineyards at Zell

Bullay on the Mosel

Typical sundials at Mosel vineyards

0 1 2 3 km

MOSEL-SAAR-RUWER
Individual sites
Bernkastel district (Middle Mosel)

Bereich Bernkastel (Mittelmosel)

GROSSLAGE VOM HEISSEN STEIN

Briedel
Weisserberg 156
Schäferlay 157
Herzchen 158
Nonnengarten 159
Schelm 160

Pünderich
Goldlay 161
Rosenberg 162
Nonnengarten 163
Marienberg 164

Reil
Goldlay 165
Falklay 166
Moullay-Hofberg 167
Sorentberg 168

GROSSLAGE SCHWARZLAY

Burg
Wendelstück 169
Hahnenschrittchen 170
Thomasberg 171
Falklay 172
Schloßberg 173

Enkirch
Edelberg 174
Monteneubel 175
Steffensberg 176
Weinkammer 177
Herrenberg 178
Zeppwingert 179
Batterieberg 180
Ellergrub 181

Starkenburg
Rosengarten 182

Traben-Trarbach
Ortsteil Trarbach
Burgberg 185
Schloßberg 186
Ungsberg 187
Hühnerberg 188
Kreuzberg 189
Taubenhaus 190

Ortsteil Traben
Gaispfad 183
Zollturm 184
Königsberg 191
Kräuterhaus 192
Würzgarten 193

Wolf
Ortsteil von Traben-Trarbach
Schatzgarten 194
Sonnenlay 195
Klosterberg 196
Goldgrube 197
Auf der Heide 198

Kinheim
Rosenberg 199
Hubertuslay 200

Lösnich
Försterlay 201
Burgberg 202

Erden
Busslay 203
Herrenberg 204
Treppchen 205
Prälat 206

Ürzig
Würzgarten 207
Goldwingert 208

Bengel
einzellagenfrei*

Bausendorf
Herzlay 209
Hubertuslay 210

Flußbach
Reichelberg 211

Wittlich
Kupp 212
Lay 213
Bottchen 214
Felsentreppchen 215
Rosenberg 216
Portnersberg 217
Klosterberg 218

Hupperath
Klosterweg 219

Dreis
Johannisberg 220

Platten
Klosterberg 221
Rotlay 222

Bullay
168 Pünderich
164 163
162 161 158
160
Reil 165 159 157
166 169 171 Briedel 156
167 170
Burg 172
173
174 175
226 223 176
227 225 177
228 224 197 198 178 Enkirch
200 Kröv 179
205 196 Wolf 180
Kinheim 194 191
199 181
Lösnich 195 193 183 182
231 Starkenburg
332 184
233 242 185 Traben-Trarbach
239 190
Wehlen 186
Graach 187
238 240 241 189 188
244 245
243 251
249 246
248 252 247
256 255 Bernkastel-Kues
261
260
259 252
253
264
265

Flußbach 211
210 209
Bausendorf
212

Hupperath 214 213
215
217 216
219 218

Wittlich

Dreis 220

Sehlem 322

Rivenich 320
Hetzerath 321 318 319
307
Bekond 328 326 327
329 330 331
328 333
Schweich 352 335 334
350 336 337 323
351 349 338
Longuich 343 339 341
353 348 Longen 342
Lörsch 344
Kenn 354 Mehring 340
Riol 345
347 346
Fell
347
347

Platten
221 222
223
229
230
234
235 236 237

Osann
283 282
Monzel
281 285
Kesten 286
287
302 301 300 298 297 299
303
304 Piesport
Niederemmel
296 295 294 293
305 308 306
309 Dhron Minheim 292
310 290 291
Neumagen 305
311
312 310 306
325 313
324
315 317
Trittenheim 314

Maring-Noviand 279
277
278
262
Brauneberg 275
Mülheim 263
266 272 274 Veldenz
273 Burgen
290 290

Wittrich
258
268 269 270 271
280 284
267

Lieser 250
248
Kues

Andel

GROSSLAGE
NACKTARSCH

Kröv
Burglay 223
Herrenberg 224
Steffensberg 225
Letterlay 226
Kirchlay 227
Paradies 228

GROSSLAGE
MÜNZLAY

**Zeltingen-Rachtig
Ortsteil Zeltingen**
Deutschherrenberg
    229
Himmelreich 230
Schloßberg 231
Sonnenuhr 232

Wehlen
Ortsteil von Bern-
kastel-Kues
Sonnenuhr 233 △
Hofberg 234
Abtei 235
Klosterhofgut 236
Klosterberg 237
Nonnenberg 238

Graach
Domprobst 239
Himmelreich 240
Abtsberg 241
Josephshöfer 242

GROSSLAGE
BADSTUBE

**Bernkastel-Kues
Ortsteil Bernkastel**
Lay 243
Matheisbildchen
    244
Bratenhöfchen 245
Graben 246
Doctor 247 △

GROSSLAGE
BEERENLAY

Lieser
Süßenberg 248
Niederberg-
    Helden 249
Rosenlay 250

GROSSLAGE
KURFÜRSTLAY

**Bernkastel-Kues
Ortsteil Bernkastel**
Johannisbrünnchen
    251
Schloßberg 252 T
Stephanus-Rosen-
    gärtchen 253

**Bernkastel-Kues
Ortsteil Kues**
Rosenberg 254
Kardinalsberg 255
Weißenstein 256

Andel
Ortsteil von Bern-
kastel-Kues
Schloßberg 252 T

Lieser
Schloßberg 258

Mülheim
Elisenberg 259 T
Sonnenlay 260
Helenenkloster 261
Amtgarten 262

Veldenz
Elisenberg 259 T
Kirchberg 263
Mühlberg 264
Grafschafter
    Sonnenberg 265
Carlsberg 266

Maring-Noviand
Honigberg 267
Klosterberg 268
Römerpfad 269
Kirchberg 270
Sonnenuhr 271

Burgen
Römerberg 272
Kirchberg 273
Hasenläufer 274

Brauneberg
Mandelgraben 275
Klostergarten 276
Juffer 277
Juffer Sonnenuhr
    278
Kammer 279
Hasenläufer 280

Osann-Monzel
Paulinslay 281
Kätzchen 282
Kirchlay 283
Rosenberg 284

Kesten
Paulinshofberger
    285
Herrenberg 286
Paulinsberg 287

Wintrich
Stefanslay 288
Großer Herrgott
    289
Sonnseite 290
Ohligsberg 291
Geierslay 292

GROSSLAGE
MICHELSBERG

Minheim
Burglay 293
Kapellchen 294
Rosenberg 295
Günterslay 299 T

Piesport
Treppchen 296
Falkenberg 297

Goldtröpfchen 298 T
Günterslay 299 T
Domherr 300
Gärtchen 301
Kreuzwingert 302
Schubertslay 303
Grafenberg 304 T
Hofberger 305 T

**Neumagen-Dhron
Ortsteil Dhron**
Goldtröpfchen 298 T
Grafenberg 304 T
Hofberger 305 T
Roterd 306
Großer Hengelberg
    307
Häschen 308

**– Ortsteil
Neumagen**
Nußwingert 309
Engelgrube 310
Laudamusberg 311
Rosengärtchen 312
Sonnenuhr 313

Trittenheim
Altärchen 314
Apotheke 315
Felsenkopf 316
Leiterchen 317

Rivenich
Niederberg 318
Geisberg 319
Rosenberg 320
Brauneberg 321 T

Hetzerath
Brauneberg 321 T

Sehlem
Rotlay 322

GROSSLAGE
ST. MICHAEL

Leiwen
Klostergarten 323
Laurentiuslay 324 T

Köwerich
Laurentiuslay
    324 T
Held 325

Klüsserath
Bruderschaft 326
Königsberg 327

Bekond
Schloßberg 328
Brauneberg 329

Thörnich
Enggaß 330
Ritsch 331
Schießlay 332

Ensch
Mühlenberg 333
St. Martin 334
Sonnenlay 335

Detzem
Würzgarten 336
Maximiner
    Klosterlay 337

Schleich
Sonnenberg 338
Klosterberg 339

Pölich
Held 340
Südlay 341

Mehring
Blattenberg 342
Goldkupp 343
Zellerberg 344 T

Lörsch
Ortsteil von Mehring
Zellerberg 344 T

Longen
Zellerberg 344 T

GROSSLAGE
PROBSTBERG

Mehring
einzellagenfrei 345

Riol
Römerberg 346

Fell
Maximiner
    Burgberg 347

Longuich
Hirschlay 348
Maximiner
    Herrenberg 349
Herrenberg 350 T

Schweich
Herrenberg 350 T
Annaberg 351
Burgmauer 352

Kenn
Held 353
Maximiner
    Hofgarten 354

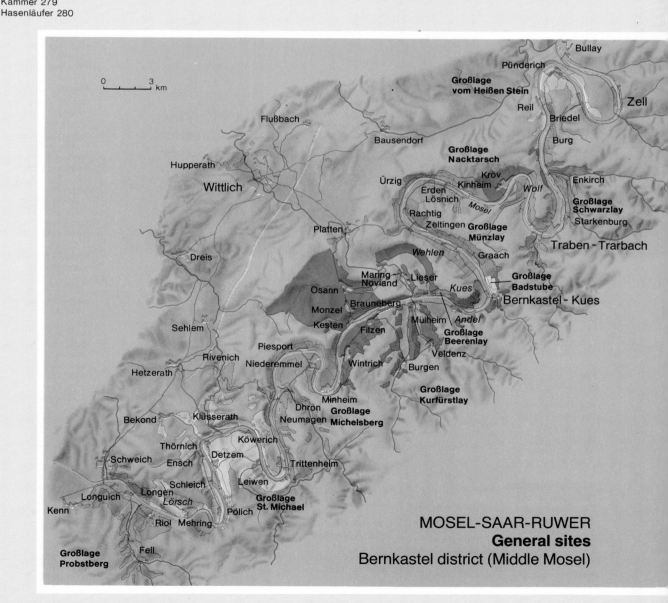

MOSEL-SAAR-RUWER
General sites
Bernkastel district (Middle Mosel)

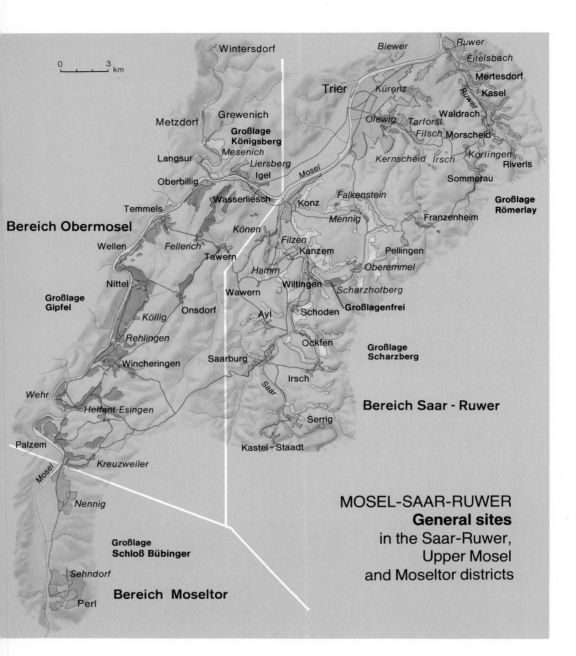

Wintersdorf

Biewer
Ruwer
Eitelsbach
Mertesdorf
Kasel
Trier
Kürenz
Waldrach
Olewig Tarforst
Filsch Morscheid
Metzdorf Grewenich
Großlage
Königsberg
Mesenich
Langsur Liersberg
Igel
Mosel
Kernscheid Irsch
Korlingen
Riveris
Oberbillig
Falkenstein
Sommerau
Wasserliesch
Großlage
Römerlay
Temmels Konz
Mennig Franzenheim

Bereich Obermosel

Wellen Könen
Filzen
Kanzem
Pellingen
Fellerich
Tawern Hamm Oberemmel
Nittel Wawern Wiltingen
Großlage Scharzhofberg
Gipfel Onsdorf Schoden Großlagenfrei
Köllig Ayl
Rehlingen Ockfen
Großlage
Scharzberg
Wincheringen Saarburg
Irsch
Wehr
Helfant-Esingen Serrig
Palzem **Bereich Saar - Ruwer**
Mosel Kastel - Staadt
Kreuzweiler

Nennig **MOSEL-SAAR-RUWER**
General sites
in the Saar-Ruwer,
Upper Mosel
Großlage and Moseltor districts
Schloß Bübinger

Sehndorf
Perl **Bereich Moseltor**

0 3 km

With vineyards in the Edingen, Godendorf, Grewenich, Langsur, Liersberg, Metzdorf, Ralingen and Wintersdorf sections not included in the individual sites.

GROSSLAGE GIPFEL

Wasserliesch
Reinig auf der Burg 500
Albachtaler 501

Oberbillig
Hirtengarten 502
Römerberg 503

Fellerich
Ortsteil von Tawern
Schleidberg 504

Temmels
St. Georgshof 505
Münsterstatt 506

Wellen
Altenberg 507

Onsdorf
Hubertusberg 508 T

Nittel
Hubertusberg 508 T
Leiterchen 509
Blümchen 510
Rochusfels 511 T

Köllig
Ortsteil von Nittel
Rochusfels 511 T

Rehlingen
Ortsteil von Nittel
Kapellenberg 512

Wincheringen
Burg Warsberg 513
Fuchsloch 514

Wehr
Ortsteil von Palzem
Rosenberg 515

Helfant und Esingen
Ortsteil von Palzem
Kapellenberg 516

MOSEL-SAAR-RUWER
Individual sites
in the Saar-Ruwer, Upper Mosel and Moseltor districts

The 30 km-long wine-growing region of the Saar starts near Konz

Bereich Moseltor

GROSSLAGE BÜBINGER

Nennig
Ortsteil von Perl
Schloßberg 520
Römerberg 521

Palzem
Karlsfelsen 517
Lay 518

Kreuzweiler
Ortsteil von Palzem
Schloß Thorner Kupp 519

With vineyards in the Bitzingen, Fisch, Kirf, Meurich, Portz, Soest, Tawern sections not included in the individual sites.

Sehndorf
Ortsteil von Perl
Klosterberg 522
Marienberg 523
with vineyards in the Oberperl section.

Perl
Quirinusberg 524
Hasenberg 525

Individual vineyard sites in Besch, Tettingen and Wochern

0 1 2 3 km

Mittelrhein

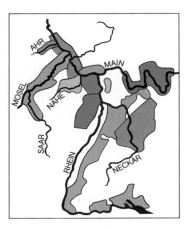

In geological terms, the part of the Rhine flowing between Bonn and Bingen is still a very young output. Originally it flowed in the direction of the Danube and Mediterranean; only during the ice-age – through breaks and convulsions of the earth's crust – did it grow into a continuous, unified stream.

Many peoples have left their mark along the historic banks of the Rhine – Kelts, Teutons, Romans, Huns, Swedes, Austrians, Prussians, Russians and Frenchmen – and from time immemorial,

Castle Stahleck near Bacharach

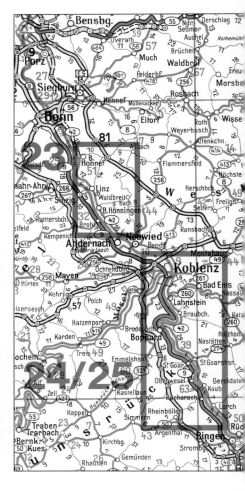

myths and legends have been woven around the river's name: the legends of the Rhinegold, of Siegfried and Hagen, of the Burgundian knights, and many more.

Today, the 1,320 km long Rhine remains a lifeline between the Alps and the North Sea: a trading route at one time, and now the most important industrial shipping route in the world, with the largest

inland-harbours, the Rhine's greatest promoter of fame has been its wine. The wide range of wines growing in the region prove the point: the Riesling wine with its definite, fruity character; the mild, palatable Silvaner; the aromatic Müller-Thurgau. Their many character-traits all stem from varying soil conditions – blue-black slate, grey-stone or quartzite.

Riesling

Main types of vine in the Mittelrhein:

Riesling	75.2%
Müller-Thurgau	11.5%

Data and facts

Geographical notes: *100 km of vineyards along both banks of the river; vineyards also stretch out on southern slopes of side valleys.*

Climate: *The often steeply-rising vineyard terraces lie sheltered from the wind and get plenty of warm sunshine. The stream's extensive surface of water acts as a "heat-reservoir".*

Soil: *mainly slaty, weathered, grey-stone soil. Small islands of loess, distributed throughout the area, make for pithy, lively wine. In the northern part of the region, towards the mountains of the Siebengebirge, some of the ground is of volcanic origin.*

Cultivated area: *A narrow ribbon of vineyards (approx. 903 ha) often broken by northern slopes; 3 Districts, 11 General Sites, 110 Individual Sites.*

Types of vine: *The Riesling leads with 679 ha, producing pithy, often astonishingly flowery wine; next come the Müller-Thurgau with 104 ha.*

Yield: *On average 1975–1977: 70,000 hl; roughly 1% of the total German must harvest; nearly all the sites are on steep inclines.*

Production structure: *84 per cent of producers are small growers with less than one ha wine-growing surface; a high percentage of growers market their own wine; roughly 25% of the harvests are taken up by wine-growers' associations; sale: predominantly bottled wine.*

Visitors' Gazetteer

Boppard: *Adelshäuser (ancient houses of the aristocracy); castle buildings formerly belonging to the Elector; Alte Burg Museum; game preserve Jakobsberg.*

Braubach: *St.-Martins-Kapelle (chapel); Marksburg castle with collection of ancient weapons.*

Kaub: *Medieval town; church; walk along the ancient town wall; Gutenfels castle; Pfalz (castle); General Blücher museum; "Stadt Mannheim" (inn), Blücher's HQ when he crossed the Rhine.*

Koblenz: *Stadttheater (theatre); Mittelrhein-Museum; Deutsches Eck (famous landmark); Schöffenhaus (court of jurors); Alte Burg (castle); Balduinsbrücke (bridge); Münzplatz (square); Schloss (palace); Kranhaus (old building); government buildings of the Elector; Feste Ehrenbreitstein (ancient fort).*

Leutesdorf: *Cloisters; castle; Wallfahrtskirche (pilgrims' church).*

Oberlahnstein: *Wenzelskapelle (chapel); old town hall; fortifications; Lahneck castle; Martinsburg (castle).*

Oberwesel with the wine-village of Engehöll: *ruins of the Minoriten Monastery; town hall; ancient fortification towers.*

Trechtinghausen: *Castles Reichenstein (Falkenburg), Rheinstein, with museum, and Sooneck.*

From Bonn to Bingen – castles and vineyards

At Königswinter, near Bonn, the most northerly part of the German wine-country begins, stretching along both sides of the river. The B42, on the right-hand bank, takes in breathtaking views. From the Drachenfels, where, according to legend, Siegfried slew the dragon, or from the Petersberg, which gives a unique view of the Rhine, making it look like three lakes, a particularly splendid panorama unfolds. The ruins of the castle of Hammerstein go back to the days of the German emperor Heinrich IV. Older still is Koblenz, founded in the 9th century BC by Drusus under the name "Confluentes" and serving as a military camp; and from the Schlossplatz (Palace Square) on the heights of Ehrenbreitstein, the Rhine, Mosel, and

---

Bereich Siebengebirge

GROSSLAGE PETERSBERG

Oberdollendorf
Ortsteil von Königswinter
Rosenhügel 1
Laurentiusberg 2
Sülzenberg 3

Niederdollendorf
Ortsteil von Königswinter
Goldfüßchen 4
Longenburgerberg 5
Heisterberg 6

Königswinter
Drachenfels 7

Rhöndorf
Ortsteil von Bad Honnef
Drachenfels 8

Bereich Rheinburgengau

GROSSLAGE BURG HAMMERSTEIN

Unkel
Berg 9
Sonnenberg 10

Kasbach
Stehlerberg 11

Linz
Rheinhöller 12

Dattenberg
Gertrudenberg 13

Leubsdorf
Weißes Kreuz 14

Bad Hönningen
Schloßberg 15

Rheinbrohl
Monte Jup 16
Römerberg 17

Hammerstein
In den Layfelsen 18
Hölle 19
Schloßberg 20

Leutesdorf
Forstberg 21
Gartenlay 22
Rosenberg 23

MITTELRHEIN
General sites
in the northern part

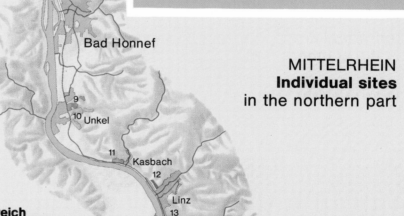

MITTELRHEIN
Individual sites
in the northern part

**MITTELRHEIN
Individual sites
in the southern part**

*Terraces on the Rhine
near Oberwesel*

**GROSSLAGE
LAHNTAL**

Fachbach
einzellagenfrei 24

Bad Ems
Hasenberg 25 T

Dausenau
Hasenberg 25 T

Nassau
Schloßberg 26

Weinähr
Giebelhöll 27

Obernhof
Goetheberg 28

Braubach
Koppelstein 33 T
Mühlberg 35
Marmorberg 36

Osterspai
Liebeneck-
Sonnenlay 37

Filsen
Pfarrgarten 38

**GROSSLAGE
MARKSBURG**

Vallendar
Rheinnieder 29 T

Urbar
Rheinnieder 29 T

**Koblenz, Ortsteil
Ehrenbreitstein**
Kreuzberg 31

Koblenz
Schnorbach
Brückstück 32

Lahnstein
Koppelstein 33 T

**GROSSLAGE
GEDEONSECK**

Rhens
König Wenzel 39
Sonnenlay 40

Brey
Hämmchen 41

Spay
Engelstein 42 T

Boppard
Engelstein 42 T
Ohlenberg 43
Feuerley 44
Mandelstein 45
Weingrube 46
Fässerlay 47
Elfenley 48

GROSSLAGENFREI

Hirzenach
Probsteiberg 49

**GROSSLAGE
BURG RHEINFELS**

**St. Goar
Ortsteil Werlau**
Rosenberg 50
Frohwingert 51
Ameisenberg 52

St. Goar
Kuhstall 53

**GROSSLAGE
LORELEYFELSEN**

Kamp-Bornhofen
Pilgerpfad 54
Liebenstein-
Sterrenberg 55 T

Kestert
Liebenstein-
Sterrenberg 55 T

Nochern
Brünnchen 56

Patersberg
Teufelstein 57

**St. Goarshausen
Ortsteile Wellmich
und Ehrental**
Burg Maus 58
Hessern 59
Burg Katz 60
Loreley Edel 61

Bornich
Rothenack 62

**GROSSLAGE
SCHLOSS
SCHÖNBURG**

Urbar
Ortsteil von Ober-
wesel
Beulsberg 63

Niederburg
Rheingoldberg 64
Bienenberg 65 T

Damscheid
Frankenhell 66
Sonnenstock 67
Goldemund 68

Oberwesel
Bienenberg 65 T
Goldemund 68 a
Sieben Jungfrauen
69
Ölsberg 70
St. Martinsberg 71
Römerkrug 73

**Oberwesel
Ortsteil Engehöll**
Bernstein 72

Dellhofen
Ortsteil von Ober-
wesel
Römerkrug 74
St. Wernerberg 75

Langscheid
Ortsteil von Ober-
wesel
Hundert 76

Perscheid
Rosental 77

**GROSSLAGE
HERRENBERG**

Dörscheid
Wolfsnack 78
Kupferflöz 79

Kaub
Roßstein 80
Backofen 81
Rauschelay 82
Blüchertal 83
Burg Gutenfels 84
Pfalzgrafenstein 85

**Bereich
Bacharach**

**GROSSLAGE
SCHLOSS
STAHLECK**

**Bacharach
Ortsteil Steeg**
Schloß Stahlberg 86
Lennenborn 87
St. Jost 88
Hambusch 89

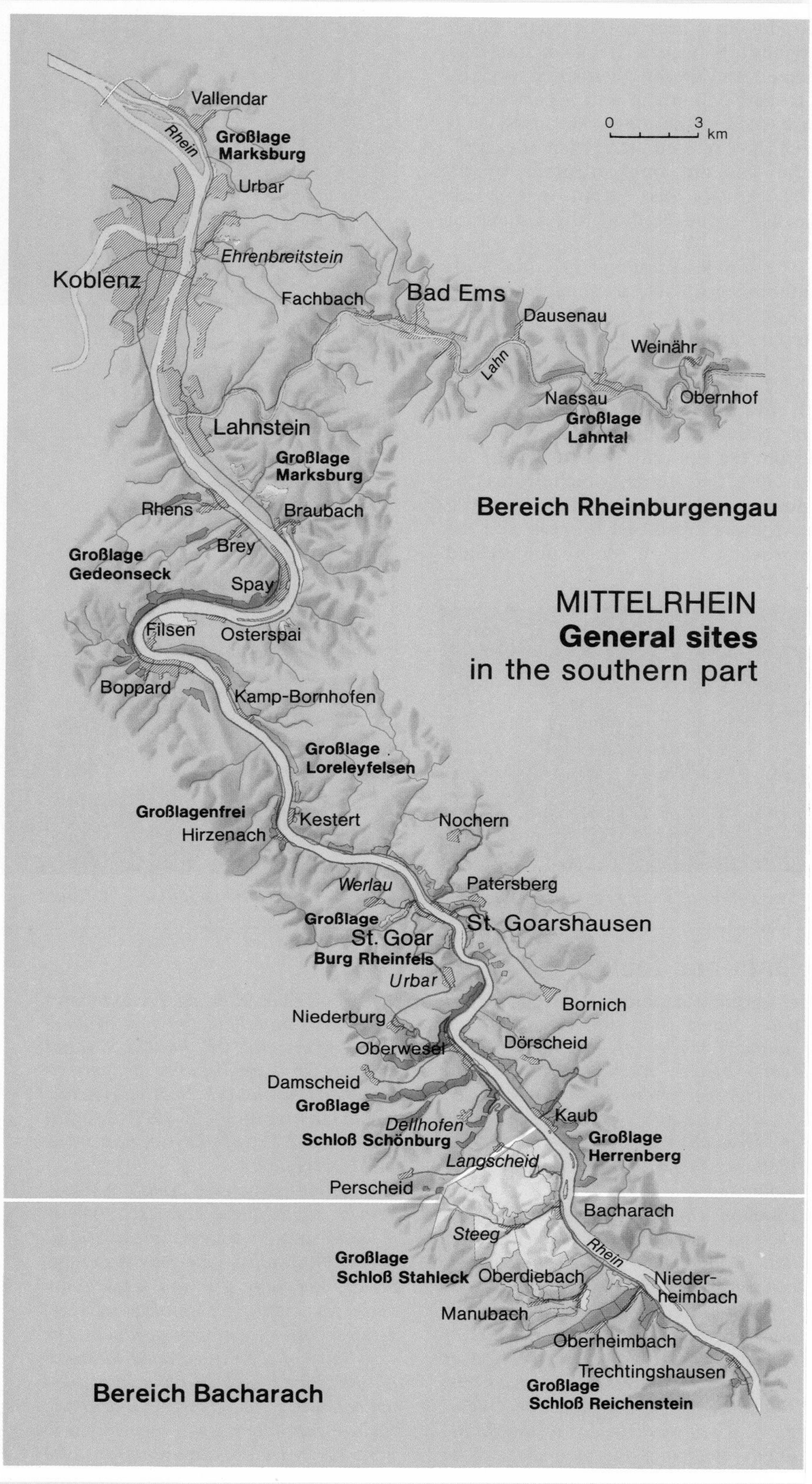

The map shows the Mittelrhein region with labels:

Vallendar

Großlage Marksburg

Urbar

Ehrenbreitstein

Koblenz

Fachbach — Bad Ems

Dausenau

Weinähr

Lahn

Nassau — Obernhof

Großlage Lahntal

Lahnstein

Großlage Marksburg

Rhens — Braubach

Brey

Großlage Gedeonseck

Spay

Filsen — Osterspai

Boppard — Kamp-Bornhofen

Bereich Rheinburgengau

MITTELRHEIN
General sites
in the southern part

0 3 km

Großlage Loreleyfelsen

Großlagenfrei
Hirzenach — Kestert — Nochern

Werlau — Patersberg

Großlage St. Goar — St. Goarshausen

Burg Rheinfels
Urbar

Niederburg — Bornich

Oberwesel — Dörscheid

Damscheid

Großlage
Dellhofen
Schloß Schönburg
Langscheid

Kaub

Großlage Herrenberg

Perscheid

Bacharach

Steeg

Großlage
Schloß Stahleck Oberdiebach

Nieder-heimbach

Manubach

Oberheimbach

Trechtingshausen

Großlage
Schloß Reichenstein

Bereich Bacharach

---

the Eifel and Hunsrück mountains can be taken in with a single glance. Braubach, with its well preserved medieval castle, lies near the Rhine's longest loop, which ends at Kamp-Bornhofen. The Loreley-Burgenstrasse (local route 103) to the legendary "Loreley" rock offers an enthralling journey past imposing castles dotted along the heights.

An alternative approach is by the Bundestrasse 9 (national route), which runs along the left river bank (from the north, change onto the "Rheingoldstrasse" at Rhens). Rhens, Boppard, St. Goar, Oberwesel, Bacharach, all mirror the spirit of their history – witnessed by countless castles and palace ruins along the way.

Castle Pfalz near Kaub

Oberwesel

Information about the Middle Rhine, and dates of its wine and vintage festivals can also be obtained from:
Mittelrhein – Burgen und Weine e.V.
Postfach
5423 Braubach
Western Germany

Bacharach
Hahn 90
Insel Heylesen Wert 91
Wolfshöhle 92
Posten 93
Mathias Weingarten 94
Kloster Fürstental 95

Manubach
Langgarten 96
St. Oswald 97
Mönchwingert 98
Heilgarten 99

Oberdiebach
Bischofshub 100
Fürstenberg 101
Kräuterberg 102
Rheinberg 103

GROSSLAGE
SCHLOSS
REICHENSTEIN

Oberheimbach
Römerberg 104
Klosterberg 105
Wahrheit 106
Sonne 107

Niederheimbach
Froher Weingarten 108
Schloß Hohneck 109
Reifersley 110
Soonecker Schloßberg 111

Trechtingshausen
Morgenbachtaler 112

Rheingau

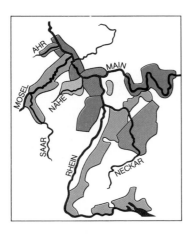

This small area at the foot of the Taunus mountains has held a particular magic throughout its history. Heads of state like Napoleon and Queen Victoria, musicians like Robert Schumann and a poet of the stature of Goethe have all loved and praised this "blessed little patch of earth". Goethe was not only attracted by its beauty. Among his output is a poem dedicated to the "Eilfer", the vintage of 1811.

The noble Riesling, reacting with inimitable sensitivity to climate and soil variations, finds growing conditions particularly favourable in the Rheingau region. In vineyards sheltered from wind by the Taunus mountains, the vines face south towards the Rhine and draw a double ration of sunshine: from the sky, and from the sun-reflecting surface of the river. Here the Rhine, which forms the boundary of the Rheingau, flows for a short distance from east to west, and the wine-growing region does not extend

Madonna with a bunch of grapes at Lorch

The cellar of wine presses at Eberbach

"Drosselgasse" at Rüdesheim

Riesling

Main types of vine in the Rheingau:

Riesling	75.4%
Müller-Thurgau	10.2%
Silvaner	4.7%

Data and facts

Geographical notes: *Between Bingen and Mainz the Rhine forms the southern border of the Rheingau; a region of only 36 kilometres of wine-growing, stretching from Lorchhausen or to Flörsheim. Vineyards, planted predominantly on southern slopes, are sheltered in the north by the Taunus mountains.*

Climate: *The Taunus mountain range shelters the vines from cold weather; mild winters and warm summers encourage the growth of vines. An average rainfall of approximately 55 mm, and more than average hours of sunshine during the growth period of May to October, have given the Rheingau the popular name of "Weingau". The broad surface of the Rhine, amply reflecting the sun, acts as an additional reservoir of warmth.*

Soil: *Quartzite and weathered slate-stone in the higher placed sites produces a pithy, elegant wine; the loam, loess and clay soil of the valley vineyards gives a full, robust type; the fruity, delicate-tasting Burgunder wine grows best in the blue phyllite-slate soil around Assmannshausen.*

Cultivated area: *2,837 ha of vineyards; 1 District, 10 General Sites, 116 Individual Sites.*

Types of vine: *Riesling predominates on approximately 2,140 ha. Müller-Thurgau occupies 289 ha and Silvaner 132 ha. On a small patch of approximately 61 ha there is Spätburgunder.*

Yield: *On average 1975–1977: 235,000 hl; about 2.5% of the German wine-must harvest.*

Production structure: *Small growers deliver their harvest to 16, mostly medium sized, producers' associations; about 500 family wine-growing enterprises, one large growers' association and a fair number of well-known wine-estates bottle their own produce. The proximity of the large industrial areas of the Rhine and Main offers good opportunities to growers marketing their own produce; sales by growers to inns, taverns and restaurants are also high. The trade takes roughly half the harvest.*

Typical characteristics of the region: *Production of top quality wine is high, especially of the Rheingauer Rieslings; much is exported; many are large wine-estates with a long tradition of wine-growing; the spring and autumn auctions of Rheingau wine are held in high esteem by experts.*

A view of Winkel

much further – barely 40 km from Lorchhausen to Hochheim.

The Wine culture of the Rhine

Originally inhabited by Kelts and already quite densely populated in Roman times, ecclesiastical princes in the Middle Ages

Roman drinking vessels found in Brömserburg Castle "Grey House", Winkel

actively encouraged viticulture in this region. The worldly "wine saint" Charlemagne did the same for the vine on the other bank of the Rhine – in his Ingelheimer Kaiserpfalz. With the founding of the first monasteries in the 12th century, the number of vineyards mentioned in documents grew rapidly.

Today the most famous, preserved monastery is probably the Cistercian monastery in Eberbach. Its foundation stone was laid in 1145, and its monumental buildings belong to the finest examples of European architecture.

By road through the "Weingau"

The Rheingauer Riesling Route takes its name from the most important vine in the region and leads the motorist away from the heavy traffic on the Rheinufer route, to the renowned wine estates and prosperous wine-growing communities between Lorchhausen and Hochheim. Light green and white signposts showing a large wine goblet show the way. First stop on the "Riesling route" is Lorch, with its painted timber houses.

Those who love red wine are drawn to Assmanshausen, the "red wine island" where a magnificent Spätburgunder grows. Bismarck was enthusiastic about Assmanshäuser red wine and particularly appreciated the "Cabinetwein" of 1858.

During holiday time visitors flock to the excellent wine-taverns in Rüdesheim's famous Drosselgasse.

The impressive ancient Roman castle of Brömserburg contains a wine-museum detailing the absorbing history of wine growing.

Geisenheim, with perhaps less ancient history to its name, has nevertheless a one hundred year-old teaching and research institute for viticulture, fruit-growing and horticulture, which is renowned throughout the scientific world.

Visitors' Gazetteer

Assmannshausen: *World-famous for its gastronomic delights; nearby: Burg Rheinstein (castle); Clemenskapelle (13c. chapel).*
Eltville: *Prince Elector's castle; church, Adelshöfe, sparkling wine cellars. State Domain; rose-gardens.*
Erbach: *Schloss Reinhartshausen; church of St. Markus; Marcobrunnen (fountain); timbered houses and ancient Patrician buildings; Mariannenaue (island in the Rhine).*
Geisenheim: *Rheingauer Dom (cathedral); Schloss Monrepos (palace). nearby: Marienthal (place of pilgrimage).*
Hallgarten: *Church with Hallgarter Madonna; Hallgarter Zange (famous viewpoint over splendid panorama).*
Hattenheim: *Church; timbered houses; Schloss Reichhartshausen; nearby: Kloster Eberbach (medieval monastery).*
Hochheim: *Church; Madonna auf dem Plan (statue); sparkling wine cellars.*
Johannisberg: *Schloss Johannisberg (formerly Benedictine monastery); St. Georgs Klause.*
Kiedrich: *"Gothic island": St. Valentin Kirche (place of pilgrimage); Kapelle St. Michael (chapel with many art-treasures, including Gregorian art).*
Lorch: *St. Martins Church; Hilchenhaus; Leprosenhaus; Castle of Nollich; in the Rhine: Isle of the Dead.*
Oestrich-Winkel: *St. Martins Church; town hall; old Rhinecrane; Gothic fountain; Basilica St. Ägidius; Graues Haus; nearby: Schloss Vollrads.*
Rauenthal: *Church; Bubenhäuser Höhe (panoramic view).*
Rüdesheim: *Castle Brömserburg with wine-museum; Boosenburg (castle); Adlerturm (tower); St. Jacob's Church; Brömershof; Drosselgasse; wine distillery; in the town-quarter of Eibingen: former Benedictine monastery; town hall; Winzerhäuser (vintagers' dwellings); Abtei St. Hildegard (convent) with church; nearby: ruins of Rossel; hunting lodge Niederwald; ruins of Ehrenfels; Niederwald monument.*

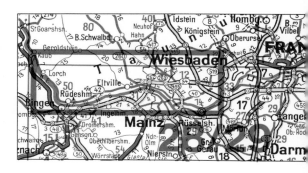

Wine in palaces and monasteries

The rarest treasures are to be found in the vast, catacomb-like wine-cellars of Schloss Johannisberg. The oldest wine dates back to 1748, but the wine history of Johannisberg is even older. Around 1100, Benedictine monks built the first monastery in the Rheingau and gave it its famous name. In 1775 the monks discovered – by accident – the secret held by grapes left to wither on the vine. A courier on his way from Fulda was waylaid and kept prisoner for days by robbers and did not arrive in time at Johannisberg with the necessary permission from the sovereign prince to harvest the grapes, which had to be left on the vine stocks, where they started to rot. But it was those grapes which produced the first Spätlese and Auslese.

St. Urban

A stone Shrine at Schloss Johannisberg

Schloss Johannisberg has had many masters in its long history, among them Napoleon. At the Congress of Vienna it was given to Emperor Franz I, who in turn presented it as a gift to his Chancellor, Prince Metternich (with the duty, incidentally still in force today, to give a tenth of the wine-harvest to the House of Habsburg).

The Graues Haus – the oldest tavern of its type in Germany – stands in Winkel where local Hasensprung or Dachsberg is available. At Mittelheim, which is linked to Winkel, there is the oldest sacred building of the Rhine region, the St. Ägidius Basilica and nearby the renowned castle, Schloss Vollrads, whose ancient tower is surrounded by water. At Oestrich, Lenchen or Klosterberg can be tasted, while the full-blooded wines of Hallgarten also offer their temptations. Every village or town in the Rheingau has its special wine to offer the traveller, among them being Hattenheim with its timbered houses, Erbach (Marcobrunnen), Schloss Reinhartshausen, Kiedrich, which has a Gothic church and particularly charming timbered dwellings or, near Kloster Eberbach, the Steinberg vineyards surrounded by a stone wall. Eltville deserves a special mention as the town of "wine and roses", once the domicile of Johannes Gutenberg, the famous German printer (1400–1468).

Rauenthaler wine, which is as strong, pithy and racy as the wine from Martinsthal, or wine from Walluf should be tried. Finally, along the Rheingauer-Riesling route, there is, of course, Hock – or wine originally said to be from Hochheim – which Queen Victoria (who said: "Good hock keeps off the doc") praised and helped make famous the world over. With its earthy taste it is a particular speciality among the Rheingau wines.

Additionally, many wine seminars are held in the region.

Information about seminars and wine festivals can be obtained from:

"Der Rheingau – Der Weingau"
Im alten Rathaus
6225 Johannisberg, Rheingau
Western Germany

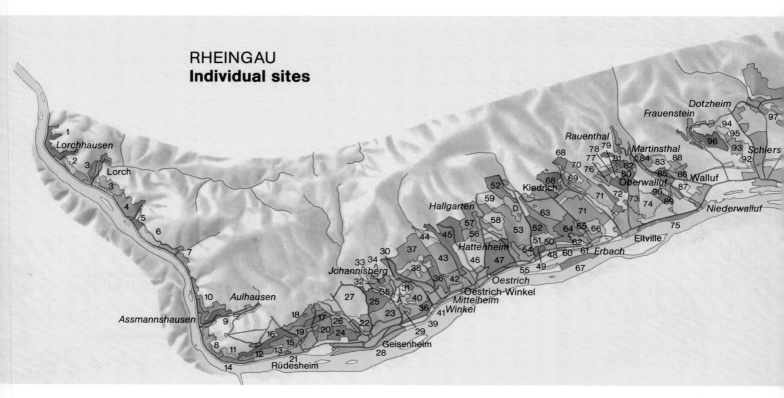

RHEINGAU
Individual sites

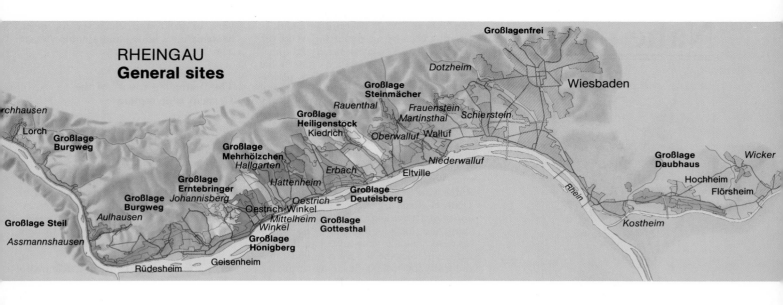

RHEINGAU
General sites

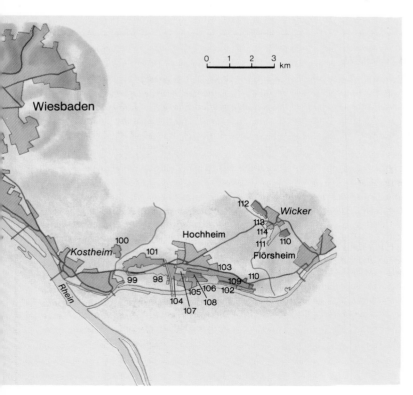

```
0   1   2   3
|___|___|___| km
```

Bereich Johannisberg

Lorchhausen
Ortsteil von Lorch
Rosenberg 1
Seligmacher 2

Lorch
Schloßberg 3
Kapellenberg 4
Krone 5
Pfaffenwies 6
Bodental-
Steinberg 7

GROSSLAGE STEIL
(Einzellagen 8–10)

Assmannshausen Aulhausen
Ortsteile von
Rüdesheim
Frankenthal 8
Höllenberg 9
Hinterkirch 10
Berg Kaiserstein-
fels 11

GROSSLAGE BURGWEG
(Einzellagen 1–7,
11–22, 24, 26, 27,
28)

Rüdesheim
Berg Roseneck 12
Berg Rottland 13
Berg Schloßberg 14

Bischofsberg 15
Drachenstein 16
Kirchenpfad 17
Klosterberg 18
Klosterlay 19
Magdalenen-
kreuz 20
Rosengarten 21

Geisenheim
Rothenberg 22
Kläuserweg 23
Fuchsberg 24
Kilzberg 25
Mäuerchen 26
Mönchspfad 27
Schloßgarten 28
Klaus 29 T

GROSSLAGE ERNTEBRINGER
(Einzellagen 23, 25,
28, 30–35, 37, 44,
A;
29, 42, 43 teilweise)

Johannisberg
Ortsteil von Geisen-
heim
Klaus 29 T
Schwarzenstein 30
Vogelsang 31
Hölle 32
Hansenberg 33
Goldatzel 34
Mittelhölle 35
Schloß Johannis-
berg (Ortsteil) A

GROSSLAGE HONIGBERG
(Einzellagen 36,
38–41, B; 29, 42,
43 teilweise)

Winkel
Ortsteil von
Oestrich-Winkel
Klaus 29 T
Gutenberg 36
Dachsberg 37

Schloßberg 38
Jesuitengarten 39
Hasensprung 40
Bienengarten 41
Schloß Vollrads
(Ortsteil) B

Mittelheim
Ortsteil von
Oestrich-Winkel
St. Nikolaus 42
Edelmann 43
Goldberg 44

GROSSLAGE GOTTESTHAL
(Einzellagen 46, 47,
C; 45 teilweise)

Oestrich
Ortsteil von
Oestrich-Winkel
Klosterg 45
Lenchen 46
Doosberg 47
Schloß Reichharts-
hausen
(Ortsteil) C

GROSSLAGE DEUTELSBERG
(Einzellagen 48–55,
60–67)

Hattenheim
Ortsteil von Eltville
Mannberg 48
Nußbrunnen 49
Wisselbrunnen 50
Hassel 51
Heiligenberg 52
Schützenhaus 53
Engelmannsberg 54
Pfaffenberg 55
Steinberg
(Ortsteil) D

GROSSLAGE MEHRHÖLZCHEN
(Einzellagen 56–58;
45 teilweise)

Hallgarten
Ortsteil von
Oestrich-Winkel
Schönhell 56
Würzgarten 57
Jungfer 58
Hendelberg 59

Erbach
Ortsteil von Eltville
Marcobrunn 60
Schloßberg 61
Siegelsberg 62
Honigberg 63
Michelmark 64
Hohenrain 65
Steinmorgen 66
Rheinhell 67

GROSSLAGE HEILIGENSTOCK
(Einzellagen 68–71)

Kiedrich
Klosterberg 68
Gräfenberg 69
Wasseros 70
Sandgrub 71

GROSSLAGE STEINMÄCHER
(Einzellagen 72–90,
92–97)

Eltville
Taubenberg 72
Langenstück 73
Sonnenberg 74
Rheinberg 75
Sandgrub 76

Rauenthal
Ortsteil von Eltville
Baiken 77
Gehrn 78
Wülfen 79
Rothenberg 80
Langenstück 81
Nonnenberg 82

Martinsthal
Ortsteil von Eltville
Wildsau 83
Langenberg 84
Rödchen 85

Niederwalluf
Ortsteil von Walluf
Berg-Bildstock 86
Walkenberg 87
Oberberg 88

Oberwalluf
Ortsteil von Walluf
Fitusberg 89
Langenstück 90

Wiesbaden
Neroberg 91
(großlagenfrei)

– Ortsteil Schier-stein
Dachsberg 92
Hölle 93

– Ortsteil Frauen-stein
Marschall 94
Homberg 95
Herrnberg 96

– Ortsteil Dotzheim
Judenkirch 97

GROSSLAGE DAUBHAUS
(Einzellagen
98–114)

Mainz
Ortsteil Kostheim
Reichesthal 98 T
Weiß Erd 99
Steig 100
Berg 101 T

Hochheim
Reichesthal 98 T
Berg 101 T
Königin Victoria-
berg 102
Hofmeister 103
Stielweg 104
Sommerheil 105
Hölle 106
Domdechaney 107
Kirchenstück 108
Stein 109
Herrnberg 110 T

Wicker
Stein 111
Mönchsgewann 112
König Wilhelms-
berg 113
Nonnenberg 114

Flörsheim
Herrnberg 110 T

Frankfurt
Lohrberger Hang*

Böddiger
(Landkreis
Melsungen)
Berg*

Nahe

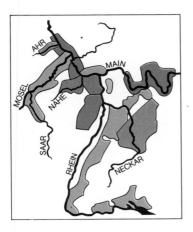

The Nahe is a small, peaceful wineland, as yet untouched by mass tourism, where the bonviveur can also relish peace and quiet.

The idyllic Nahe valley offers noble wines and romantic, out-of-the-way places. It enjoys a temperate climate. The small tributaries to right and left of the Nahe help to create a landscape as richly varied as are the wines that grow within it. According to the site where the vines are planted, there are similarities to Mosel, Rheingau or Palatinate wines, for Nahe wine combines the fruity, racy taste of Rhine wine with the lively, pithy aroma of a Mosel. Each of the varied soil conditions – quartzite, slate, coloured sandstone, loam and loess – influences the wine's taste, so that the wine-lover can find the right type of wine for every mood: light and fruity for ordinary, everyday drinking, wine of a stronger character for quiet, contemplative hours, and a noble vintage wine for festive occasions.

The "sampling room" of the German wine regions

Enthusiasts have declared the Nahe to be their "wine-sampling room" because of the proliferation of romantic wine villages and their hospitable inns and taverns.

The first wine-growing communities appear along the B48 in the direction of Bad Kreuznach from Bingerbrück: Münster-Sarmsheim, Laubenheim, Langenlonsheim, Bretzenheim, and by turning right just after Sarmsheim, the road passes near many restful little wine villages, among them being Dorsheim, Rümmels-

The Nahe region near Niederhausen

Müller-Thurgau

Main types of vine in the Nahe:

Müller-Thurgau	31.0%
Silvaner	24.3%
Riesling	22.5%

Data and facts

Geographical notes: *The wine-growing region extends upstream from the Rhine estuary near Bingen as far as Kirn, and then spreads through the many small valleys of the Guldenbach and Gräfenbach, and those of the Glan and Alsenz rivers.*

Climate: *The sheltering Soonwald (forest) in the north-west and the heat-retaining hilly countryside of the east assure a temperate climate, free from hard winter frosts.*

Soil: *The soil consists of quartzite and slate along the Nahe's lower reaches; of porphyr, melaphyr and coloured sandstone along its middle and upper reaches; and in the vicinity of Bad Kreuznach additionally of weathered clay, sandstone, loess and loam soil.*

Cultivated area: *4,469 ha, interspersed with other agricultural land, 2 Districts, 7 General Sites, 327 Individual Sites.*

Types of vine: *80% of the cultivation is divided between three major types: Müller-Thurgau (1,384 ha); Silvaner (1,087 ha); Riesling (1,005 ha). Morio-Muskat and some newly evolved types, while some of the red wine species are only of local significance.*

Yield: *On average 1975–1977: 415,000 hl, it amounts to 4.4% of the German must harvest.*

Production structure: *Some larger wine estates, but mainly mixed middle-class and peasant smallholdings; winegrowers' co-operatives market 20% of yield. The rest is taken up by wine traders, partly active as growers, or connected with growers' associations.*

Typical characteristics of the region: *The wine festival "Rund um die Naheweinstrasse" is the only German wine festival embracing a whole region.*

The "Fausthaus", an historical Inn

Houses on the bridge at Bad Kreuznach

Steep, rock formations at Norheim

heim and Windesheim – although nearly all the place-names end in "heim" in the Nahe region, each town and village offers its own personal brand of traditional hospitality.

The Naheweinstrasse starts immediately after Bad Kreuznach, the centre of the Nahegau. This is a German region where very little rain falls. Spring starts early and autumn is long – ideal conditions for viticulture. Bad Kreuznach itself is famous for its thermal springs (Nahe wine can additionally aid therapy, by helping to make the cure as agreeable as possible to the patient!)

The six hundred year-old bridge at Bad Kreuznach carries unusual Dutch-style houses, while the historical Fausthaus, where many tempting Nahe wines can be sampled, also merits a visit. Beyond, lies the lovely scenery between the Nahe, the Alsenz and the Glan rivers.

The Naheweinstrasse runs alongside the peacefully flowing river, where some of the villages have been connected with viticulture for the last 2000 years. History relates that the Roman legionaries brought vines to the Nahe, because they did not want to be without their favourite drink. Ancient Roman tools, wine-jugs, sculp-

tures, and mosaic-floors remain as witnesses to these early times. In the Middle Ages, monks and ecclesiastical princes spread the knowledge of viticulture far and wide, and sometimes knights even fought battles over Nahe wine.

An area full of discoveries

At Bad Münster am Stein, or Sobernheim, all the nuances of Nahe wine can be savoured and typical local dishes such as Spiessbraten or Winzerplatte with home-made sausage enjoyed. A particularly pleasant characteristic of Nahe wine is the richness and subtle variety in taste and aroma offered by the Rieslings, the Silvaners and the Müller-Thurgaus.

In late August, local inhabitants drink Federweisser, a milky-white, still fermenting – and strong – young wine.

Only a few minutes drive from Bad Münster am Stein stand the porphyr rocks of the "Rotenfels", the steepest rock-face in Germany outside the Alps, and somewhat similar to rock formations in the Dolomites.

Historically interesting places abound: The castle of Ebernburg, at the mouth of the Alsenz river, is an impressive fortress built in the 11th century. Under Franz von Sickingen (1481–1523) it came to be called "Herberge der Gerechtigkeit" ("refuge of justice"). It has seen many crowned heads and famous men, and its name is honoured in German history as a focal point of the idea of a free German State.

The castle near medieval Meisenheim is one of many along the valley of the river Glan. The wine-growing community of Odernheim, mentioned in documents from 976 AD, enjoyed considerable prosperity in the 15th century, and profited for a long time from the viticultural efforts of the monastery and pilgrim centre of Disibodenberg.

Much more can be learned about the history and countryside of the region by attending a weekend seminar for wine-lovers which includes a tour through wine-cellars and sampling.

More detailed information, also about the wine festival "Rund um die Naheweinstrasse", can be obtained from:

Weinland Nahe e.V.
Kornmarkt 6
6550 Bad Kreuznach
Western Germany

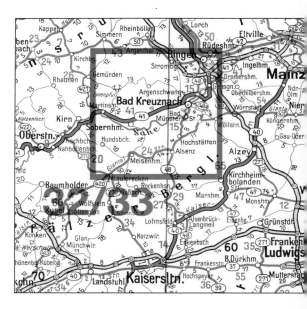

Visitors' Gazetteer

Bad Kreuznach: *Kauzenburg mit Bergfried (castle); Nahebrücke (ancient bridge: 1300 AD) with houses; Nikolauskirche (church 1266 AD); ancient Roman mosaic floor; Dr.-Karl-Geib-Museum.*

Bad Münster am Stein: *Nearby: ascent to the Rheingrafenstein; to the south lies the wine-village Ebernburg with the Sickingerschloss (8th century); to the north-west Rotenfels (highest rock face outside Alps).*

Meisenheim: *Ancient towngate near the Glanbrücke (bridge); Herzog-Wolfgang-Haus; town hall; Meisenbrunnen (fountain).*

Monzingen: *Particularly beautiful timbered houses, such as the "Alte Haus" (1589); late Gothic church.*

Odernheim: *Town hall (1541); Pfalz-Zweibrückener Schlösschen (small palace); ascent to the Disibodenberg; old monastery ruins.*

Sobernheim: *Early Christian church (976); old patrician houses.*

Waldböckelheim: *Kurmainzische Schaffnerei (steward's offices under the ancient electorate of Mainz); ruins of castle Böckelheim.*

Vineyards
by the middle reaches of the Nahe

Bereich Kreuznach

GROSSLAGE SCHLOSSKAPELLE

Bingen
Ortsteil Bingerbrück
Hildegardisbrünnchen 1
Klostergarten 2 T
Abtei Ruppertsberg 3 T
Römerberg 4 T

Weiler
Klostergarten 2 T
Abtei Ruppertsberg 3 T
Römerberg 4 T

Münster-Sarmsheim
Römerberg 4 a
Rheinberg 5
Kapellenberg 6
Dautenpflänzer 7
Trollberg 8
Pittersberg 9
Liebehöll 10
Steinkopf 11
Königsschloß 12

Rümmelsheim
Steinköpfchen 13
(Burg Layen)
Schloßberg 14
(Burg Layen)
Hölle 15
(Burg Layen)
Rothenberg 16
(Burg Layen)
Johannisberg 17

Waldlaubersheim
Domberg 18
Bingerweg 19
Alteburg 20

Hörnchen 21
Lieseberg 22
Otterberg 23

Genheim
Ortsteil von Waldalgesheim
Rossel 24

Eckenroth
Felsenberg 25
Hölle 26

Schweppenhausen
Steyerberg 27
Schloßgarten 28

Windesheim
Saukopf 29
Sonnenmorgen 30
Hölle 31
Rosenberg 32
Preiselberg 33
Hausgiebel 34
Schäfchen 35
Römerberg 36
Fels 37

Guldental, Ortsteile Heddesheim und Waldhilbersheim
Apostelberg 38
Honigberg 39

St. Martin 40
Sonnenberg 41
Teufelsküche 42
Hölle 43
Hipperich 44
Rosenteich 45

Dorsheim
Burgberg 46
Honigberg 47
Goldloch 48
Pittermännchen 49
Klosterpfad 50
Laurenziweg 51
Jungbrunnen 52
Nixenberg 53
Trollberg 54

Laubenheim
Vogelsang 55
Karthäuser 56
St. Remigiusberg 57
Fuchsen 58
Junker 59
Hörnchen 60
Krone 61

GROSSLAGE SONNENBORN

Langenlonsheim
Löhrer Berg 62
Bergborn 63
Lauerweg 64
Königsschild 65
Rothenberg 66
Steinchen 67
St. Antoniusweg 68

GROSSLAGE PFARRGARTEN

Schöneberg
Schäfersley 69
Sonnenberg 70

Spabrücken
Höll 71

Dalberg
Schloßberg 72
Ritterhölle
Sonnenberg 74

Hergenfeld
Mönchberg 75
Sonnenberg 76
Herrschaftsgarten 77

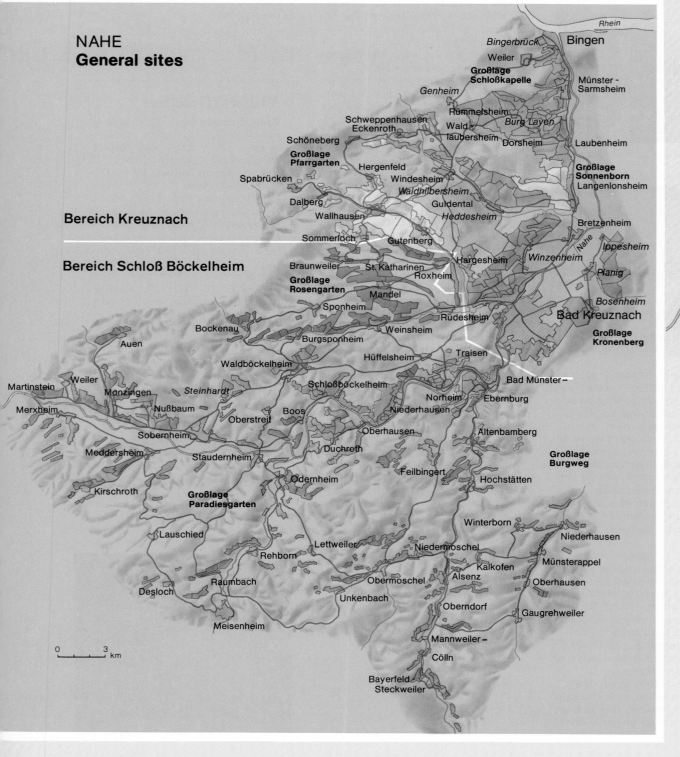

NAHE
General sites

0   3 km

32

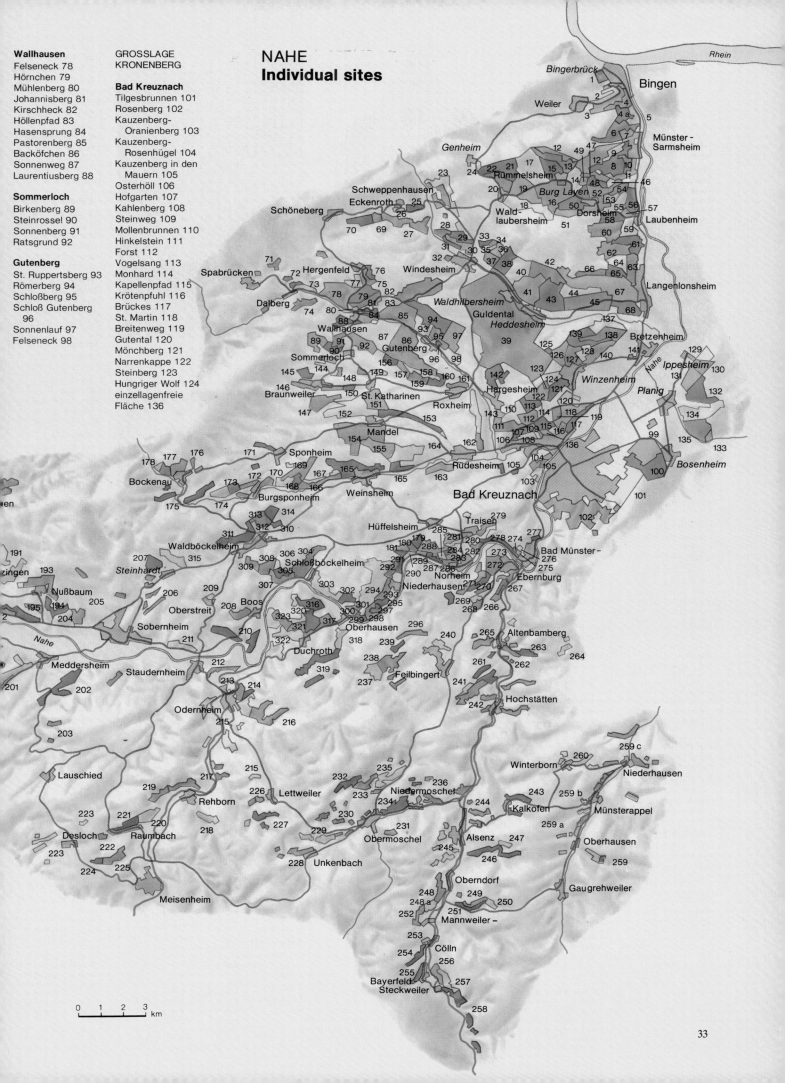

NAHE
Individual sites

Wallhausen
Felseneck 78
Hörnchen 79
Mühlenberg 80
Johannisberg 81
Kirschheck 82
Höllenpfad 83
Hasensprung 84
Pastorenberg 85
Backöfchen 86
Sonnenweg 87
Laurentiusberg 88

Sommerloch
Birkenberg 89
Steinrossel 90
Sonnenberg 91
Ratsgrund 92

Gutenberg
St. Ruppertsberg 93
Römerberg 94
Schloßberg 95
Schloß Gutenberg 96
Sonnenlauf 97
Felseneck 98

GROSSLAGE
KRONENBERG

Bad Kreuznach
Tilgesbrunnen 101
Rosenberg 102
Kauzenberg-
 Oranienberg 103
Kauzenberg-
 Rosenhügel 104
Kauzenberg in den
 Mauern 105
Osterhöll 106
Hofgarten 107
Kahlenberg 108
Steinweg 109
Mollenbrunnen 110
Hinkelstein 111
Forst 112
Vogelsang 113
Monhard 114
Kapellenpfad 115
Krötenpfuhl 116
Brückes 117
St. Martin 118
Breitenweg 119
Gutental 120
Mönchberg 121
Narrenkappe 122
Steinberg 123
Hungriger Wolf 124
einzellagenfreie
Fläche 136

0 1 2 3 km

An ancient building in Monzingen · The grape harvest below the Rotenfels

Vineyards as far as the eye can see in the Nahe

34

Rheinhessen

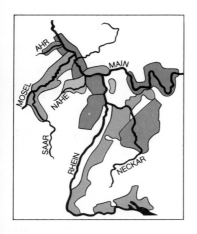

The Rheinhessen landscape seen from Harxheim

Rheinhessen does not lie politically in the federal state of Hessen (Hesse) but in the state of Rheinland-Pfalz. Framed by the glistening Nahe and the sweeping flow of the Rhine, it lies like a peaceful island. Spring, with its snow-white fruit-tree blossoms, or autumn, when a mild, golden sun moves from hill to hill, lighting up the valleys in a blaze of warm colours, provide an unforgettably beautiful wine country.

Sheltered from bad weather in the west by the Hunsrück mountains and the Pfälzer Wald (forest), and in the north and east by the Taunus mountains and the forest of Odenwald, the vines flourish in a mild, temperate climate. Rheinhessen and Rheinpfalz are the two largest and most productive wine regions in Germany; Rheinhessen holds first place in the export market, and not simply because of the popularity in Britain and America of the famous Liebfraumilch. Varying soil conditions, different types of vine and sites encourage the growing of a wide range of wines, from palatable table wines to the highest quality.

The wines of Rheinhessen have a very particular style, yet admirers of delicate, harmonious wines will find their taste catered for there, as do those who prefer more robust, fruity types.

Along the Rhine from Bingen, and across the hills

"Bingium" was the name of the Roman fortress in Drusus' days, standing where the castle of Burg Klopp today serves as Bingen's town hall. In the castle's tower is the Bingen Museum, where the region's history can be traced. In Bingen, the wine-lovers particularly appreciate Schlossberg, Schwätzerchen and Scharlachberg: robust wines of a piquant flavour which grow well in the quartzite-slate or porphyr soil of Bingen's countryside.

Poetry has strong associations with Rheinhessen. Goethe wrote his famous

"wine sermon" for the consecration ceremony of the St. Rochus chapel after it had been rebuilt. The internationally-known German Symbolist poet, Stefan George, was born in Bingen. The house still stands there.

The wine and sparkling wine cellars of the area offer a very wide variety of interest

St. Rochus Chapel

at this the intersection of four wine-regions; Nahe, Mittelrhein, Rheinhessen, and Rheingau on the other side of the Rhine. The German wine-trade and its allied industries is never more in stronger evidence.

On the B9 from Bingen towards Mainz is the red wine town of Ingelheim where relics dating back to Charlemagne's "Kaiserpfalz", a Carolingian bath, and an ancient Roman aquaduct can be seen. Eating also offers unusual pleasures – at asparagus time – while Portugieser provides a refreshing drink, as does Spät-burgunder. Frühburgunder also flourishes at Ingelheim.

Another 15 km on is the 2000 year-old "golden" city of Mainz, where wine is

Scheurebe

Main types of vine in Rheinhessen:

Müller-Thurgau	33.8%
Silvaner	24.3%
Scheurebe	6.7%
Riesling	4.9%
Portugieser	4.0%

The "Beautiful Lady of Mainz"
(c. 1510), Mainz Cathedral

and always has been a way of life as well as a marketable commodity. History abounds: the cathedral, many churches and museums and the places where Johannes Gutenberg (1400–1468), the great printmaster lived and worked. Refreshment can be had at the many wine taverns.

Bundesstrasse 9 along the banks of the Rhine – top quality wines grow here – leads to Laubenheim, Bodenheim, and Nackenheim, where the German author and playwright Carl Zuckmayer was born; his "Der fröhliche Weinberg" (The Merry Vineyard) is a play of importance. As a native of Rheinhessen, Zuckmayer characterized the wines of his homeland as "laughing wines" and thought that of all the "little" wines (Schoppenweine), those from Rheinhessen were the most amiable and the most wholesome – such as the typical wines of Nackenheim, Nierstein and Oppenheim, which grow on red sandstone and sandy clay soil. Guntersblum is

The Nierstein wine festival...

... with a valiant knight

another area that has known viticulture since Roman days from where the country road runs parallel to Bundesstrasse 9 on its way to Worms, via Alsheim, Mettenheim and Osthofen, passing, en route, the enchanting view of vineyards across the Rhine valley from the top of a vineyard.

How "Monk" turned into "Milch"

Although 65% of the town of Worms was a victim of the war, traces of many epochs in its long history have survived: remnants of the old city walls; the cathedral; noteworthy churches; the oldest synagogue in Germany; and, of course, Worms' world-famous wine association with "Liebfrauenmilch". The name goes back to the vineyards of the Liebfrauenstift, a monastery where monks made wine, and "Minch", which meant monk, was slowly changed to "Milch" (milk).

A 17th-century wine press at Ockenheim

Data and facts

Geographical notes: *Three towns, Bingen, Mainz and Worms, form a large triangle of wine-growing land. In the north and the east the Rhine is a natural border.*
Climate: *Taunus (mountain range) and Odenwald in the north and the east keep cold winds off.*
Soil: *The Rhine basin near Mainz – once covered by the sea – shows various types of soil formed by sediments and weathering processes. The inter-glacial periods were marked in this region by gigantic sandstorms, depositing loess, which today forms the greater part of the soil. These various soils give the nuances of a mild, flowery, bouquet to the wine – the main characteristic of Rheinhessen wine.*

Deep loam soil

Cultivated area: *Rheinhessen, with a cultivated area of 22,565 ha is one of the two largest Anbaugebiete in Germany. A continuous ribbon of vineyards lies alongside the Rhine, and there are large islands of wine-growing areas in the hilly countryside. 3 districts, 23 General Sites, and approximately 435 Individual Sites.*
Types of vine: *Traditionally, the Silvaner used to be the major vine in this region (5,492 ha), but today the Müller-Thurgau (7,618 ha) has overtaken it. On the heavier marl soil the Riesling's pithy, racy wines flourish (1,096 ha). Those grown on the lower, new, red sandstone soil along the Rhine are of a particularly fine, spicey character. The Alzeyer Scheurebe (1,516 ha) and Morio-Muscat (1,127 ha) are today gaining in importance. The Portugieser (897 ha) has its established place and produces smooth, palatable red wine, but the best red wine is the blue Spätburgunder (90 ha) of Ingelheim. New vines are also strongly represented, including Faber (540 ha), Bacchus (397 ha), Huxelrebe (342 ha), Perle (118 ha), Karner (326 ha) and Siegerrebe (122 ha).*
Yield: *On average 1975–1977: 2.2m hl; Rheinhessen produces 23.3% of the total German must harvest.*
Production structure: *Mainly peasant smallholdings, plus a number of largish wine-estates; large-scale wine cellars run by the wine-trade, and local growers' co-operatives undertake marketing. Near towns and big transit routes the number of growers marketing their own produce increases.*

A view of the Katherinenkirche of Oppenheim

History of the "Wonnegau"

Old wine traditions have been retained especially in the small, picturesque villages away from the Rheinstrasse, in Westhofen, for instance, or, in a northerly direction, at Bechtheim, where viticulture has flourished since Carolingian times. The name alone of this Bereich promises pleasure: Wonnegau – "Wonne" means "bliss". History can be traced elsewhere: further south in Flörsheim-Dalsheim, there is an ancient town wall; in Mölsheim, a Renaissance palace. A hearty "Winzerfrühstück" (vintager's breakfast) can be had in the unchanged old part of the city of Alzey, which lies north. In neighbouring Albig, Bornheim and Gau-Odernheim, quality wine grows on the southern slopes. Armsheim, which has one of the most beautiful village churches in Rheinhessen, is also within easy distance.

Relaxing over wine

Rich in tradition – dedicated to progress

The Zentralkellerei (central wine cellar) of the Rhenish wine-growers' co-operatives lies in the centre of the hilly country of Gau-Bickelheim. 5000 small wine-growers deliver their produce to this modern wine cellar which can accommodate 28 mill. litres of wine in casks. It is open to visitors. Good wines flourish all over the area. Neu-Bamberg, with an ancient arch-tower at its entrance, its ruined castle and prehistoric site provides an excellent place to rest – and sample wine.

Returning to Mainz the route goes through Worrstadt, a well-known wine town, which has ancient ramparts and a famous old fountain. There were human settlements here as far back as 4000 BC, and the place was fortified even before it received its name in 779 AD.

An easy detour to the river Selz, offers the opportunity to visit Elsheim, Schwabenheim or Gross-Winternheim. Wine grows everywhere and tastes a little different, according to immediate growing conditions. Variations are particularly great – and pleasurable – in Rheinhessen, because newly developed types of vine have been introduced.

You can obtain more information about Rheinhessen – also about its vintage festivals – from:

Rheinhessenweine e.V.
117er Ehrenhof 5
6500 Mainz
Western Germany

Visitors' Gazetteer

Alzey: *Town Hall; Nikolaikirche (church); town wall; Hexenturm (witches' tower); watch-tower on the Wartberg; museum in the Burggrafenamt.*
Bingen: *Burg Klopp (castle) with museum in castle-tower; Rochuskapelle (chapel); Mäuseturm (mouse-tower).*
Bodenheim: *Town hall; chapel of Maria Oberndorf.*
Dalsheim: *700 years old city wall with seven towers.*
Dittelsheim-Hessloch: *Wine-castle on Kloppberg.*
Guntersblum: *Church with Norman tower; Adelshöfe; ancient wine-cellars.*
Ingelheim: *Remnants of Kaiserpfalz and medieval ramparts; Burgkirche (castle-church).*
Laubenheim: *Old dwellings; baroque church; Schott'sche Villa (Richard Wagner).*
Mainz: *Cathedral of St. Martin; Diözesanmuseum (museum); Gutenbergmuseum; Stephanskirche (church); former Prince Elector's palace; Zeughaus (arsenal).*
Nackenheim: *Town hall (timbered buildings); church; museum.*
Neu-Bamberg: *Historical buildings; castle-ruin (1251).*
Nierstein: *Signal tower; mountain church of St. Kilian; famous wine-cellars.*
Oppenheim: *Gautor (arch); Luther house; town hall; Katharinen Museum.*
Worms: *Cathedral; St.-Paulus-Kirche (church and monastery); St.-Martin-Kirche (church); Liebfrauenkirche (church); Luther monument; Andreasstift Museum.*

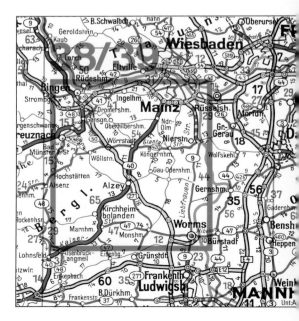

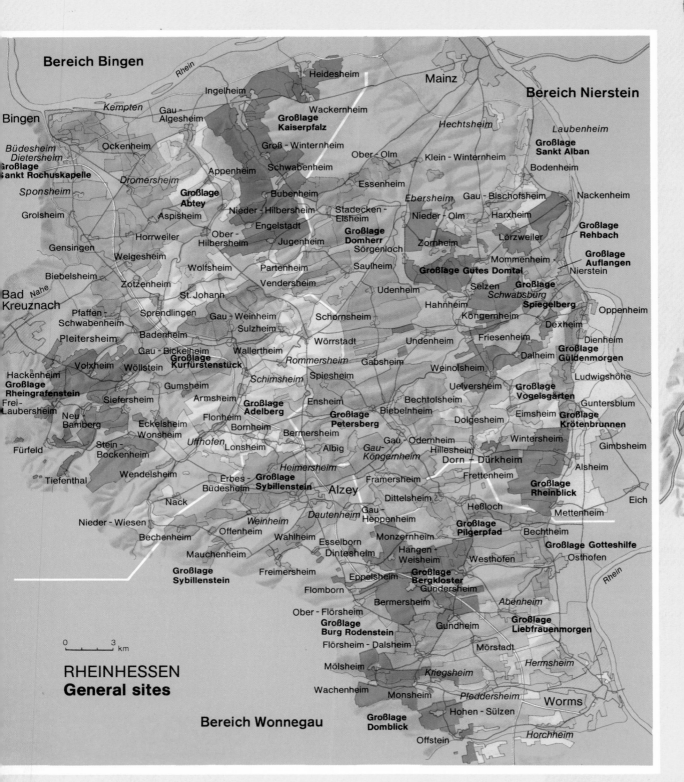

Bereich Bingen

Bereich Nierstein

Bereich Wonnegau

Bingen

Mainz

Worms

Bad Kreuznach

RHEINHESSEN
General sites

Großlage Kaiserpfalz

Großlage Abtey

Großlage Domherr

Großlage Sankt Rochuskapelle

Großlage Rheingrafenstein

Großlage Kurfürstenstück

Großlage Adelberg

Großlage Petersberg

Großlage Sybillenstein

Großlage Sybillenstein

Großlage Burg Rodenstein

Großlage Bergkloster

Großlage Domblick

Großlage Sankt Alban

Großlage Rehbach

Großlage Auflangen

Großlage Spiegelberg

Großlage Gutes Domtal

Großlage Güldenmorgen

Großlage Vogelsgärten

Großlage Krötenbrunnen

Großlage Rheinblick

Großlage Pilgerpfad

Großlage Gotteshilfe

Großlage Liebfrauenmorgen

0 ___ 3 km

Bingen
Büdesheim
Dietersheim
Sponsheim
Grolsheim
Gensingen
Bad Kreuznach
Hackenheim
Frei-Laubersheim
Fürfeld
Tiefenthal

1
7
8
67
66
68
70
69
71
72
73
81
77
76 a
75
74
Fürfeld
Tiefentha

RHEINHESSEN
Individual sites

Sankt Johann
Klostergarten 54
Steinberg 55
Geyersberg 56

Wolfsheim
Götzenborn 57
Osterberg 58
Sankt Kathrin 59

Partenheim
Sankt Georgen 60
Steinberg 61

GROSSLAGE
RHEINGRAFEN-
STEIN

Pleitersheim
Sternberg 62

Volxheim
Mönchberg 63
Alte Römerstraße
64 T
Liebfrau 65

Hackenheim
Klostergarten 66
Sonnenberg 67
Galgenberg 68
Gewürzgarten 69
Kirchberg 70

Freilaubersheim
Alte Römerstraße 64 T
Kirchberg 70 a
Fels 71
Rheingrafenberg 72
Reichskeller 73

Tiefenthal
Graukatz 74

Fürfeld
Kapellenberg 75
Eichelberg 76
Steige 77

Stein-Bockenheim
Sonnenberg 78

Wonsheim
Sonnenberg 78 a
Hölle 79
Martinsberg 85 T

Neu-Bamberg
Eichelberg 76 a
Kletterberg 80
Kirschwingert 81
Heerkretz 82

Siefersheim
Heerkretz 82 a
Goldenes Horn 83
Höllberg 84
Martinsberg 85 T

Wöllstein
Haarberg-Katzensteg 86
Ölberg 87
Äffchen 88
Hölle 89

Eckelsheim
Kirchberg 90
Eselstreiber 91
Sonnenköpfchen 92

GROSSLAGE ADELBERG

Nieder-Wiesen
Wingertsberg 93

Nack
Ahrenberg 94

Wendelsheim
Heiligenpfad 95
Steigerberg 96

Flonheim
Pfaffenberg 97
Bingerberg 98
La Roche 99
Rotenpfad 100
Klostergarten 101
Geisterberg 102 T

Erbes-Büdesheim
Geisterberg 102 T
Vogelsang 103

Bornheim
Hähnchen 104
Hütte-Terrassen 105
Kirchenstück 106
Schönberg 107 T

Lonsheim
Schönberg 107 T
Mandelberg 108

Bermersheim v. d. H.
Klostergarten 109
Hildegardisberg 110

Armsheim
Goldstückchen 111
Geiersberg 112
Leckerberg 113

Ensheim
Kachelberg 114 a

Wörrstadt
Kachelberg 114
Rheingrafenberg 115

Sulzheim
Greifenberg 116
Honigberg 117
Schildberg 118

GROSSLAGE KURFÜRSTEN-STÜCK

Gumbsheim
Schloßhölle 119 T

Gau-Bickelheim
Bockshaut 120 T
Saukopf 121
Kapelle 122

Wallertheim
Vogelsang 123
Heil 124

Wöllstein
Schloßhölle 119 T
Bockshaut 120 T

Gau-Weinheim
Wißberg 125
Kaisergarten 126
Geyersberg 127

Vendersheim
Sonnenberg 128
Goldberg 129

GROSSLAGE KAISERPFALZ

Jugenheim
St. Georgenberg 130
Goldberg 131
Hasensprung 132
Heiligen-häuschen 133

Engelstadt
Adelpfad 134
Römerberg 135

Bubenheim
Kallenberg 136
Honigberg 137

Schwabenheim
Sonnenberg 138
Schloßberg 139 a
Klostergarten 140

Ingelheim
(mit Ortsteil Groß-Winternheim)
Schloßberg 139
Klosterbruder 141
Bockstein 142
Heilig-häuschen 143
Schloß Westerhaus 144
Sonnenhang 145
Rheinhöhe 146
Sonnenberg 147
Burgberg 148
Kirchenstück 149
Täuscherspfad 150
Horn 151
Pares 152
Steinacker 153
Höllenweg 154
Rotes Kreuz 155
Lottenstück 156
Rabenkopf 157

Wackernheim
Rabenkopf 157 a
Schwalben 158
Steinberg 159

Heidesheim
Geißberg 160
Steinacker 161
Höllenberg 162

Bereich Nierstein

GROSSLAGE SANKT ALBAN

Mainz
Ortsteil Hechtsheim
Kirchenstück 163

– Ortsteil Lauben-heim
Johannisberg 164
Edelmann 165
Klosterberg 166

– Ortsteil Ebers-heim
Sand 167
Hüttberg 168
Weinkeller 169

Bodenheim
Mönchspfad 170
Burgweg 171
Ebersberg 172
Heitersbrünnchen 173
Reichsritterstift 174
Westrum 175
Hoch 176
Kapelle 177
Leidhecke 178
Silberberg 179
Kreuzberg 180

Gau-Bischofsheim
Glockenberg 181
Pfaffenweg 182
Kellersberg 183
Herrnberg 184

Harxheim
Börnchen 185
Schloßberg 186
Lieth 187

Lörzweiler
Ölgild 188
Hohberg 189

GROSSLAGE DOMHERR

Klein-Winternheim
Geiershöll 190
Villenkeller 191
Herrgottshaus 192

Ober-Olm
Kapellenberg 193

Essenheim
Teufelspfad 194
Römerberg 195

Stadecken-Elsheim
Bockstein 196
Tempelchen 197
Blume 198
Lenchen 199
Spitzberg 200

Saulheim
Probstey 201
Schloßberg 202
Hölle 203
Haubenberg 204
Pfaffengarten 205
Heiligenhaus 206

Udenheim
Goldberg 207
Sonnenberg 208
Kirchberg 209

Schornsheim
Mönchspfad 210
Ritterberg 211
Sonnenhang 212

Gabsheim
Dornpfad 213
Kirchberg 214
Rosengarten 215

With vineyards in the Budenheim, Mainz-Finthen and Mainz-Drais sections not included in the individual sites.

GROSSLAGE GUTES DOMTAL

Nieder-Olm
Klosterberg 216
Sonnenberg 217
Goldberg 218

Lörzweiler
Königstuhl 219

Nackenheim
Schmitts-kapellchen 220

Nierstein
Pfaffenkappe 221

Dexheim
Doktor 222

Dalheim
Steinberg 223
Kranzberg 224
Altdörr 225

Weinolsheim
Hohberg 226
Kehr 227

Friesenheim
Altdörr 225 a
Bergpfad 228
Knopf 229

Undenheim
Goldberg 230

Köngernheim
Ortsteil von Gau-Odernheim
Goldgrube 231

Selzen
Rheinpforte 232
Gottesgarten 233
Osterberg 234

Hahnheim
Knopf 235
Moosberg 236

Sörgenloch
Moosberg 236 a

Zornheim
Vogelsang 237
Guldenmorgen 238
Mönchbäumchen 239
Dachgewann 240
Pilgerweg 241

Mommenheim
Osterberg 234 a
Silbergrube 242
Kloppenberg 243

GROSSLAGE SPIEGELBERG

Nackenheim
Engelsberg 244
Rothenberg 245

Nierstein
Rosenberg 246
Klostergarten 247
Findling 248
Kirchplatte 249
Schloß Hohen-rechen 250
Ebersberg 251
Bildstock 252
Brückchen 253
Paterberg 254
Hölle 255

GROSSLAGE REHBACH

Nierstein
Pettenthal 256
Brudersberg 257
Hipping 258
Goldene Luft 259

GROSSLAGE AUFLANGEN

Nierstein
Kranzberg 260
Zehnmorgen 261
Bergkirche 262
Glöck 263
Ölberg 264
Heiligenbaum 265
Orbel 266
Schloß Schwabs-burg 267

GROSSLAGE GÜLDENMORGEN

Oppenheim
Daubhaus 268
Zuckerberg 269
Herrenberg 270 T
Sackträger 271
Schützenhütte 272
Kreuz 273 T
Gutleuthaus 274

The Roman heritage

The Romans were again principally responsible for introducing change to this particular area when they settled there in 58 B.C. Both banks of the river were constantly fought over; Romans and Teutons fought for them; while the Franconians, Alemans and Saxons occupied the left bank. Mass migration brought constant change: Attila the Hun drove his hordes through these lands. The Nibelungen saga, still very much alive in Worms and

A view of Schloss Alzey

Dienheim
Herrenberg 270 T
Kreuz 273 T
Falkenberg 275
Siliusbrunnen 276
Höhlchen 277
Tafelstein 278 T

Uelversheim
Tafelstein 278 T

GROSSLAGE KRÖTENBRUNNEN

Oppenheim
Schloßberg 279
Schloß 280 T
Paterhof 281 T
Herrengarten 282 T

Dienheim
Schloß 280 T
Paterhof 281 T
Herrengarten 282 T

Ludwigshöhe
Honigberg 283

Guntersblum
Steinberg 284
Sonnenhang 285
Sonnenberg 286
Eiserne Hand 287
Sankt Julianen-brunnen 288

Gimbsheim
Sonnenweg 289
Liebfrauenthal 290

Alsheim
Goldberg 291 T

Eich
Goldberg 291 T

Mettenheim
Goldberg 291 T

Hillesheim
Altenberg 292
Sonnheil 293

Wintersheim
Frauengarten 294

Dolgesheim
Kreuzberg 295
Schützenhütte 296

Alzey, originated in those far-off days.

After a "golden age" under Charlemagne in the 9th century the Normans came, to be followed a few decades later, by the Hungarians. Then, in the 13th century, robber-barons held sway over the Rhine, right up to the time of Rudolf von Hapsburg, who brought peace back to the region.

Rheinhessen wine has survived

Nothing in Rheinhessen has survived all the upheavals of its history as well as its viticulture. It has not only survived, but developed into a unique culture. Throughout the ages, people found wine to be the only stable thing in an ever-changing environment and protected it.

Archaeological finds prove that the Romans brought viticulture to Rheinhessen in approximately the 2nd century AD and extant documents show that by the 8th century a number of well-tended vineyards existed. Although Charlemagne probably did not personally introduce viticulture, he certainly did much to encourage and expand it, especially around Ingelheim in the "Kaiserpfalz" (Emperor's Palatinate). Much merit is due to the monasteries, whose role in viticulture history is a truly great one; but the special characteristics of Rheinhessen's wine are due, first and foremost, to the untiring work of the vintner. "He who is not a vintner is not a true Rhinehessian" the local proverb goes, and, travelling through the countryside between Bingen and Worms, or going into the hilly hinterland confirms that there is hardly an inhabitant in the region who is not at least a part-time vintner.

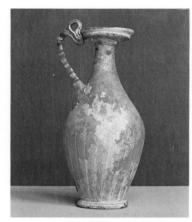

Roman finds at Mainz:
1. "Good Health" beaker;
2. Glass jug; 3. Glass beakers
with coloured knobs

Rheinpfalz

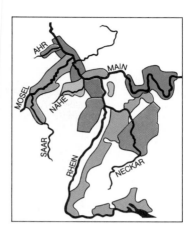

The Deutsche Weinstrasse (German wine route) applies to the north-south route stretching along the foot of the Haardt mountain range from Bockenheim to the Deutsches Weintor (German wine gate) near Schweigen on the borders of Alsace It is the oldest wine-lovers' "walk" – 80 km long and established for at least 2000 years; along it lie places whose fame is proclaimed on wine-bottle labels throughout the world.

The idea of the Deutsche Weinstrasse – the original name has been in existence for the last 40 years – has been taken up by other German wine-growing regions, but the first wine route retains its historical reputation.

From the Zeller Schnepfenflug in the Zell valley, via the Forster Mariengarten to the Nussdorfer Bischofskreuz and the Bergzaberner Kloster Liebfrauenberg can be found noble Riesling, fragrant Müller-Thurgau, fruity Silvaner, flowery Gewürztraminer and spicy Morio-Muskat wines. The Rheinpfalz boasts the whole range of wines from quality wines for daily consumption to Trockenbeerenauslese.

In Charlemagne's days the Pfalz (Palatinate) was already the most important supplier of table as well as "Coronation" wines; and long before the Romans had realized the potential of the warm, porous soil for viticulture. Thus, the Rhenish Palatinate became the "wine-cellar" of Charlemagne's "Holy Roman Empire". There is a marked "southern atmosphere" about the region: much sunshine and an average annual temperature of 11 degrees centigrade encourage a subtropical vegetation with fig, almond, chestnut and lemon trees, sweet-corn and tobacco.

The inhabitants of the region are cheerful and hospitable, and this mood is reflected in the taverns, inns and restaurants. Local fare is particularly succulent: Pfälzer Saumagen mit Sauerkraut (sow's stomach with sauerkraut) and seasonal Martinsgans (goose), or roast hare served with chestnuts and brussel sprouts on the one hand; while other regional delicacies are a special potato soup followed by damson cake. Pfälzer Zweibelkuchen (onion pastry) and the famous white Palatinate cheese.

At grape harvest time, a special wine is offered – Federweisser, milky white, full of vitamins because at the height of fermentation, and deemed to be extremely nutritious.

From the Zellertal to the Mittelhaardt

The German wine route starts at Bockenheim, where the annual poetry competition of the Palatinate is held, and where a good red wine, or a remarkably good Riesling are available. The Zellertal, a valley lying a little farther to the north, produces substantial, spicy white wines from the heavy soil around Zell, Niefernheim and Harxheim.

Neuleiningen

Bockenheim, once fortified, has seen many sieges in the course of history. The ruins of the castle Emichsburg, a Renaissance portal, and a clock-tower still bear witness to its beleaguered past.

The wine-enthusiast will also be rewarded by visiting the small neighbouring villages, among them the more remote Kindenheim.

Centre of the Unterhaardt region is Grünstadt, once the residence of the Counts of Leiningen. Around Grünstadt, Dirmstein, Kirchheim and Grosskarlbach the vineyards mainly produce white wines, but also some velvety red ones.

South-west of Grünstadt, there is the picturesque medieval hill village of Neuleiningen with its ancient town wall and

Wine cavern at Edesheim/ Southern wine route
A Pfalz recipe: (for sow's stomach)

Müller-Thurgau

Main types of vine in the Rheinpfalz:

Müller-Thurgau	24.5%
Silvaner	20.0%
Riesling	13.7%
Portugieser	10.3%

Pfälzer Saumagen
zubereitet nach einem alten Kallstadter Rezept

Ein kleiner Saumagen aus frischer Schlachtung (für ca. 12 Personen), der vom Metzger schon gereinigt zu beziehen ist, wird gut gewässert. 750 g mageren Schweinebauch ohne Schwarte und 750 g mageren Schweinevorderschinken ohne Knochen und Schwarte in 1 cm große Würfel schneiden, ebenso 750 g geschälte Kartoffeln. Die Kartoffeln in Wasser einmal aufkochen. Schweinebauch, Schweinevorderschinken, Kartoffelwürfel, 1000 g feines helles Bratwurstbrät, 2-3 eingeweichte Brötchen, wenn der Saumagen besonders zart gewünscht wird, 4-6 Eier, gut mischen und mit Salz, Pfeffer, Muskat und Majoran abschmecken. Die Masse in den Saumagen füllen, jedoch nicht zu prall, da dieser sonst leicht aufplatzt. Die 3 Magenöffnungen abbinden. Nun muß der Magen gut 3 Stunden in heißem Wasser ca. 80° ziehen, keinesfalls darf er kochen. Er muß dabei frei schwimmen und öfter gedreht werden. Danach kurz abtropfen, eventuell (aber nicht unbedingt) knusprig nachbraten.
Der Saumagen wird mit Weinkraut und Bauernbrot serviert. Am besten schneidet man ihn am Tisch in Scheiben und legt sie vor.
Gekrönt wird das Mahl durch Kallstadter Saumagen Riesling im Glase. Wohl bekomm's!

Bockenheim

towers, and its castle ruins. During the peasant wars the castle was saved from destruction only to fall a victim of the wars of Louis XIV.

From Grünstadt a walking tour can be made through the Leininger valley, starting at Sausenheim and following the Eckbach stream. After about 10 km the splendid castle ruins of Altleiningen – the oldest ancestral seat of the Counts of Leiningen – come into view.

Drink and eat Saumagen

From Altleiningen the Peterskopf hill can be reached by a high footpath. An avenue of almond trees leads down again via Leistadt, leading finally to the cheerful town of Kallstadt, where not only the world-famous wine called Saumagen grows, but where Saumagen (sow's stomach) is also served as a local sausage speciality.

In neighbouring Freinsheim, the visitor can view the splendid remnants of a medieval town: its heavy iron gate and tower, baroque town hall, late Gothic church with Renaissance portal, and the town's fortifications. Its vineyards, which grow noble wines, complete the authentic ambience.

Germany's greatest wine festival

A few kilometers further along the Weinstrasse – via Ungstein – lies Bad Dürkheim framed by the forested heights of the Haardt mountains and a broad ribbon of encircling vineyards. Here, Spielberg and Rittergarten are popular drinks.

The Bad Dürkheim Wurstmarkt (Sausage Market), Germany's greatest wine festival, takes place annually, in September. It is the most famous event in the Rhenish Palatinate. The friendly aroma of wine and sausages fills the air, aided by the happy Pfälzer whose high spirits are reflected in the enormous festival wine-

cask, holding 1.7 mill. litres of wine!

Bad Dürkheim also has an impressive cultural heritage: the Schlosskirche (palace church) with crypt and chapel, and, especially the ruins of the Limburg monastery nearby, which had been built on the foundations of the ancestral castle of the Salian emperors. Between Bad Dürkheim and Ungstein a Roman villa is still extant.

The old town gate at Freinsheim

Familiar wine place-names

South of Bad Dürkheim are some familiar wine names: Wachenheim, at the foot of the ruins of castle Wachtenburg, where not only reputed wines are produced, but also almonds, figs and edible chestnuts ripen amid flowering mulberry trees.

Forst, with its noble vintage wines, offers the tourist a charming little street play, on the "Lätare" Sunday of the church calendar: the "Hansel-Fingerhut-Spiel" – a tussle between summer and winter.

Deidesheim – where each house on its famous Feigengasse sports its own fruit-bearing fig tree – holds an annual goat auction on Whit Tuesday, a time-honoured event going back almost 600 years, which started as a tribute paid by the cloth-weaving town of Lambrecht for grazing rights, and was subsequently endorsed by Napoleon himself. Deidesheim will please the gourmet as well as the lover of wine with its excellent inns and restaurants.

Comfortable inns are also to be found

Data and facts

Geographical notes: *A continuous girdle of vineyards, 6 to 10 km wide and 80 km long, runs along the crest of the Haardt mountain range and the Pfälzer Wald (forest region), beginning south of Worms and ending at the border of Alsace.*
Climate: *On the western rim of the upper Rhine region, sheltered by the Wasgau, Haardt and Donnersberg mountain ranges, a mild climate, ideal for viticulture, predominates.*
Soil: *From the weathered, coloured sandstone deposits, to the widely dispersed "islands" of shell-limestone, granite, porphyr and slate, the region shows a great variety of soil conditions, producing a spicey, fruity wine.*
Cultivated area: *One of the largest, compact vine-growing areas in Germany, with 21,338 ha. 2 Districts, 26 General Sites, approximately 335 Individual Sites.*
Types of vine: *Almost half of the white wine production comes from the Müller-Thurgau (5,227 ha) and the Silvaner (4,272 ha). The Riesling (2,919 ha) produces a fruity wine. The Morio-Muskat vine grows on 1,619 ha. Kerner, a new type of Riesling style (1,178 ha) can be found increasingly. Of red wine types, the Portugieser (2,195 ha), gives warm, mild wine.*
Yield: *On average 1975–1977: 2.4m hl, nearly 28.5% of German must harvest.*
Production structure: *Two-thirds of production is in the hands of small-holders; one-third is run by full-time wine growers; privately owned small vineyards predominate. Approximately 27% of the grape harvest is taken by wine-growers' co-operatives. 20 to 25% is marketed by the wine-estates, and the rest sold to the trade by individual growers.*

A timbered house at Kallstadt

in Ruppertsberg which produces outstanding wines from vineyards that were probably tilled in Roman times, as the remnants of an ancient Roman fort seem to indicate. In Königsbach the red wine vies in excellence with the Dürkheimer, while Gimmeldingen boasts the Meerspinne.

Haardt and Mussbach's soil and climate are particularly favourable, and produce not only the Mandelring and the Letten, but also figs and lemons and various sub-tropical trees. Wine lovers particularly appreciate the Mussbacher Eselshaut, a wine that Charlemagne also must have enjoyed.

Neustadt, stronghold of Palatinate wine

Neustadt is the wine metropolis of the Rhenish Palatinate, the seat of the region's teaching and research institute for viticulture and fruit-growing. In October, at grape harvest time, the Wine Queen of the Palatinate and also the German Wine Queen are chosen there.

A Gothic church with tombs of the Palatinate Electors emphasises Neustadt's importance in the Middle Ages. The Count Palatinate, Johann Casimir, founded a college of Calvinist theology, and the Neustädter Bible, published at that time, is respected by members of the Reformed Church.

Twenty-five km away at Speyer, is the Kaiserdom, a cathedral in romanesque style, the crypt of which contains the tombs of eight German emperors, and also the unique Wine Museum. Housed in the historical museum of the Palatinate, it shows the development of 2000 years of viticulture. Exhibits include coopers' tools, drinking vessels and many other utensils.

Roman amphora containing 1,600 year-old wine

View from Slevogt-Hof

The most fascinating exhibit is a glass amphora – found in a Roman sarcophagus – which, under a thick layer of resin and oil, still contains a residue of liquid, golden wine.

History and wine are strongly interlinked

The Hambach quarter of Neustadt has an important place in the history of German democracy.

The Hambacher Schloss (Maxburg) castle recalls the Hambacher Fest in 1832, when the first German democratic republican mass-meeting took place and made Hambacher Schloss the birthplace of German democracy.

Below Hambacher castle, which offers a magnificent panoramic view of the Rhine plain, lies Neustadt-Diedesfeld where the Bereich Mittelhaardt/Deutsche Weinstrasse ends.

In the sunshine of the Southern Wine Route

In Maikammer, one of the largest German wine-growing communities, the Bereich of Südliche Weinstrasse (southern wine route) begins. From here the charming St. Martin can be reached. On this Saint's feastday, November 11, the traditional Martins Spiel is performed in front of the church.

From Schloss Ludwigshöhe near Edenkoben, the summer residence of the Bavarian King Ludwig I ("the most beautiful square mile of my realm") a chair-lift rises to the "Aussichtsterrasse der Deutschen Weinstrasse" ("viewpoint of the German wine-route").

Below the Rietburg is Rhodt, where the 300 year-old vineyard of Traminer Wingert, the oldest in Germany, lies at the outskirts, towards Edesheim.

Burrweiler produces the Burrweiler Schäwer, a wine that grows on slaty soil. Gleisweiler has a landscape similar to upper Italy with sub-tropical vegetation, while the fortress architect of Louis XIV built himself a "sun-temple" there. He also built the octagonal fortress of Landau, which remained a fortified town for 200 years; today it is a charming garden-city and the wine metropolis of the Südliche Weinstrasse. In the autumn, a procession of Landau peasants and vintners celebrate the Fest des Federweissen (Federweissen Festival).

In Nussdorf, a district of Landau, the peasant's house still stands from which the signal for the start of the peasants' uprising in 1525 was given.

Frankweiler

Visitors' Gazetteer

Annweiler: *Former imperial fortress.*
Bad Bergzabern: *Health resort; thermal baths; historical town centre.*
Bockenheim: *Remnants of the Emichsburg castle; ancient fortified church; Katzenstein (pagan place of worship); Heiligenkirche (church) 2.5 km.*
Deidesheim: *Medieval market-square with beautiful old town hall and church; Andreasbrunnen (fountain); hospital with Gothic church; Feigengasse; Gasthaus "Zur Kanne" (inn).*
Bad Dürkheim: *Gothic palace church; Johanniskirche (church), with crypt and tombs of the Counts of Leiningen; thermal springs; casino; walking tour to the ruins of castle Hardenburg and ruins of the Limburg monastery, and to the Brunholdistuhl and Heidenmauer.*
Edenkoben: *Local museum; Weinlehrpfad; Heilsbruck, former convent of Cistercian nuns; Kropsburg (castle); wine festival of the Südliche Weinstrasse in September.*
Edesheim: *Large, representative wine-sampling cellar of the Südliche Weinstrasse.*

Freinsheim: *Iron gate; baroque town hall; late Gothic church with Renaissance portals.*
Grünstadt: *Oberhof, former residence of the Counts of Leiningen; Martinskirche (church); national park.*
Maikammer-Alsterweiler: *At foot of the Kalmit, highest point of Haardt mountain range (683 m); beautiful timbered houses; well-preserved triptych in Alsterweiler chapel.*
St. Martin: *Interesting buildings: ancient corner houses; antiques; above the town: Kropsburg (castle).*
Rhodt unter Rietburg: *Picturesque wine village; Weinschlössel (small palace, around 1780) with valuable picture-gallery; St.-Georgs-Kirche (church, 13th century).*
Schweigen-Rechtenbach: *Deutsches Weintor (German wine-gate); Weinlehrpfad (wine study trail).*
Speyer: *Altpörtel (town gate); town hall; Dreifaltigkeitskirche (church); Kaiserdom (cathedral); wine museum.*
Wachenheim: *Ruins of castle Wachtenburg; deerpark near the forestry house of Rotsteig.*

Leinsweiler

Neighbouring Siebeldingen has the Federal Institute for Viticulture, housed in the Geilweilerhof. Best known among the newly-developed strains is Morio-Muskat, a cross between Silvaner and Weissburgunder.

A land of castles

If the regions of Unterhaardt and Mittelhaardt contain a sizeable number of castles, the Südliche Weinstrasse has even more. Above Eschbach, the turrets and ramparts of the Madenburg tower like some fantastic, oriental city. A little further west lies Annweiler and the Trifels, where the emperors of the Hohenstaufen dynasty kept the Reich's insignia – crown, sceptre and the imperial orb – and where Richard Coeur-de-Lion was held prisoner.

The way to Leinsweiler passes through

Birkweiler. After a detour through the extensive viticultural community of Ilbesheim, Klingenmünster is reached. Ruins there are of one of the oldest fortified castles in the Rhenish Palatinate.

Bad Bergzabern, the spa centre on the Weinstrasse, displays the full magnificence of its sub-tropical vegetation; sweet corn, tobacco and lemons are among the products of its mild climate; and, of course, wine.

Just a few kilometers further on, Dörrenbach, with its timbered houses and its fortified church, readily conjures up a picture of the Middle Ages.

In Schweigen-Rechtenbach the Deutsche Weinstrasse ends at the wine-gate, erected in 1936.

Information is available from:
"Rheinpfalz-Weinpfalz" e.V.
Friedrich-Ebert-Strasse 11–13
6730 Neustadt/Weinstrasse
Western Germany.

On the wine path at Edenkoben

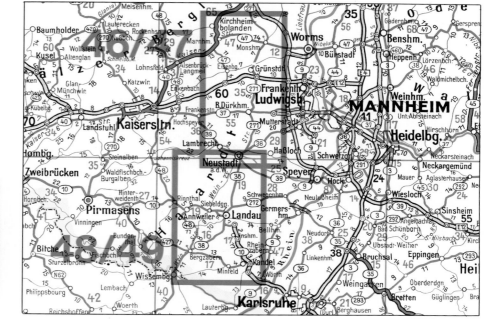

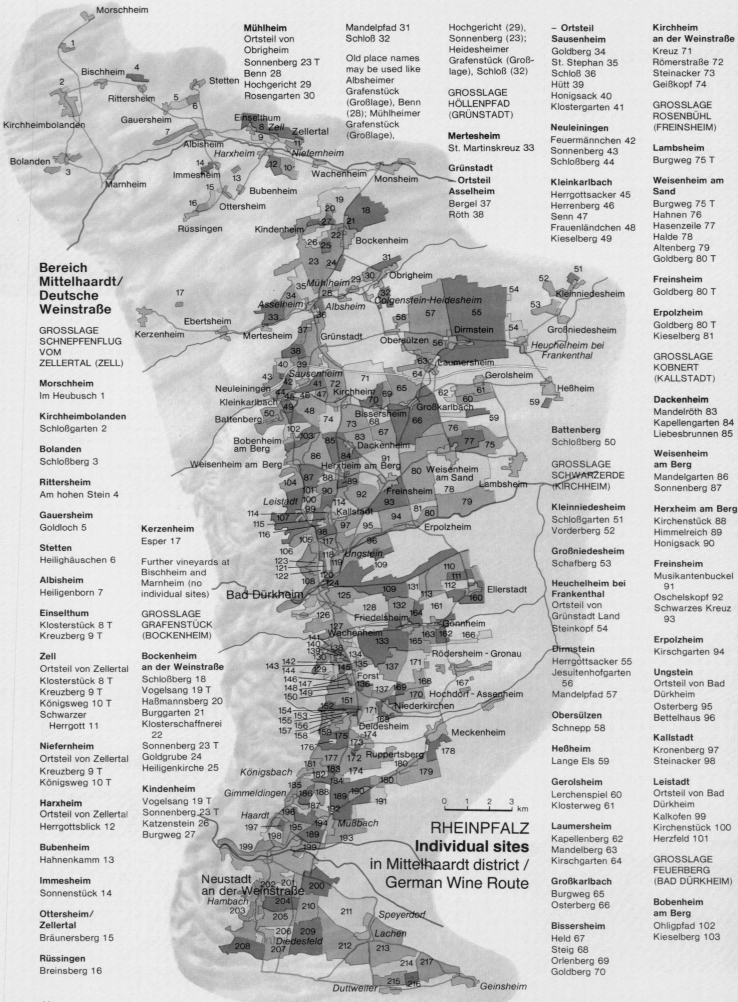

Mühlheim
Ortsteil von Obrigheim
Sonnenberg 23 T
Benn 28
Hochgericht 29
Rosengarten 30

Mandelpfad 31
Schloß 32
Old place names may be used like Albsheimer Grafenstück (Großlage), Benn (28); Mühlheimer Grafenstück (Großlage),

Hochgericht (29), Sonnenberg (23); Heidesheimer Grafenstück (Großlage), Schloß (32)

GROSSLAGE HÖLLENPFAD (GRÜNSTADT)

Mertesheim
St. Martinskreuz 33

**Grünstadt
– Ortsteil Asselheim**
Bergel 37
Röth 38

– Ortsteil Sausenheim
Goldberg 34
St. Stephan 35
Schloß 36
Hütt 39
Honigsack 40
Klostergarten 41

Neuleiningen
Feuermännchen 42
Sonnenberg 43
Schloßberg 44

Kleinkarlbach
Herrgottsacker 45
Herrenberg 46
Senn 47
Frauenländchen 48
Kieselberg 49

Kirchheim an der Weinstraße
Kreuz 71
Römerstraße 72
Steinacker 73
Geißkopf 74

GROSSLAGE ROSENBÜHL (FREINSHEIM)

Lambsheim
Burgweg 75 T

Weisenheim am Sand
Burgweg 75 T
Hahnen 76
Hasenzeile 77
Halde 78
Altenberg 79
Goldberg 80 T

Freinsheim
Goldberg 80 T

Erpolzheim
Goldberg 80 T
Kieselberg 81

GROSSLAGE KOBNERT (KALLSTADT)

Dackenheim
Mandelröth 83
Kapellengarten 84
Liebesbrunnen 85

Weisenheim am Berg
Mandelgarten 86
Sonnenberg 87

Herxheim am Berg
Kirchenstück 88
Himmelreich 89
Honigsack 90

Freinsheim
Musikantenbuckel 91
Oschelskopf 92
Schwarzes Kreuz 93

Erpolzheim
Kirschgarten 94

Ungstein
Ortsteil von Bad Dürkheim
Osterberg 95
Bettelhaus 96

Kallstadt
Kronenberg 97
Steinacker 98

Leistadt
Ortsteil von Bad Dürkheim
Kalkofen 99
Kirchenstück 100
Herzfeld 101

GROSSLAGE FEUERBERG (BAD DÜRKHEIM)

Bobenheim am Berg
Ohligpfad 102
Kieselberg 103

Bereich Mittelhaardt/ Deutsche Weinstraße

GROSSLAGE SCHNEPFENFLUG VOM ZELLERTAL (ZELL)

Morschheim
Im Heubusch 1

Kirchheimbolanden
Schloßgarten 2

Bolanden
Schloßberg 3

Rittersheim
Am hohen Stein 4

Gauersheim
Goldloch 5

Stetten
Heilighäuschen 6

Albisheim
Heiligenborn 7

Einselthum
Klosterstück 8 T
Kreuzberg 9 T

Zell
Ortsteil von Zellertal
Klosterstück 8 T
Kreuzberg 9 T
Königsweg 10 T
Schwarzer Herrgott 11

Niefernheim
Ortsteil von Zellertal
Kreuzberg 9 T
Königsweg 10 T

Harxheim
Ortsteil von Zellertal
Herrgottsblick 12

Bubenheim
Hahnenkamm 13

Immesheim
Sonnenstück 14

Ottersheim/ Zellertal
Bräunersberg 15

Rüssingen
Breinsberg 16

Kerzenheim
Esper 17

Further vineyards at Bischheim and Marnheim (no individual sites)

GROSSLAGE GRAFENSTÜCK (BOCKENHEIM)

Bockenheim an der Weinstraße
Schloßberg 18
Vogelsang 19 T
Haßmannsberg 20
Burggarten 21
Klosterschaffnerei 22
Sonnenberg 23 T
Goldgrube 24
Heiligenkirche 25

Kindenheim
Vogelsang 19 T
Sonnenberg 23 T
Katzenstein 26
Burgweg 27

Kleinniedesheim
Schloßgarten 51
Vorderberg 52

Großniedesheim
Schafberg 53

Heuchelheim bei Frankenthal
Ortsteil von Grünstadt Land
Steinkopf 54

Dirmstein
Herrgottsacker 55
Jesuitenhofgarten 56
Mandelpfad 57

Obersülzen
Schnepp 58

Heßheim
Lange Els 59

Gerolsheim
Lerchenspiel 60
Klosterweg 61

Laumersheim
Kapellenberg 62
Mandelberg 63
Kirschgarten 64

Großkarlbach
Burgweg 65
Osterberg 66

Bissersheim
Held 67
Steig 68
Orlenberg 69
Goldberg 70

---

0 1 2 3 km

RHEINPFALZ
Individual sites
in Mittelhaardt district / German Wine Route

**Weisenheim
am Berg**
Vogelsang 104

Kallstadt
Annaberg 105
Kreidkeller 106

Bad Dürkheim
Herrenmorgen 107
Steinberg 108
Nonnengarten 109

Ellerstadt
Sonnenberg 110
Dickkopp 111
Bubeneck 112

Gönnheim
Martinshöhe 113

**GROSSLAGE
SAUMAGEN
(KALLSTADT)**

Kallstadt
Nill 114
Kirchenstück 115
Horn 116

**GROSSLAGE
HONIGSÄCKEL
(UNGSTEIN)**

Ungstein
Ortsteil von Bad
Dürkheim
Weilberg 117
Herrenberg 118
Nußriegel 119

**GROSSLAGE
HOCHMESS
(BAD DÜRKHEIM)**

Ungstein
Ortsteil von Bad
Dürkheim
Michelsberg 120 T

Bad Dürkheim
Michelsberg 120 T
Spielberg 121
Rittergarten 122
Hochbenn 123

**GROSSLAGE
SCHENKENBÖHL
(WACHENHEIM)**

Bad Dürkheim
Abtsfronhof 124
Fronhof 125
Fuchsmantel 126 T

Wachenheim
Fuchsmantel 126 T
Königswingert 127
Mandelgarten 128
Odinstal 129
Schloßberg 130

**GROSSLAGE
SCHNEPFENFLUG
AN DER
WEINSTRASSE
(FORST AN DER
WEINSTRASSE)**

Friedelsheim
Kreuz 131
Schloßgarten 132
Bischofsgarten
133 T

Wachenheim
Bischofsgarten
133 T
Luginsland 134

**Forst
an der Weinstraße**
Bischofsgarten
133 T
Süßkopf 135
Stift 136

Deidesheim
Letten 137

**GROSSLAGE
MARIENGARTEN
(FORST AN DER
WEINSTRASSE)**

Wachenheim
Böhlig 138
Belz 139
Rechbächel 140
Goldbächel 141
Gerümpel 142
Altenburg 143

**Forst
an der Weinstraße**
Musenhang 144
Pechstein 145
Jesuitengarten 146
Kirchenstück 147
Freundstück 148
Ungeheuer 149
Elster 150

Deidesheim
Herrgottsacker 151
Mäushöhle 152
Kieselberg 153
Kalkofen 154
Grainhübel 155
Hohenmorgen 156
Leinhöhle 157
Langenmorgen 158
Paradiesgarten 159

**GROSSLAGE
HOFSTÜCK
(DEIDESHEIM)**

Ellerstadt
Kirchenstück 160

Gönnheim
Sonnenberg 161
Mandelgarten 162
Klostergarten 163

Friedelsheim
Rosengarten 164
Gerümpel 165

**Hochdorf-
Assenheim**
Fuchsloch 166 T

**Rödersheim-
Gronau**
Fuchsloch 166 T

Niederkirchen
Osterbrunnen 168
Klostergarten 169
Schloßberg 170

Deidesheim
Nonnenstück 171

Ruppertsberg
Linsenbusch 172
Hoheburg 173
Gaisböhl 174
Reiterpfad 175
Spieß 176
Nußbien 177

Meckenheim
Wolfsdarm 178
Spielberg 179
Neuberg 180

**GROSSLAGE
MEERSPINNE
(NEUSTADT AN DER
WEINSTRASSE
ORTSTEIL
GIMMELDINGEN)**

**Königsbach
an der Weinstraße**
Ortsteil von
Neustadt an der
Weinstraße
Ölberg 181
Idig 182
Jesuitengarten 183
Reiterpfad 184

**Gimmeldingen an
der Weinstraße**
Ortsteil von
Neustadt an der
Weinstraße
Bienengarten 185
Kapellenberg 186
Mandelgarten 187
Schlössel 188

**Mußbach
an der Weinstraße**
Ortsteil von
Neustadt an der
Weinstraße
Eselshaut 189
Glockenzehnt 190
Kurfürst 191
Spiegel 192
Bischofsweg 193
Johannitergarten
194

**Haardt
an der Weinstraße**
Ortsteil von
Neustadt an der
Weinstraße
Mandelring 195
Herzog 196
Herrenletten 197
Bürgergarten 198

**Neustadt
an der Weinstraße**
Mönchgarten 199

**GROSSLAGE
REBSTÖCKEL
(NEUSTADT AN DER
WEINSTRASSE,
ORTSTEIL
DIEDESFELD)**

**Neustadt
an der Weinstraße**
Grain 200
Erkenbrecht 201

**Hambach
an der Weinstraße**
Ortsteil von
Neustadt an der
Weinstraße
Kaiserstuhl 202
Kirchberg 203
Feuer 204
Schloßberg 205

**Diedesfeld
an der Weinstraße**
Ortsteil von
Neustadt an der
Weinstraße
Ölgässel 206
Johanniskirchel 207
Paradies 208

Diedesfeld
Ortsteil von
Neustadt an der
Weinstraße
Berg 209

**GROSSLAGE
PFAFFENGRUND
(NEUSTADT AN DER
WEINSTRASSE,
ORTSTEIL
DIEDESFELD)**

**Hambach
an der Weinstraße**
Ortsteil von
Neustadt an der
Weinstraße
Römerbrunnen 210

Lachen/Speyerdorf
Ortsteil von
Neustadt an der
Weinstraße
Langenstein 211
Lerchenböhl 212
Kroatenpfad 213

Duttweiler
Ortsteil von
Neustadt an der
Weinstraße
Kreuzberg 214
Mandelberg 215
Kalkberg 216

Geinsheim
Ortsteil von
Neustadt an der
Weinstraße
Gässel 217

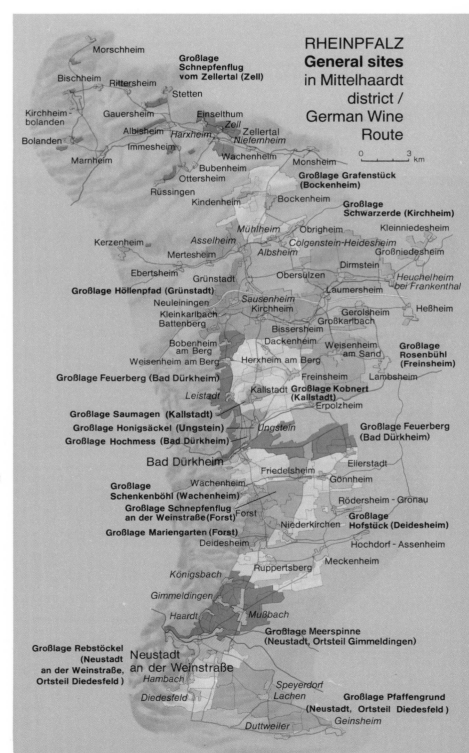

RHEINPFALZ
General sites
in Mittelhaardt
district /
German Wine
Route

0   3
km

Bereich Südliche Weinstraße

GROSSLAGE MANDELHÖHE (MAIKAMMER)

Maikammer
Alsterweiler
  Kapellenberg 218
Kirchenstück 219
Immengarten 220
Heiligenberg 221

Kirrweiler
Römerweg 222
Mandelberg 223
Oberschloß 224

GROSSLAGE SCHLOSS LUDWIGSHÖHE (EDENKOBEN)

St. Martin
Kirchberg 225
Baron 226
Zitadelle 227

Edenkoben
Bergel 228
Heilig Kreuz 229
Klostergarten 230
Heidegarten 231
Kirchberg 232
Blücherhöhe 233
Mühlberg 234
Schwarzer Letten 235
Kastaniengarten 236

GROSSLAGE ORDENSGUT (EDESHEIM)

Rhodt unter Rietburg
Klosterpfad 237
Schloßberg 238
Rosengarten 239

Weyher in der Pfalz
Michelsberg 240
Heide 241

Hainfeld
Letten 242
Kapelle 243
Kirchenstück 244

Edesheim
Forst 245
Mandelhang 246
Schloß 247
Rosengarten 248

GROSSLAGE TRAPPENBERG (HOCHSTADT)

Böbingen
Ortelberg 249

Altdorf
Gottesacker 250
Hochgericht 251

Venningen
Doktor 252

Groß- und Kleinfischlingen
Kirchberg 253

Freimersheim
Bildberg 254

Essingen
Roßberg 255
Sonnenberg 256
Osterberg 257

Ottersheim
Kahlenberg 258

Knittelsheim
Gollenberg 259 T

Bellheim
Gollenberg 259 T

Bornheim
Neuberg 261

Hochstadt
Roter Berg 262

Zeiskam
Klostergarten 263 T

Lustadt
Klostergarten 263 T

Weingarten
Schloßberg 264

Schwegenheim
Bründelsberg*

Römerberg (bei Speyer)
Schlittberg*
Alter Berg*
Narrenberg*

Vineyards without site names in sections Gommersheim (22 ha) and Offenbach (0.6 ha).

GROSSLAGE BISCHOFSKREUZ (WALSHEIM)

Burrweiler
Altenforst 265
St. Annaberg 266
Schäwer 267
Schloßgarten 268

Gleisweiler
Hölle 269

Flemlingen
Herrenbuckel 270
Vogelsprung 271
Zechpeter 272

Böchingen
Rosenkranz 273

Nußdorf
Ortsteil von Landau in der Pfalz
Herrenberg 274
Kaiserberg 275
Kirchenstück 276

Walsheim
Forstweg 277
Silberberg 278

Roschbach
Simonsgarten 279
Rosenkränzel 280

Knöringen
Hohenrain 281

Dammheim
Ortsteil von Landau in der Pfalz
Höhe 282

GROSSLAGE KÖNIGSGARTEN (GODRAMSTEIN)

Landau in der Pfalz
Altes Löhl 283

Godramstein
Ortsteil von Landau in der Pfalz
Klostergarten 284
Münzberg 285

Frankweiler
Kalkgrube 286
Biengarten 287

Albersweiler
Latt 288
(St. Johann)
Kirchberg 289

Siebeldingen
Mönchspfad 290
Im Sonnenschein 291
Rosenberg 292 T

Birkweiler
Rosenberg 292 T
Kastanienbusch 293
Mandelberg 294

Ranschbach
Seligmacher 295 T

Arzheim
Ortsteil von Landau
Rosenberg 292 T
Seligmacher 295 T

6 hectares of vineyards without site names in the Gräfenhausen section

GROSSLAGE HERRLICH (ESCHBACH)

Leinsweiler
Sonnenberg 296 T

Eschbach
Hasen 297

Göcklingen
Kaiserberg 298

Ilbesheim
Sonnenberg 296 T
Rittersberg 299

Wollmesheim
Ortsteil von Landau in der Pfalz
Mütterle 300

Mörzheim
Ortsteil von Landau in der Pfalz
Pfaffenberg 301

Impflingen
Abtsberg 302

Insheim
Schäfergarten 303 T

Rohrbach
Schäfergarten 303 T

Herxheim bei Landau in der Pfalz
Engelsberg 304

Herxheimweyher
Am Gaisberg 305

GROSSLAGE KLOSTER LIEBFRAUENBERG (BAD BERGZABERN)

Klingenmünster
Maria Magdalena 306

Göcklingen
Herrenpfad 307 T

Heuchelheim-Klingen
Herrenpfad 307 T

Rohrbach
Mandelpfad 308 T

Billigheim-Ingenheim
Mandelpfad 308 T
(Billigheim)
Venusbuckel 309
(Billigheim)
Sauschwänzel 310
(Billigheim)
Steingebiß 311
(Appenhofen)
Pfaffenberg 312
(Ingenheim)
Rosenberg 313 T
(Mühlhofen)

Steinweiler
Rosenberg 313 T

Winden
Narrenberg 314 T

Hergersweiler
Narrenberg 314 T

Barbelroth
Kirchberg 315

Oberhausen
Frohnwingert 316

Niederhorbach
Silberberg 317

Gleiszellen-Gleishorbach
Kirchberg 318
Frühmess 319

Neustadt an der Weinstraße

Großlage Mandelhöhe (Maikammer)

Maikammer

Großlage Schloß Ludwigshöhe (Edenkoben)

St. Martin

Kirrweiler

Großlage Ordensgut (Edesheim)

Edenkoben

Rhodt

Venningen

Altdorf

Böbingen

Gommersheim

Großlage Bischofskreuz (Walsheim)

Weyher

Groß-

Freimersheim

Freisbach

Hainfeld

Edesheim

Kleinfischlingen

Burrweiler

Flemlingen

Weingarten

Gleisweiler

Roschbach

Essingen

Hochstadt

Großlage Königsgarten (Goldramstein)

Frankweiler

Böchingen

Walsheim

Knöringen

Lustadt

Albersweiler

Godramstein

Nußdorf

Zeiskam

Siebeldingen

Dammheim

Bornheim

Birkweiler

Großlage Trappenberg (Hochstadt)

Ranschbach

Queichheim

Offenbach an der Queich

Knittelsheim

Großlage Herrlich (Eschbach)

Arzheim

Landau in der Pfalz

Ottersheim

Bellheim

Leinsweiler

Ilbesheim

Wollmesheim

Eschbach

Mörzheim

Impflingen

Göcklingen

Insheim

Heuchelheim - Klingen

Appenhofen

Rohrbach

Herxheimweyher

Klingenmünster

Ingenheim Billigheim -

Herxheim

Gleiszellen - Gleishorbach

Pleisweiler - Oberhofen

Niederhorbach

Steinweiler

Großlage Kloster Liebfrauenberg (Bad Bergzabern)

Bad Bergzabern

Kapellen-

Barbelroth

Winden

Druisweiler

Dörrenbach

Oberhausen Hergersweiler

Oberotterbach

Dierbach

Rechtenbach

Vollmersweiler

Kandel

Niederotterbach

Minfeld

Schweigen

Freckenfeldt

Schweighofen

Schaidt

Steinfeld

Großlage Guttenberg (Schweigen)

Kapsweyer

0   3 km

RHEINPFALZ
General sites
Southern Wine
Route district

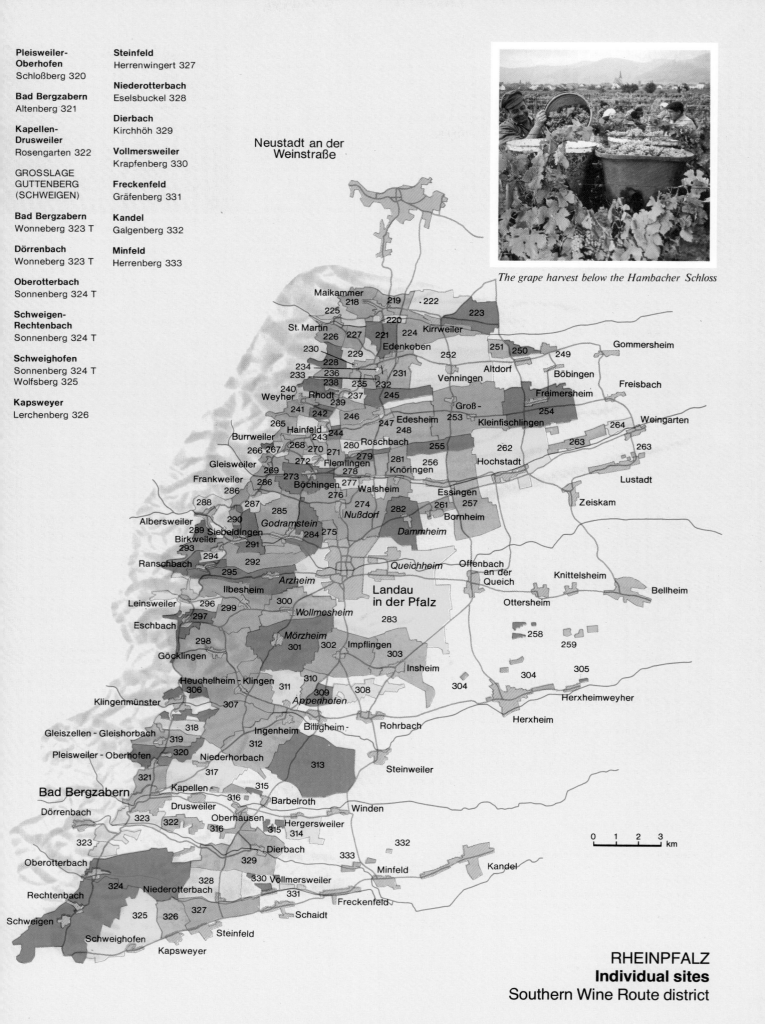

Pleisweiler-
Oberhofen
Schloßberg 320

Bad Bergzabern
Altenberg 321

Kapellen-
Drusweiler
Rosengarten 322

GROSSLAGE
GUTTENBERG
(SCHWEIGEN)

Bad Bergzabern
Wonneberg 323 T

Dörrenbach
Wonneberg 323 T

Oberotterbach
Sonnenberg 324 T

Schweigen-
Rechtenbach
Sonnenberg 324 T

Schweighofen
Sonnenberg 324 T
Wolfsberg 325

Kapsweyer
Lerchenberg 326

Steinfeld
Herrenwingert 327

Niederotterbach
Eselsbuckel 328

Dierbach
Kirchhöh 329

Vollmersweiler
Krapfenberg 330

Freckenfeld
Gräfenberg 331

Kandel
Galgenberg 332

Minfeld
Herrenberg 333

Neustadt an der
Weinstraße

The grape harvest below the Hambacher Schloss

Maikammer 218 219 .222
225   220   223
St. Martin 226 227 221 224 Kirrweiler
230   229   Gommersheim
234 228   231 251 250 249
233 236   Altdorf   Böbingen
240 238 235 232 Venningen   Freisbach
Weyher Rhodt 237 245   Freimersheim
241 242 239   Groß - 254
265   246 247 Edesheim 253 Weingarten
Burrweiler Hainfeld 243 244 248 Kleinfischlingen 264
266 267 268 270 271 280 Roschbach 255 262 263
Gleisweiler 269 272 278 279 281 256   263
Frankweiler 286 273 Flemlingen Knöringen Hochstadt   Lustadt
288   287 Böchingen 277   Essingen   Zeiskam
Albersweiler 285 276 Walsheim 261 257
290   Godramstein 274 282   Bornheim
289 Siebeldingen 284 275 Nußdorf Dammheim
Birkweiler 293 291   Dammheim
Ranschbach 294   Queichheim Offenbach   Knittelsheim
295   292   an der Queich
Arzheim 300   Landau Ottersheim   Bellheim
Ilbesheim   in der Pfalz
Leinsweiler 296 299   Wollmesheim 283
Eschbach 297   258
298   Mörzheim 301 302 Impflingen 259
Göcklingen   303   304 305
Heuchelheim - Klingen 310   Insheim   Herxheimweyher
306   311 309 308   304
Klingenmünster 307 Appenhofen   Herxheim
318   Ingenheim Billigheim -   Rohrbach
Gleiszellen - Gleishorbach 319   312   Steinweiler
Pleisweiler - Oberhofen 320 Niederhorbach 313
321   317   Winden
Bad Bergzabern Kapellen - 315
Dörrenbach 316 Barbelroth 332
323   322 Oberhausen 315 314 333 Kandel
323   316 Dierbach Minfeld
Oberotterbach 329   Freckenfeld
324 Niederotterbach 328 330 Vollmersweiler
Rechtenbach 325 326 327 331 Schaidt
Schweigen
Schweighofen   Steinfeld
Kapsweyer

0 1 2 3
km

RHEINPFALZ
Individual sites
Southern Wine Route district

49

Hessische Bergstraße

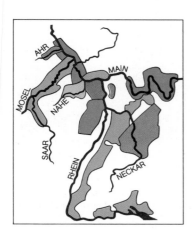

"The spring garden of Germany". This anonymous remark about the Bergstrasse conveys the early blossoming peach, almond and cherry trees announcing the spring's arrival in Germany. The Bergstrasse's mild climate is most beneficial to the vine.

The earthy acidity and fragrant heartiness of Bergstrasse wine give it very particular virtues. Although only a small region, different soil conditions make for wines of a purposefully individualistic character. To sample superb Riesling, Silvaner or Müller-Thurgau – which often win prizes – entails an enjoyable climb up to the ancient Roman "strata montana". The wine of the Zwingenberg, Bensheim and Heppenheim regions was mentioned in documents 1200 years ago. Rewarding visits are recommended to Alsbach, the ancient little town of Zwingenberg, Auerbach, Bensheim or Heppenheim at the foot of the Starkenburg castle – built in 1065, where typical wine taverns offer warm hospitality.

Germany's spring garden

Further information, also about vintage festivals can be obtained from:
Weinbauverband
Hessische Bergstrasse e.V.
Königsberger Strasse 4
6148 Heppenheim/Bergstrasse
Western Germany

Main types of vine in Hess. Bergstrasse

Riesling	52.3%
Müller-Thurgau	19.3%
Silvaner	10.0%

Data and facts

Geographical notes: *Situated between Zwingenberg and Heppenheim; also, Odenwälder Weininsel east of Darmstadt.*
Climate: *The Odenwald forest is a shield against rough easterly weather conditions; south and west facing vineyards get most sunshine and, especially during the vegetation period, the right amount of rain.*
Soil: *Not too heavy soil, with varying degrees of loess content, gives the wine its fine, fragrant character.*

Cultivated area: *350 ha, with 2 Districts, 3 General Sites and 22 Individual Sites.*
Types of vine: *Riesling (147 ha); Müller-Thurgau (54 ha); Silvaner (28 ha); wines are of a fine, fruity character, delicately acid.*
Yield: *On average 1975–1977: 31,000 hl, 0.3% of a normal German must harvest.*
Production structure: *Small undertakings, privately run.*

Visitors' Gazetteer

Bensheim: *Schloss Schönberg (palace); old houses of aristocracy.*
Heppenheim: *Market place with Marienbrunnen (fountain); town hall tower with glockenspiel; nearby: Starkenburg castle (1065).*
Lorsch: *Remnants of Carolingian monastery (8th century).*
Zwingenberg: *Remnants of fortifications; church (approx. 1200).*

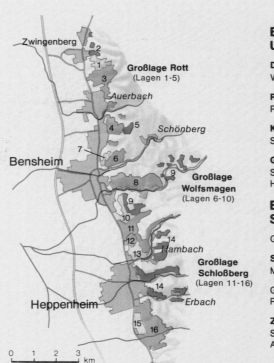

Bereich Umstadt	Bensheim-Auerbach
Dietzenbach Wingertsberg*	Höllberg 3 Fürstenlager 4
Roßdorf Roßberg*	**Bensheim-Schönberg** Herrnwingert 5
Klein-Umstadt Stachelberg*	GROSSLAGE WOLFSMAGEN
Groß-Umstadt Steingerück* Herrnberg*	**Bensheim** Kalkgasse 6 Kirchberg 7 Steichling 8
Bereich Starkenburg	Hemsberg 9 Paulus 10
GROSSLAGENFREI	GROSSLAGE SCHLOSSBERG
Seeheim Mundklingen*	**Heppenheim** (including Erbach and Hambach)
GROSSLAGE ROTT	Stemmler 11 Centgericht 12
Zwingenberg Steingeröll 1 Alte Burg 2	Steinkopf 13 Maiberg 14 Guldenzoll 15 Eckweg 16

Franken

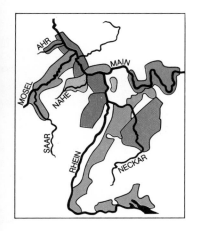

The romantic beauties of the Franconian lands attract hundreds of thousands of visitors each year. Countless picturesque wine-growing communities live on the banks of the river Main and in the Steigerwald region where impressive ancient town walls, towers, town halls and lovely old timbered houses – and Franconian wines – have been appreciated for centuries.

This most manly of wines likes to reveal its true identity gradually. The flagon-shaped Franconian wine bottle (called a Bocksbeutel) emphasises that the wine it holds is different from all other wines, and this anticipation is subsequently confirmed by taste and aroma. Sometimes hearty, sometimes earthy or fruity, it affirms the soil-type on which it has grown. The typical flavour of this very individual wine opens up a wide range of nuances: the Würzburger Silvaner is pithy

Framed by vineyards: Repperndorf

and fiery; wine from the Steigerwald is more powerful; while the Müller-Thurgau from the Main region has a mild flowery aroma. Adherents of Franconian wine include Goethe who wrote: "... to me, none other tastes as good", and such faithfulness to Franconian wine is not unusual.

Visitors' Gazetteer

Aschaffenburg: *Basilica; town hall; theatre; church; palace; Pompejanum.*
Bamberg: *Cathedral; Benedictine monastery St. Michael; Carmelite monastery; Stephansberg.*
Castell: *Palace gardens of the Princes of Castell-Castell.*
Dettelbach: *36 ancient towers; pilgrims church; town hall; wooden bridge between church towers.*
Eibelstadt: *Ancient town wall; Baroque town hall; late Gothic church.*
Homburg: *Zehntscheuer (Gothic building); Pippinsturm (tower); on the Burgberg.*
Iphofen: *Ancient town gates; Veitskirche (late Gothic church); beautiful old town hall.*
Kitzingen: *Renaissance town hall; Gothic church; two towers: Falterturm and Marktturm; remnants of town fortifications; Main bridge.*
Ochsenfurt: *St. Andreaskirche (church with works by Brenck and Riemenschneider); late Gothic town hall; Palatium; Michaelskapelle (chapel); Kreuzkirche (church); Wolfgangskapelle (chapel); local museum, with Brückenschlössle; Greising house: with museum of national costumes.*
Rödelsee: *Old palace of Crailsheim, in front of it an oak wine-press.*
Volkach: *Town hall; pilgrims' church of St. Maria im Weingarten; Riemenschneider's "Madonna with Rosary"; Pieta of the 15th century; Schelfenhaus with local museum.*
Würzburg: *"Residence"; cathedral; old Main bridge; market square; town hall; Juliusspital and Stift Haug (charitable institutions); Bürgerspital (charitable institution); Marienfeste (castle with museum); St. Burkard (monastery church); pilgrims' church "Kappelle" (B. Neumann); ancient Adelshöfe (houses of aristocracy).*

Silvaner

Main types of vine in Franken:

Müller-Thurgau	46.3%
Silvaner	31.4%

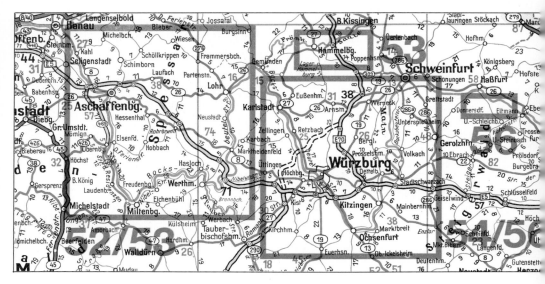

Bereich Mainviereck

GROSSLAGE REUSCHBERG

Hörstein
Ortsteil von Alzenau
Abtsberg 1
übr. Rebflächen 2

GROSSLAGENFREI

Wasserlos
Ortsteil von Alzenau
Schloßberg 3
Luhmännchen 3 a

Michelbach
Ortsteil von Alzenau
Steinberg 4
Apostelgarten 5

Aschaffenburg
Pompejaner 6

Obernau
Sanderberg 7

Rottenberg
Gräfenstein 7 a

GROSSLAGE HEILIGENTHAL

Großostheim
Reischklingeberg 8
Harstell 9

With vineyards in the Wenigumstadt section

GROSSLAGENFREI

Großwallstadt
Lützeltalerberg 10

Rück
Ortsteil von Elsenfeld
Johannisberg 11
Jesuitenberg 12

Erlenbach am Main
Hochberg 13

Klingenberg am Main
Hochberg 14
Schloßberg 15

Großheubach
Bischofsberg 16

Engelsberg
Ortsteil von Großheubach
Klostergarten 17

Miltenberg
Steingrübler 18

Bürgstadt
Mainhölle 19
Centgrafenberg 20

Dorfprozelten
Predigtstuhl 21

Kreuzwertheim
Kaffelstein 22

Bereich Maindreieck

GROSSLAGENFREI

Homburg am Main
Kallmuth 23
Edelfrau 24

Lengfurt
Alter Berg 25
Oberrot 26

Erlenbach (bei Marktheidenfeld)
Krähenschnabel 27

Marktheidenfeld
Kreuzberg 27 a

FRANKEN
Individual sites
at Aschaffenburg

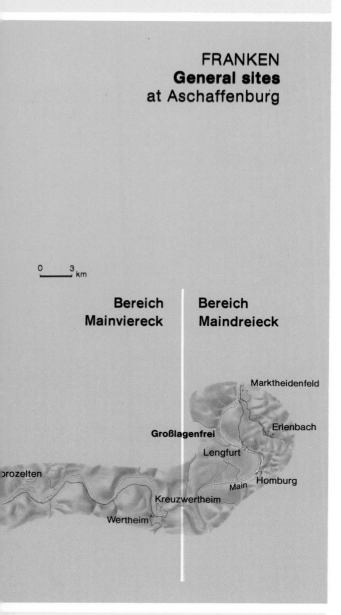

FRANKEN
General sites
at Aschaffenburg

0 3 km

Bereich Mainviereck | **Bereich Maindreieck**

Marktheidenfeld

Erlenbach

Großlagenfrei

Lengfurt

Homburg

Main

Kreuzwertheim

Wertheim

rozelten

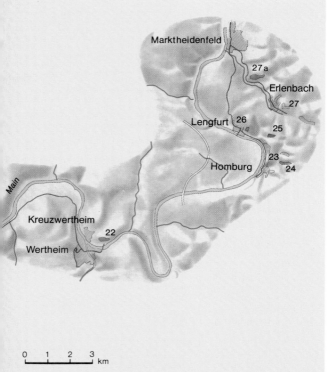

Marktheidenfeld

27 a

Erlenbach

27

Lengfurt 26

25

Homburg 23

24

Main

Kreuzwertheim

22

Wertheim

0 1 2 3 km

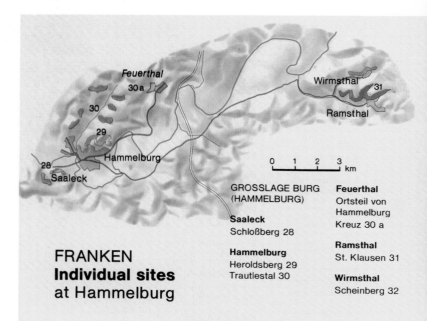

Feuerthal

30 a

30

Wirmsthal

31

29

Ramsthal

28

Hammelburg

Saaleck

0 1 2 3 km

FRANKEN
Individual sites
at Hammelburg

GROSSLAGE BURG (HAMMELBURG)

Saaleck
Schloßberg 28

Hammelburg
Heroldsberg 29
Trautlestal 30

Feuerthal
Ortsteil von
Hammelburg
Kreuz 30 a

Ramsthal
St. Klausen 31

Wirmsthal
Scheinberg 32

Without monasteries – no Frankenwein

Wine historians are not certain whether the Franconians brought
wine with them from the Rhine, or whether they found that viticulture already existed when they advanced into the region from the
west and gave it its name. Early documents (between 775 and 780)
mention a number of vineyards: near Münnerstadt, in the Grabfeld
area, near Halsheim on the Wern river, near Hammelburg,
Klingenberg, and also around Würzburg.

The Irish missionary St. Kilian – patron Saint of vintagers –
brought Christianity to the region, and soon afterwards the bishoprics
of Eichstätt and Würzburg were founded by Bonifatius.

The Würzburger Bürgerspital (hospital) plays a most important
part in the history of Franconian wine. Founded in 1319 as a
charitable institution, vineyard after vineyard was added to its
property as gifts, "for the refreshment and invigoration of the sick
and the weak". The hospital's wine-estate grew and became a
forerunner of high quality viticulture. To this day, Franconian wine
is often referred to as Steinwein, a name given to it after the Lage
called Stein, where the Bürgerspital (and the two other large
Würzburg wine-estates) has owned vineyards for centuries. In addition
to a great number of wine-estates, there are also many small vintage
undertakings which market their own produce. Efficient wine-
growers' co-operatives take up to 50% of the annual must harvest.

St. Kilian with the Marienberg fortress at Würzburg in the background

53

GROSSLAGE
ROSSTAL
(KARLSTADT)

Gössenheim
Arnberg 33

Karlburg
Ortsteil von
Karlstadt
einzellagenfreie
Rebflächen 34

Gambach
Ortsteil von
Karlstadt
Kalbenstein 35

Mühlbach
einzellagenfreie
Rebflächen 36

Laudenbach
einzellagenfreie
Rebflächen 37

Eußenheim
First 38

Stetten
Stein 39

Arnstein
einzellagenfreie
Rebflächen 40

Karlstadt
Im Stein 41

Himmelstadt
Kelter 42

Retzstadt
Langenberg 43

GROSSLAGE
RAVENSBURG
(THÜNGERSHEIM)

Retzbach
Ortsteil von
Zellingen
Benediktusberg 44

Thüngersheim
Johannisberg 45
Scharlachberg 46

Güntersleben
Sommerstuhl 47

Erlabrunn
Weinsteig 48

Oberleinach
einzellagenfreie
Rebflächen 49

Veitshöchheim
Wölflein 50

GROSSLAGENFREI

Veitshöchheim
Sonnenschein 51

Rimpar
Kobersberg 52

Böttigheim
Wurmberg*

Würzburg
Pfaffenberg 53

Stein 54
Stein/Harfe 55
Schloßberg 56
Innere Leiste 57
Abtsleite 58
Kirchberg 59

GROSSLAGE
EWIG LEBEN

Randersacker
Teufelskeller 60
Sonnenstuhl 61
Pfülben 62
Marsberg 63

GROSSLAGE
ÖLSPIEL

Sommerhausen
Steinbach 64
Reifenstein 65

Kleinochsenfurt
Ortsteil von
Ochsenfurt
einzellagenfreie
Rebflächen 65 a

GROSSLAGE
TEUFELSTOR

Eibelstadt
Kapellenberg 66
Mönchsleite 67

Randersacker
Dabug 68

GROSSLAGENFREI

Tauberrettersheim
Königin*

Röttingen
Feuerstein*

Bergtheim
Harfenspiel 69

Frickenhausen
Fischer 70
Kapellenberg 71
Markgraf
   Babenberg 72

Gaibach
Schloßpark 97 a

GROSSLAGE
HOFRAT
(KITZINGEN)

Segnitz
Zobelsberg 73
Pfaffensteig 74

Marktbreit
Sonnenberg 75

Sulzfeld
Maustal 76
Cyriakusberg 77

Kitzingen
Wilhelmsberg 78

Repperndorf
Kaiser Karl 79

Buchbrunn
Heißer Stein 80

Mainstockheim
Hofstück 81

GROSSLAGE
HONIGBERG

Dettelbach
Berg-Rondell 82
Sonnenleite 83

Bibergau
Ortsteil von
Dettelbach
einzellagenfreie
Rebflächen 84

GROSSLAGE
KIRCHBERG
(VOLKACH)

Neuses a. Berg
Glatzen 85

Escherndorf
Ortsteil von Volkach
Fürstenberg 86
Berg 87
Lump 88

Sommerach
Katzenkopf 89
Rosenberg 90

Vogelsburg
Ortsteil von Volkach
Pforte 92 a

Nordheim
Vögelein 91
Kreuzberg 92

Astheim
Ortsteil von Volkach
Karthäuser 93

Krautheim
Sonnenleite 94

Obervolkach
Landsknecht 95

Rimbach
einzellagenfreie
Rebflächen 96

Gaibach
Kapellenberg 97

Volkach
Ratsherr 98

Untereisenheim
Sonnenberg 99

Obereisenheim
Höll 100

Stammheim
Eselsberg 101

Wipfeld
Zehntgraf 102

also vineyards in
the sections Neu-
setz, Köhler (Orts-
teil von Volkach)
and Fahr

GROSSLAGENFREI

Hallburg
Ortsteil von Volkach
Schloßberg 103

Kitzingen
Eherieder Berg 103 a

Obernbreit
Kanzel 103 b

Frankenwinheim
Rosenberg 104

Zeilitzheim
Heiligenberg 104 a

Schweinfurt
Peterstirn*
Mainleite*

Mainberg
Ortsteil von
Schonungen
Schloß*

Bereich
Steigerwald

GROSSLAGE
SCHILD
(ABTSWIND)

Abtswind
Altenberg 105

Greuth
Bastel 105 a

GROSSLAGE
HERRENBERG

Castell
Bausch 106
Honart 107
Kirchberg 108
Feuerbach 109
Kugelspiel 110
Reitsteig 111
Schloßberg 112
Trautberg 113

GROSSLAGE
SCHLOSSBERG
(RÖDELSEE)

Kleinlangheim
Wutschenberg 114

Wiesenbronn
Wachhügel 115
Geißberg 115 a

Großlangheim
Kiliansberg 116

Rödelsee
Schwanleite 117
Küchenmeister 118

Sickershausen
Ortsteil von
Kitzingen
Storchenbrünnle 119

also vineyards in
the sections
Mainbernheim and
Hoheim (Ortsteil von
Kitzingen)

GROSSLAGE
BURGWEG
(IPHOFEN)

Iphofen
Julius-Echter-Berg
   120
Kronsberg 133
Kalb 121

Markt Einersheim
Vogelsang 122

Willianzheim
einzellagenfreie
Rebflächen 122 a

Gössenheim
33

Gambach

35

34

Eußenheim

38

Karlburg

40

Karlstadt

Mühlbach

Arnstein

36

39

Stetten

37

Laudenbach

41

Himmelstadt

42

Retzstadt

Retzbach

43

44

Main

45

Thüngersheim

47

46 Güntersleben

52

Oberleinach

48

Rimpar

49 Erlabrunn

51

50

Veitshöchheim

53

53

55 54

54

56

57

Würzbur

58
60

59

Ran
ack

62

Heidingsfeld

59

Eibelstad

54

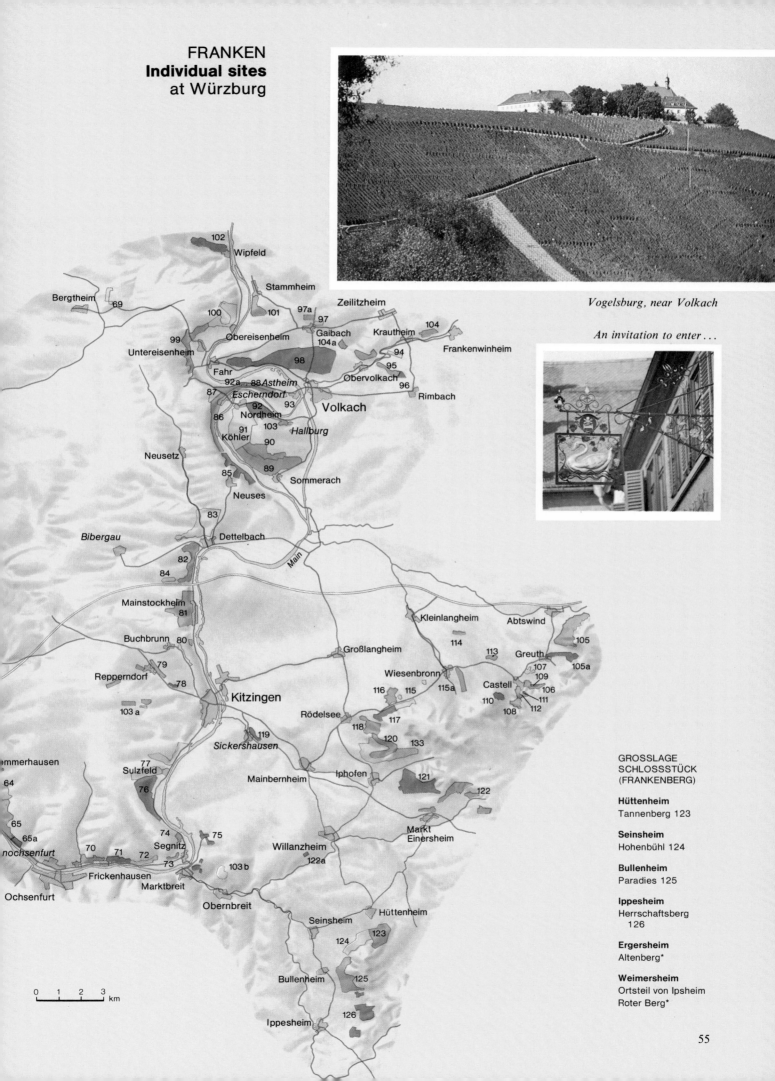

FRANKEN
Individual sites
at Würzburg

Vogelsburg, near Volkach

An invitation to enter ...

GROSSLAGE
SCHLOSSSTÜCK
(FRANKENBERG)

Hüttenheim
Tannenberg 123

Seinsheim
Hohenbühl 124

Bullenheim
Paradies 125

Ippesheim
Herrschaftsberg
126

Ergersheim
Altenberg*

Weimersheim
Ortsteil von Ipsheim
Roter Berg*

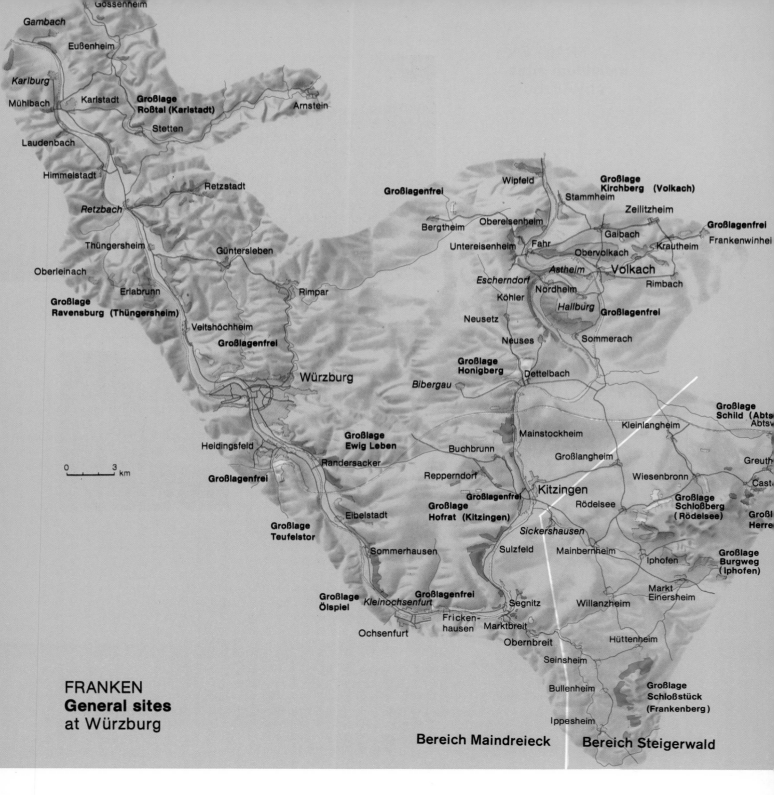

FRANKEN
General sites
at Würzburg

Gambach
Gossenheim
Eußenheim
Karlburg
Mühlbach
Karlstadt
Großlage Roßtal (Karlstadt)
Stetten
Arnstein
Laudenbach
Himmelstadt
Retzstadt
Retzbach
Thüngersheim
Güntersleben
Oberleinach
Erlabrunn
Rimpar
Großlage Ravensburg (Thüngersheim)
Veitshöchheim
Großlagenfrei
Würzburg
Wipfeld
Großlagenfrei
Bergtheim
Obereisenheim
Großlage Kirchberg (Volkach)
Stammheim
Zeilitzheim
Untereisenheim
Fahr
Galbach
Großlagenfrei Frankenwinhel
Obervolkach
Krautheim
Astheim
Volkach
Escherndorf
Köhler
Nordheim
Rimbach
Neusetz
Hallburg
Großlagenfrei
Neuses
Sommerach
Großlage Honigberg
Dettelbach
Bibergau
Großlage Schild (Abts
Abtsw
Mainstockheim
Kleinlangheim
Großlage Ewig Leben
Buchbrunn
Großlangheim
Greuth
Randersacker
Repperndorf
Wiesenbronn
Cast
Kitzingen
Großlagenfrei
Großlagenfrei
Heidingsfeld
Rödelsee
Großlage Schloßberg (Rödelsee)
Großlage Hofrat (Kitzingen)
Eibelstadt
Großl Herre
Sickershausen
Großlagenfrei
Großlage Teufelstor
Sulzfeld
Mainbernheim
Großlage Burgweg (Iphofen)
Sommerhausen
Iphofen
Großlage Ölspiel
Großlagenfrei
Kleinochsenfurt
Markt Einersheim
Segnitz
Willanzheim
Frickenhausen
Marktbreit
Ochsenfurt
Obernbreit
Hüttenheim
Seinsheim
Großlage Schloßstück (Frankenberg)
Bullenheim
Ippesheim

FRANKEN
General sites
at Würzburg

Bereich Maindreieck   **Bereich Steigerwald**

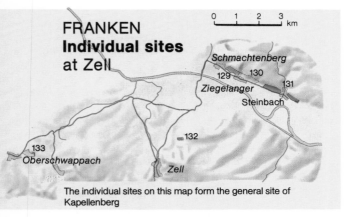

FRANKEN
Individual sites
at Zell

Schmachtenberg
129   130
Ziegelanger   131
Steinbach
132
133
Oberschwappach
Zell

The individual sites on this map form the general site of Kapellenberg

GROSSLAGE
KAPELLENBERG

Schmachtenberg
Ortsteil von Zeil am
Main
Eulengrund 129

Ziegelanger
Ortsteil von Zeil am
Main
Ölschnabel 130

Steinbach
Nonnenberg 131

Zell am Ebersberg
Ortsteil von
Kretzgau
Kronberg 132

Oberschwappach
Ortsteil von
Kretzgau
Sommertal 133

GROSSLAGENFREI

Zeil am Main
Mönchshang*

Eltmann
Schloßleite*

Altmannsdorf
Sonnenwinkel*

Michelau
Vollburg*

Oberschwarzach
Herrenberg*

Handthal
Stollberg*

Kammerforst
Ortsteil von
Breitbach
Teufel*

Prichsenstadt
Krone*

Martinsheim
Langenstein*

Ipsheim
Burg Hoheneck*

Tiefenstockheim
Stiefel*

Gerolzhofen
Arlesgarten*

Donnersdorf
Falkenberg*

Dingolshausen
Köhler*

56

Strong wine and lovely Madonnas

From the west, the Frankfurt-Nuremberg autobahn to the Spessart region passes Wasserschloss Mespelbrunn (palace) before reaching Würzburg, near the Franconian Saale, or the Tauber river. From the north the autobahn goes from Kassel via Hammelburg, and its vineyards, to Mainfranken. A round trip can be mapped out taking in not only wine but also – and unexpectedly – many beautiful Madonnas. At Würzburg – Tilman Riemenschneider's town – the route going in the direction of Randersacker is sometimes shown as Bocksbeutelstrasse (B13); via Randersacker, where the garden-house of Balthasar Neumann can be seen, the road arrives

The wine cellar at the Würzburg "Residence"

The wine press hall in the Main-Franconian museum

quickly at Eibelstadt with its ancient town wall, Sommerhausen, a small market town, and Ochsenfurt, a typical, old Franconian town. In Frickenhausen, to the south of the Maindreieck (Main triangle), the picturesque little Valentinus chapel arises from the midst of vineyards.

Along the way, attractive wrought iron inn signs, invite the visitor to enter for a refreshing glass of Frankenwein at Kitzingen, for example, the centre of the southern part of the Maindreieck, or Iphofen – an important viticulture centre in the Steigerwald region – with its quaint arches and towers and its medieval aspect.

Excellent Frankenwein can also be found in Rödelsee, Wiesenbronn, or Castell. Knowledge of wine-lore can be supplemented by visiting the first Bavarian

"Maria of the Rosary", Volkach

wine study trail in Abtswind, where newly-cultivated and re-named vineyards abound. Returning to Würzburg via Wiesentheid, Sommerach, Volkach, Nordheim and Escherndorf, Gothic, Renaissance and Baroque art treasures can be discovered as well as delicious wine.

Data and facts

Geographical notes: *The Franconian wine-growing area lies between Aschaffenburg and Schweinfurt; vineyards face south, on hilly slopes in the Main valleys, and valleys of the Main's tributaries; there are also some sites on the western side of the Steigerwald.*

Climate: *On gentle slopes and steep inclines in the narrow river valleys, as well as on the sheltered western and southern sites of the Steigerwald, climatic conditions are favourable to viticulture; a continental climate of dry warm summers and cold winters makes precautions against frosts necessary.*

Soil: *The three Bereiche have separate types of soil. In the Bereich of Mainviereck and on the slopes of the Spessart, there is mainly weathered, coloured sandstone soil. In the Maindreieck, shell limestone predominates,*

Shell limestone soil

together with clay and loess soil, resulting in pithy, fruity wine. The Bereich Steigerwald, with weathered, red marl soil, gives wine with an earthy and spicy flavour.

Cultivated area: *During the Middle Ages it was almost ten times as large as today; now concentrated – with 3,403 ha – on sites with the most favourable climatic conditions. 3 Districts, 17 General Sites, approximately 157 Individual Sites.*

Types of vine: *The classic Franconian vine was, until recently, the Silvaner (1,067 ha); but during the last few years the Müller-Thurgau has overtaken it (1,576 ha). Riesling follows with 106 ha, and there is now a whole range of new types such as Scheurebe (150 ha), Perle (50 ha), Kerner (180 ha), Rieslaner (36 ha), Bacchus (60 ha). Red wine, on just 48 ha, ranks as a speciality.*

Yield: *On average 1975–1977: 350,000 hl. Franconia produces 3.7% of the German must harvest.*

Production structure: *Mainly small undertakings are in contact with wine-growers' co-operatives; a few large wine estates.*

Roughly 50% of Franconia's wine production is marketed today by nine wine-growers' co-operatives.

View of Sommerhausen

Baroque and Rococo antiquities have also been preserved at Veitshöchheim, while Würzburg has art treasures belonging to many different epochs. The collections of the Mainfränkische Museum in the fortress of Marienberg include rare exhibits of the region's centuries-old viticulture. Many more interesting sights and places await the visitor: the impressive Juliusspital, and the "Käppele"; the Dom (cathedral), the old university and the old residence of the princes. In spring, summer or autumn Franconia offers a breathtaking opportunity to sample wine.

Details about 50 or more Franconian wine festivals and further ideas for a wine-journey can be obtained from:

Frankenwein-Frankenland e.V.
Postfach 764
8700 Würzburg 2
Western Germany

Württemberg

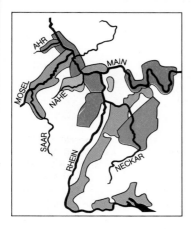

Viticultural areas extend mainly along rivers. On the Mosel, Rhine, Nahe and Ahr, vineyards climb up steep inclines that rise from the river banks; but in the side valleys there are hardly any vines. Not so in Württemberg. There are exhilarating Riesling, Silvaner, Trollinger and Müller-Thurgau species which grow on the slopes of the Neckar valley through which the Swabian wine-route runs; but wines of equal excellence can also be found in the side valleys of the Neckar, in the Remstal and Enztal, and in the Kocher, Jagst and Tauber valleys.

Even where no river marks a valley – in the Bottwartal alongside the Burgenstrasse, at the foot of the Stromberg mountain, as well as in the Zabergäu district – Frühburgunder, Spätburgunder, Schwarzriesling and the rare Lemberger grapes (grown only in Württemberg) flourish.

Despite its extensive growing area,

The river Neckar near Mundelsheim

Württemberger wine is hardly known outside the country. The reason is not hard to discover: in Württemberg, consumption of wine is almost three times as large as its production; and as the Swabian lives by the precept "you should never wait until you're thirsty", the drinking of the daily quarter carafe (which quickly becomes a three-quarter one) is a necessary routine.

Visiting Württemberg to sample the locally grown wine provides the opportunity to seek out rarer taverns still linked to a bakery where traditions are preserved and where the advice of the first President of the German Federal Republic, an old Swabian, who said: "He who pours ('säuft') wine down his gullet sins – he who drinks wine, prays!", is put to good use.

Spätzle or Knöpfle?

Swabian food has many specialities. Spätzle, which look like bent noodles and Knöpfle, a sort of tiny dumpling. The ingredients, however, are exactly the same.

A "weekly itinerary of the stomach", which Karl J. Weber drew up in his *Demokritos* in 1843 states: "The true

Trollinger

Main types of vine in Württemberg:

Riesling	21.7%
Trollinger	21.0%
Müller-Thurgau	14.8%
Schwarzriesling (Müller grape)	10.2%

View of Heilbronn from the Stauffenberg

Swabian eats noodles on Monday, Hutzle On Tuesday, Knöpfle on Wednesday, Spätzle on Thursday, Friday steamed Grundbirn (potatoes), Saturday pancakes, and Sunday Brätle and Salätle (roast and salad)".

The Swabian wine-route offers many worthwhile excursions:

In the north this wine-route starts with the Himmelreich (heavenly realm) at Gundelsheim and runs along the shores of the Neckar to the Zuckerle (sugar) region near Bad Cannstadt; on the way there are numerous delightful wine villages and towns offering plenty of interest: castles, churches, timbered houses, at Bad Wimpfen, for instance, a medieval town, and Bad Friedrichshall, famous for its 500 years old Wasserschloss (water castle).

The route to Heilbronn takes in Weinsberg, or, a little further east into the Kocher valley, where wine grows mainly around Ingelfingen, Griesbach and Niedernhall, and Jagsttal, famous for its connection with Götz von Berlichingen, a valiant knight. Alternative travel along the Burgenstrasse leads to the Hohenloher countryside and the Tauber valley.

By turning eastward again into the Bottwar valley, after visiting the lower Enz valley, splendid examples of medieval architecture can be savoured, as well as the sumptuous wines. Both can be sampled at Marbach and Ludwigsburg, before reaching Esslingen to make an excursion into the Rems valley, where great wines grow. Inns and taverns are in plentiful supply along the route.

Further information – also about dates of wine and vintage festivals – can be obtained from:

"Werbegemeinschaft Württembergischer Weingärtnergenossenschaft," Heilbronnersstrasse 41 7000 Stuttgart 1 Western Germany

(Continued on page 62)

Spätzle, a speciality of Württemberg

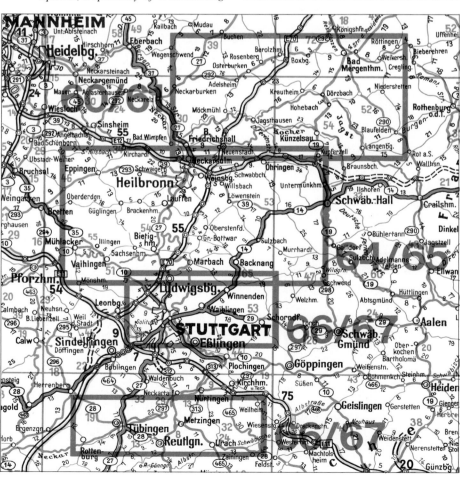

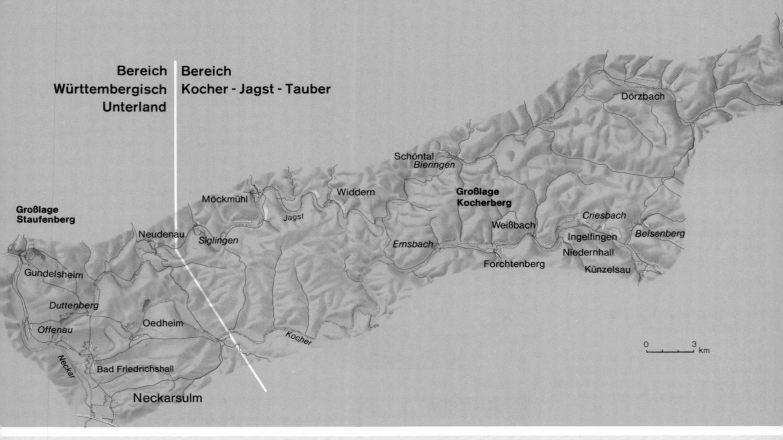

WÜRTTEMBERG
General sites
in the district of Kocher-Jagst-Tauber

Bad Mergenthe
Markels

Bereich
**Württembergisch
Unterland**

Bereich
Kocher - Jagst - Tauber

Dörzbach

Schöntal
Bieringen

**Großlage
Staufenberg**

Möckmühl

Widdern

**Großlage
Kocherberg**

Jagst

Weißbach

Criesbach

Neudenau

Siglingen

Ernsbach

Ingelfingen

Belsenberg

Niedernhall

Gundelsheim

Forchtenberg

Künzelsau

Duttenberg

Oedheim

Offenau

Kocher

0   3
        km

Neckar

Bad Friedrichshall

Neckarsulm

*These figures from the
Ludwigsburg porcelain makers are
replicas of originals dating from the 1770s*

Möckmühl 16

Widdern
16

16

17

Jagst

18

Neudenau

Siglingen

Gundelsheim

Duttenberg

22

19

Oedheim

Offenau

19

Kocher

Neckar

Bad Friedrichshall

Neckarsulm

60

Bereich Kocher-Jagst-Tauber

GROSSLAGE TAUBERBERG

Bad Mergentheim Ortsteil Markelsheim
Mönchsberg 1 T
Probstberg 2 T

Weikersheim
Hardt 3
Schmecker 4
Karlsberg 5

– Ortsteil Elpersheim
Mönchsberg 1 T
Probstberg 2 T

– Ortsteil Laudenbach
Schafsteige 6 T

– Ortsteil Haagen
Schafsteige 6 T

– Ortsteil Schäftersheim
Klosterberg 4 a

Niederstetten
Schafsteige 6 T

– Ortsteil Wermutshausen
Schafsteige 6 T

– Ortsteil Vorbachzimmern
Schafsteige 6 T

– Ortsteil Oberstetten
Schafsteige 6 T

GROSSLAGE KOCHERBERG

Dörzbach
Altenberg 7

Künzelsau
Hoher Berg 8 T

– Ortsteil Belsenberg
Heiligkreuz 9

Ingelfingen
Hoher Berg 8 T

– Ortsteil Criesbach
Hoher Berg 8 T
Sommerberg 10
Burgstall 11 T

Niedernhall
Hoher Berg 8 T
Burgstall 11 T
Engweg 12 T

Weißbach
Engweg 12 T
Altenberg 13

Forchtenberg
Flatterberg 14 T

– Ortsteil Ernsbach
Flatterberg 14 T

Schöntal Ortsteil Bieringen
Schlüsselberg 15

Widdern
Hofberg 16 T

Möckmühl
Hofberg 16 T
Ammerlanden 17

Neudenau Ortsteil Siglingen
Hofberg 16 T

WÜRTTEMBERG
Individual sites
in the district of Kocher-Jagst-Tauber

Ingelfingen from the air
(Aerial photo: SW-P1640)

Each kilometre brings historical interest

No matter which direction is taken in Württemberg, the land is full of historical places and remnants of ancient cultures. Archaeological finds near Steinheim dating back to the Ice Age prove that some very early settlements existed. Fossilized grape-pips found in an early Stone Age settlement near Weinsberg seem to indicate that viticulture existed even then.

The monastery of Lorsch, on the Bergstrasse, owned vineyards on the Michaelsberg as far back as 793, and one thousand years of viticulture have been documented in Benningen, Marbach, Steinheim, Schwaigern and Mockmühl.

Faithful women save a town's men

With the advent of German emperors and kings, the establishment of castles and Pfalzen (fortified palace seat) commenced. It was a Hohenstaufen emperor, Konrad III, who beleaguered Weinsberg in 1140. He granted the women safe conduct out of the town, allowing them to carry away their "dearest possession". Later, the women emerged through the town gate – carrying their husbands on their backs.

A never-to-be-forgotten wine

In 1147 Cistercian monks came to the Salzach valley. According to legend, they were led to a fountain by a mule, and so called their monastery "Maulbronn" (mule-fountain). After the Reformation it became the school of a Protestant religious order. Famous Swabians like Johannes Kapler, Friedrich Hölderlin and Hermann Hesse, were educated there. Elffingerberg used to belong to the monastery, and got its name ("Eleven

Eros on a Roman ceramic fragment

Fingers Mountain") from the fact that the monks wished they had eleven fingers: at Lent they were only allowed to dip their fingers into a bowl of wine, and then to lick them!

Freedom and independence

In the Rems valley (Remstal) at Beutelsbach, where a potent Riesling grows, the "Armer Konrad" peasant uprising, which the Swabian writer Wilhelm Hauff describes in his novel *Lichtenstein*, started in 1514. Schorndorf, only a few kilometres deeper into the Rems valley, is remarkable in another way. In the Middle Ages the people managed to raise 5% of the total sum of "Landessteuern" (regional taxes) from the proceeds of viticulture.

The great peasant uprising of 1525 left some deep scars on Württemberg, however. Castles Gundelsheim, Weinsberg and Neckarsulm fell victim to the freedom fighters of those days. The earliest German democratic constitution was drawn up in Tübingen in 1514 – and the "Free Imperial Cities" (Freie Reichstädte) it created always remained a thorn in the side of the Württemberger dukes.

Revolutionary expediency sometimes has its draw-backs. In 1349, the free men of Esslingen let 459,000 litres of young wine pour into the alleys, as they sacked the Württemberger town of Strümpfelbach!

Strümpfelbach

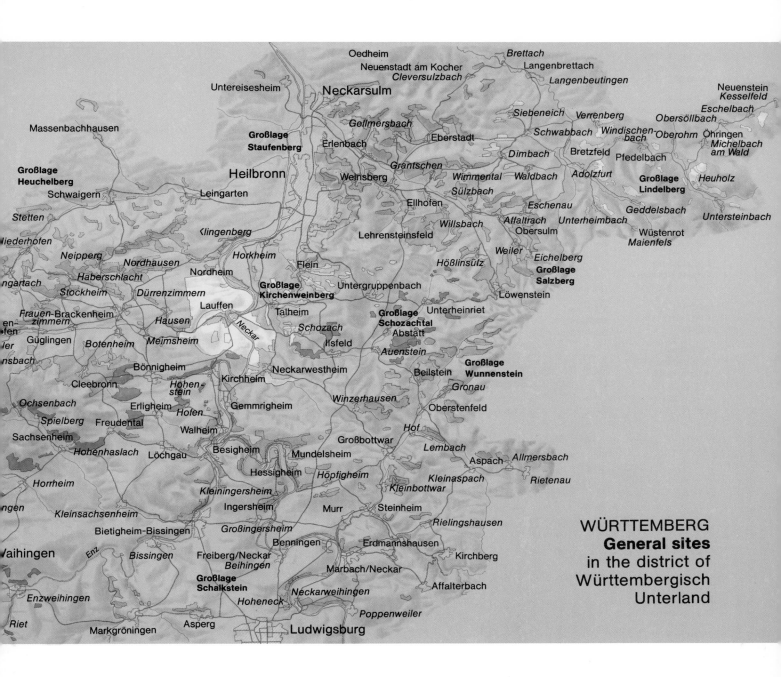

WÜRTTEMBERG
General sites
in the district of
Württembergisch
Unterland

(Map labels:)

Massenbachhausen

Oedheim
Neuenstadt am Kocher
Cleversulzbach

Brettach
Langenbrettach
Langenbeutingen

Neuenstein
Kesselfeld
Eschelbach
Obersöllbach

Untereisesheim
Neckarsulm

Siebeneich Verrenberg
Schwabbach Windischen-
bach Oberohrn Öhringen
Michelbach
am Wald

Gellmersbach
Erlenbach Eberstadt
Dimbach Bretzfeld Pfedelbach

**Großlage
Staufenberg**

Heuholz

**Großlage
Heuchelberg**
Schwaigern

Heilbronn
Leingarten

Grantschen
Weinsberg Wimmental Waldbach Adolzfurt
Sülzbach

**Großlage
Lindelberg**

Stetten

Klingenberg
Ellhofen
Eschenau
Affaltrach Unterheimbach

Geddelsbach

Untersteinbach

Niederhofen
Neipperg Nordhausen
Haberschlacht
Stockheim Dürrenzimmern

Horkheim
Lehrensteinsfeld
Willsbach
Obersulm

Wüstenrot
Maienfels

Weiler Eichelberg

Flein

Hößlinsülz

**Großlage
Salzberg**

ngartach
Frauen-Brackenheim
zimmern
Güglingen Botenheim Meimsheim
nsbach

Nordheim
Lauffen

Neckar

**Großlage
Kirchenweinberg**
Talheim
Schozach
Ilsfeld

Untergruppenbach

Löwenstein

Hausen

**Großlage
Schozachtal**
Abstatt

Unterheinriet

Auenstein

enfen
ler

Bönnigheim
Hohen-
stein
Kirchheim
Neckarwestheim

**Großlage
Wunnenstein**
Beilstein

Cleebronn
Erligheim Hofen
Ochsenbach
Spielberg Freudental
Sachsenheim
Walheim
Gemmrigheim
Winzerhausen

Gronau
Oberstenfeld

Hof

Hohenhaslach Löchgau
Besigheim
Mundelsheim
Großbottwar
Lembach

Horrheim
Hessigheim Höpfigheim
Kleinaspach

Aspach Allmersbach
Rietenau

Kleiningersheim
Kleinbottwar

ngen
Kleinsachsenheim
Ingersheim
Murr Steinheim

Bietigheim-Bissingen
Großingersheim
Rielingshausen

Vaihingen
Enz
Bissingen
Benningen
Erdmannshausen
Freiberg/Neckar
Beihingen
Kirchberg
Marbach/Neckar

**Großlage
Schalkstein**
Neckarweihingen
Affalterbach
Enzweihingen
Hoheneck

Riet
Markgröningen Asperg
Poppenweiler
Ludwigsburg

– Ortsteil Horkheim
Stiftsberg 27 T

Talheim
Stiftsberg 27 T

GROSSLAGE
LINDELBERG

**Neuenstein
Ortsteil Kesselfeld**
Schwobajörgle 30 T

– Ortsteil
Eschelbach
Schwobajörgle 30 T

– Ortsteil
Obersöllbach
Margarete 31 T

**Öhringen
Ortsteil Michelbach
am Wald**
Margarete 31 T
Dachsteiger 32 T

– Ortsteil
Verrenberg
Goldberg 33 T
Verrenberg 35

Pfedelbach
Goldberg 33 T

– Ortsteil
Untersteinbach
Dachsteiger 32 T

– Ortsteil **Heuholz**
Dachsteiger 32 T
Spielbühl 34

– Ortsteil **Harsberg**
Dachsteiger 32 T

– Ortsteil **Oberohrn**
Dachsteiger 32 T

– Ortsteil
Windischenbach
Goldberg 33 T

**Wüstenrot
Ortsteil Maienfels**
Schneckenhof 36 T

Bretzfeld
Goldberg 33 T

– Ortsteil
Geddelsbach
Schneckenhof 36 T

– Ortsteil
Unterheimbach
Schneckenhof 36 T

– Ortsteil **Adolzfurt**
Schneckenhof 36 T

– Ortsteil
Siebeneich
Himmelreich 37 T
Schloßberg 38 T

– Ortsteil
Schwabbach
Schloßberg 38 T

– Ortsteil **Dimbach**
Schloßberg 38 T

– Ortsteil **Waldbach**
Schloßberg 38 T

**Langenbrettach
Ortsteil
Langenbeutingen**
Himmelreich 37 T

GROSSLAGE
SALZBERG

Eberstadt
Sommerhalde 39
Eberfürst 40

Weinsberg
Althälde 41 T

– Ortsteil
Grantschen
Wildenberg 42

– Ortsteil
Wimmental
Altenberg 43 T

Ellhofen
Althälde 41 T
Altenberg 43 T

Lehrensteinsfeld
Althälde 41 T
Steinacker 44
Frauenzimmer 45

**Obersulm
– Ortsteil Sülzbach**
Altenberg 43 T

– Ortsteil **Willsbach**
Dieblesberg 46 T
Zeilberg 47 T

– Ortsteil **Affaltrach**
Dieblesberg 46 T
Zeilberg 47 T

– Ortsteil **Eschenau**
Paradies 48

– Ortsteil
Eichelberg
Hundsberg 49 T

– Ortsteil **Weiler**
Hundsberg 49 T
Schlierbach 50

Löwenstein
Nonnenrain 51
Wohlfahrtsberg 52
Altenberg 43 a

– Ortsteil
Hößlinsülz
Dieblesberg 46 T
Zeilberg 47 T

GROSSLAGE
SCHOZACHTAL

Abstatt
Sommerberg 53 T
Burgberg 54 T
Burg Wildeck 55

Löwenstein
Sommerberg 53 T

**Untergruppenbach
Ortsteil
Unterheinriet**
Sommerberg 53 T

Ilsfeld
Rappen 56

– Ortsteil **Auenstein**
Burgberg 54 T
Schloßberg 57

GROSSLAGE
WUNNENSTEIN

Beilstein
Wartberg 58
Steinberg 59
Schloßwengert 60

Oberstenfeld
Forstberg 61 T
Lichtenberg 62 T
Harzberg 63 T

– Ortsteil **Gronau**
Forstberg 61 T

Ilsfeld
Lichtenberg 62 T

Großbottwar
Lichtenberg 62 T
Harzberg 63 T

– Ortsteil
Winzerhausen
Lichtenberg 62 T
Harzberg 63 T

– Ortsteile
Hof und Lembach
Lichtenberg 62 T
Harzberg 63 T

Steinheim
Lichtenberg 62 T

– Ortsteil
Kleinbottwar
Lichtenberg 62 T
Oberer Berg 64 T
Süßmund 65
Götzenberg 66

**Ludwigsburg
Ortsteil Hoheneck**
Oberer Berg 64 T

GROSSLAGE
KIRCHENWEIN-
BERG

Heilbronn
Sonnenberg 67 T
Altenberg 68 T

**Brackenheim
Ortsteil Neipperg**
Vogelsang 79 T
Grafenberg 81 T
Schloßberg 82 T
Steingrube 88

**Eppingen
Ortsteil Kleingartach**
Vogelsang 79 T
Grafenberg 81 T

**Heilbronn
Ortsteil
Klingenberg**
Schloßberg 82 T
Sonntagsberg 83 T

Nordheim
Grafenberg 81 T
Sonntagsberg 83 T
Ruthe 84 T
Gräfenberg 87

– Ortsteil
Nordhausen
Sonntagsberg 83 T

– Ortsteil
Haberschlacht
Dachsberg 86 T

– Ortsteil
Botenheim
Ochsenberg 93

Cleebronn
Michaelsberg 94 T

Güglingen
Michaelsberg 94 T
Kaiserberg 95 T

– Ortsteil
Frauenzimmern
Michaelsberg 94 T
Kaiserberg 95 T

– Ortsteil Weiler
Hohenberg 97 T

Zaberfeld
Hohenberg 97 T

**Burgbronn
Ortsteil Leonbrunn**
Hahnenberg 98 T

– Ortsteil
Ochsenburg
Hahnenberg 98 T

Flein
Sonnenberg 67 T
Altenberg 68 T
Eselsberg 69

Untergruppenbach
Schloßberg 70

Talheim
Sonnenberg 67 T
Schloßberg 70 a
Hohe Eiche 71

Lauffen
Katzenbeißer 72
Riedersbückele 73
Jungfer 74

Neckarwestheim
Herrlesberg 75

**Ilsfeld
Ortsteil Schozach**
Schelmenklinge 76
Roter Berg 77

GROSSLAGE
HEUCHELBERG

Massenbachhausen
Krähenberg 78

Leingarten
Vogelsang 79 T
Leiersberg 80
Grafenberg 81 T

Brackenheim
Schloßberg 82 T
Mönchsberg 83 a T
Zweifelberg 84
Wolfsaugen 85
Dachsberg 86 T

– Ortsteil
Dürrenzimmern
Mönchsberg 83 a

– Ortsteil Hausen
Vogelsang 79 a
Staig 89
Jupiterberg 90

– Ortsteil
Meimsheim
Katzenöhrle 91

– Ortsteil
Stockheim
Altenberg 92

– Ortsteil
Eibensbach
Michaelsberg 94 T

Schwaigern
Vogelsang 79 T
Grafenberg 81 T
Ruthe 84 T
Sonnenberg 96 T

– Ortsteil Stetten
Sonnenberg 96 T

– Ortsteil
Niederhofen
Vogelsang 79 T
Grafenberg 81 T

Pfaffenhofen
Hohenberg 97 T

GROSSLAGE
STROMBERG

Oberderdingen
Kupferhalde 99

Sternenfels
König 100

Knittlingen
Reichshalde 101 T

Ötisheim
Sauberg 104

– Ortsteil
Freudenstein
Reichshalde 101 T

Maulbronn
Reichshalde 101 T
Eilfingerberg 102
(Eilfingerberg-)
Klosterstück 103

– Ortsteil
Mühlhausen
Halde 106 T

Vaihingen
Halde 106 T

**Mühlacker
Ortsteil Lienzingen**
Eichelberg 105

– Ortsteil Roßwag
Halde 106 T
Forstgrube 108 T

– Ortsteil
Enzweihingen
Höllisch Feuer 107

– Ortsteil
Gündelbach
Wachtkopf 110
Steinbachhof 111

Massenbachhausen
78
79
Schwaigern
Leingarten
96
Stetten
79
80
79
79
79
81
81
83
Niederhofen
84 a
87
81
88
81
Neipperg
90
79
81
86
82
88
89
Haberschlacht
84
79 a
Nordhaus
83 a
Eppingen Kleingartach
79
92
66
83 a
79
90
Stockheim
95
94
Dürrenzimmern
Hausen
85
99
95
94
Brackenheim
91
La
Oberderdingen
Burgbronn
Ochsenburg
97
97
84
79
90
100
Leonbronn
98
Pfaffenhofen Güglingen
Botenheim
Meimsheim
Zaberfeld
Weiler
97
94
91
Sternenfels
Eibensbach
93
99
94
94
91
Bönnigheim
114
101
Freudenstein
115
Cleebronn
119
Hohenste
Knittlingen
116
Häfnerhaslach
Ochsenbach
118
101
Diefenbach
117
Erligheim
He
101
Spielberg
Freudental
118
103
Maulbronn
110
111
114
121
102
105
Mittelhaslach
Hohenhaslach
120
Wa
Schützingen
113
Löchgau
112
Gündelbach
121
Besigh
113
Horrheim
Lienzingen
112
104
Ötisheim
Ensingen
Kleinsachsenheim
121
Illingen
108
Mühlacker
Mühlhausen
106
Vaihingen
121
Bietigh
Roßwag
106
Enz
Bissingen
Bissing
107
Enzweihingen
129
128
114
Riet
Markgröningen
Aspe

WÜRTTEMBERG
Individual sites
in the district of
Württembergisch Unterland

– Ortsteil Ensingen
Schanzreiter 112 T

– Ortsteil Horrheim
Klosterberg 113 T

– Ortsteil Riet
Kirchberg 114 T

Illingen
Halde 106 T
Forstgrube 108 T
Schanzreiter 112 T

– Ortsteil Schützingen
Heiligenberg 115 T

Sternenfels
Ortsteil Diefenbach
König 116

Sachsenheim
Ortsteil Häfnerhaslach
Heiligenberg 115 T

– Ortsteil Hohenhaslach
Klosterberg 113 T
Kirchberg 114 T

– Ortsteil Ochsenbach
Liebenberg 117 T

– Ortsteil Spielberg
Liebenberg 117 T

– Ortsteil Kleinsachsenheim
Kirchberg 114 T

Freudental
Kirchberg 114 T

Erligheim
Lerchenberg 118 T

Bönnigheim
Kirchberg 114 T
Sonnenberg 119

– Ortsteil Hohenstein
Kirchberg 114 T

– Ortsteil Hofen
Lerchenberg 118 T

Kirchheim
Kirchberg 114 T

GROSSLAGE SCHALKSTEIN

Gemmrigheim
Wurmberg 120 T
Felsengarten 121 T

Walheim
Wurmberg 120 T
Felsengarten 121 T

Besigheim
Wurmberg 120 T
Felsengarten 121 T

Hessigheim
Wurmberg 120 T
Felsengarten 121 T
Käsberg 122 T

Mundelsheim
Käsberg 122 T
Mühlbächer 123
Rozenberg 124

Steinheim, Ortsteil Höpfigheim
Königsberg 125

Murr
Neckarhälde 126 T

Ingersheim, Ortsteil Kleiningersheim
Schloßberg 127 T

– Ortsteil Großingersheim
Schloßberg 127 T

Freiberg/Neckar Ortsteil Beihingen
Neckarhälde 126 T

Benningen
Neckarhälde 126 T

Marbach
Neckarhälde 126 T

Erdmannhausen
Neckarhälde 126 T

Ludwigsburg Ortsteil Hoheneck
Neckarhälde 126 T

– Ortsteil Neckarweihingen
Neckarhälde 126 T

– Ortsteil Poppenweiler
Neckarhälde 126 T

Affalterbach
Neckarhälde 126 T

Asperg
Berg 128 T

Markgröningen
Berg 128 T
Sankt Johännser 129

Bietigheim-Bissingen Ortsteil Bissingen
Felsengarten 121 T

– Ortsteil Bietigheim
Felsengarten 121 T

Löchgau
Felsengarten 121 T

Steinheim
Burgberg 130

Kirchberg
Kelterberg 131 T

Marbach/Neckar Ortsteil Rielingshausen
Kelterberg 131 T

Aspach Ortsteil Kleinaspach
Kelterberg 131 T

– Ortsteil Allmersbach
Alter Berg 132

– Ortsteil Rietenau
Güldenkern 133

WÜRTTEMBERG
General sites
at Stuttgart

Hertmannsweiler
Winnenden
Bürg
Großlage Kopf (gelb)
Baach
Hanweiler
Neustadt
Breuningsweiler
Mühlhausen
Neckar
Waiblingen
Korb
Kleinheppach
Zuffenhausen
Münster
Fellbach
Beinstein
Großheppach
Großlage Wartbühl (braun)
Remshalden
Feuerbach
Bad Cannstadt
Endersbach
Weinstadt
Geradstetten
Hebsack
Gerlingen
Rommelshausen
Kernen
Grunbach
Beutelsbach
Rems
Winterbach
Schorndorf
Stuttgart
Untertürkheim
Stetten
Schnait
Rotenberg
Strümpfel-bach
Aichelberg
Gaisburg
Uhlbach
Obertürkheim
Aichwald
Wangen
Großlage Sonnenbühl (dunkelgrün)
Großlage Weinsteige (hellgrün)
Rohracker
Degerloch
Hedelfingen
Eßlingen

0   3 km

66

Bereich Remstal – Stuttgart

GROSSLAGE WEINSTEIGE

Gerlingen
Bopser 134

Stuttgart
Mönchhalde 135 T
Kriegsberg 136

– Ortsteil Feuerbach
Berg 137 T

– Ortsteil Degerloch
Scharrenberg 138

– Ortsteil Bad Cannstatt
Mönchhalde 135 T
Berg 137 T
Steinhalde 139 T
Zuckerle 140 T
Halde 141
Herzogenberg 142 T
Mönchberg 143 T

– Ortsteil Mühlhausen
Steinhalde 139 T
Zuckerle 140 T

– Ortsteil Münster
Berg 137 T
Steinhalde 139 T
Zuckerle 140 T

– Ortsteil Zuffenhausen
Berg 137 T

– Ortsteil Untertürkheim
Herzogenberg 142 T
Mönchberg 143 T
Altenberg 144
Gips 145 T
Wetzstein 146 T
Schloßberg 147 T

– Ortsteil Rotenberg
Schloßberg 147 T

– Ortsteil Uhlbach
Schloßberg 147 T
Steingrube 148
Götzenberg 149

– Ortsteil Gaisburg
Abelsberg 150

– Ortsteil Wangen
Berg 137 T

– Ortsteil Hedelfingen
Lenzenberg 151 T

– Ortsteil Rohracker
Lenzenberg 151 T

– Ortsteil Obertürkheim
Kirchberg 152 T
Ailenberg 153 T

Fellbach
Herzogenberg 142 T
Mönchberg 143 T
Gips 145 T
Wetzstein 146 T
Goldberg 154
Lämmler 155
Hinterer Berg 156

Eßlingen
Kirchberg 152 T
Ailenberg 153 T
Lerchenberg 157
Schenkenberg 158

GROSSLAGE KOPF

Korb
Sommerhalde 159
Berg 160 T
Hörnle 161 T

– Ortsteil Kleinheppach
Greiner 162

Waiblingen
Hörnle 161 T

– Ortsteil Neustadt
Söhrenberg 163

– Ortsteil Beinstein
Großmulde 164

Winnenden
Berg 160 T
Holzenberg 165 T
Roßberg 166

– Ortsteil Hanweiler
Berg 160 T

– Ortsteil Breuningsweiler
Holzenberg 165 T

– Ortsteil Bürg
Schloßberg 167

Weinstadt, Ortsteil Großheppach
Wanne 168

Remshalden Ortsteil Grunbach
Berghalde 169

Winterbach
Hungerberg 170

Schorndorf
Grafenberg 171

GROSSLAGE WARTBÜHL

Winnenden
Haselstein 172 T

– Ortsteil Hertmannsweiler
Himmelreich 173 T

– Ortsteil Baach
Himmelreich 173 T

– Ortsteil Breuningsweiler
Haselstein 172 T

– Ortsteil Hanweiler
Maien 174

Korb
Steingrüble 175 T

– Ortsteil Kleinheppach
Steingrüble 175 T

Weinstadt, Ortsteil Großheppach
Steingrüble 175 T
Zügernberg 177

– Ortsteil Beutelsbach
Sonnenberg 176 T
Altenberg 178 T
Käppele 179

– Ortsteil Schnait
Sonnenberg 176 T
Altenberg 178 T

– Ortsteil Endersbach
Wetzstein 180
Happenhalde 181

– Ortsteil Strümpfelbach
Gastenklinge 182
Nonnenberg 183

Remshalden Ortsteil Grunbach
Klingle 184

– Ortsteil Geradstetten
Sonnenberg 176 T
Lichtenberg 185 T

– Ortsteil Hebsack
Lichtenberg 185 T

Aichwald Ortsteil Aichelberg
Luginsland 186

Kernen Ortsteil Stetten
Pulvermächer 187
Lindhälder 188
Brotwasser 189
Häder 190 T

– Ortsteil Rommelshausen
Häder 190 T

Waiblingen
Steingrüble 175 T

GROSSLAGE SONNENBÜHL

Weinstadt Ortsteil Beutelsbach
Burghalde 192 T

– Ortsteil Schnait
Burghalde 192 T

– Ortsteil Strümpfelbach
Altenberg 193

– Ortsteil Endersbach
Hintere Klinge 194

Gerlingen
134

Kernen Ortsteil Stetten
Mönchberg 195 T

– Ortsteil Rommelshausen
Mönchberg 195 T

Bereich Bayerischer Bodensee

GROSSLAGE LINDAUER SEEGARTEN

Nonnenhorn
Seehalde*
Sonnenbüchel*

With vineyards in the Bodolz, Lindau and Wasserburg sections.

Tübingen
Unterjesingen
199
198
Wurmlingen
Hirschau
Wendelsheim
199
Neckar
Rottenburg
199
199

WÜRTTEMBERG
Individual sites
at Stuttgart

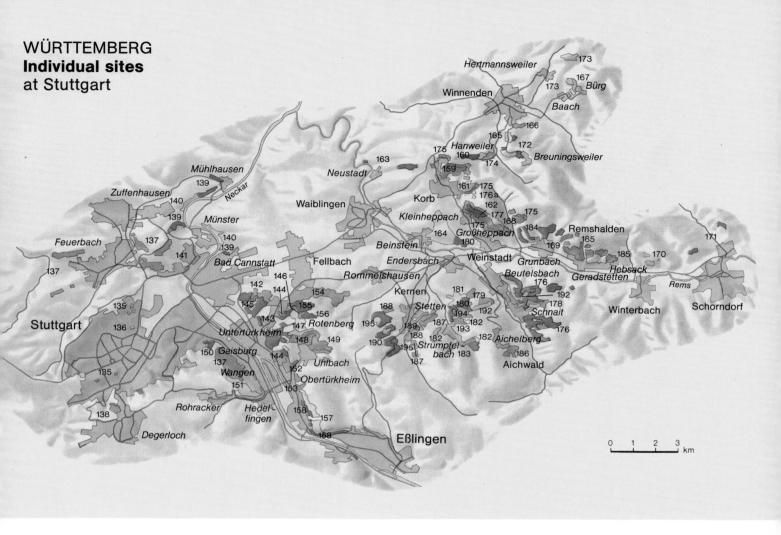

WÜRTTEMBERG
Individual sites
at Tübingen – Reutlingen

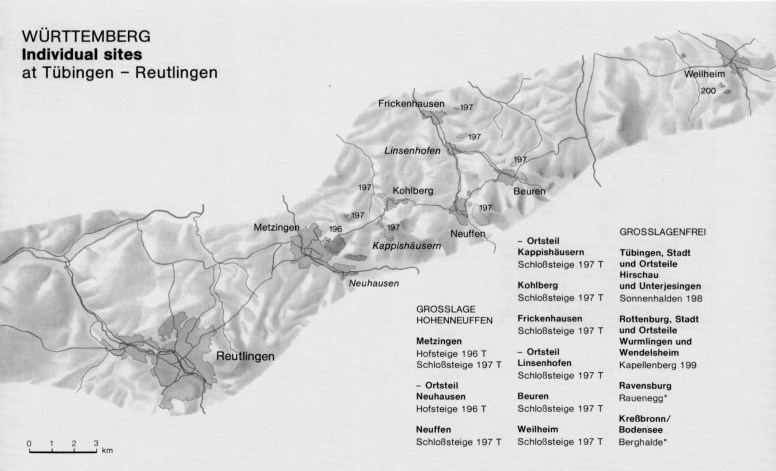

GROSSLAGE
HOHENNEUFFEN

Metzingen
Hofsteige 196 T
Schloßsteige 197 T

– Ortsteil
Neuhausen
Hofsteige 196 T

Neuffen
Schloßsteige 197 T

– Ortsteil
Kappishäusern
Schloßsteige 197 T

Kohlberg
Schloßsteige 197 T

Frickenhausen
Schloßsteige 197 T

– Ortsteil
Linsenhofen
Schloßsteige 197 T

Beuren
Schloßsteige 197 T

Weilheim
Schloßsteige 197 T

GROSSLAGENFREI

**Tübingen, Stadt
und Ortsteile
Hirschau
und Unterjesingen**
Sonnenhalden 198

**Rottenburg, Stadt
und Ortsteile
Wurmlingen und
Wendelsheim**
Kapellenberg 199

Ravensburg
Rauenegg*

**Kreßbronn/
Bodensee**
Berghalde*

67

Baden

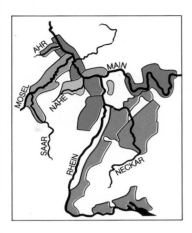

Ravensburg castle near Sulzfeld/Kraichgau

At the mention of Baden wine, wine-lovers usually think of the Kaiserstühler, or the Markgräfler or, perhaps, wine from Ortenau; but wine is grown in seven Badener districts, each one producing a different and typical kind, which can best be sampled by travelling the Badische Weinstrasse (Baden wine route) whose signposts feature a bunch of grapes along the way.

Badisches Frankenland, a land of Madonnas

The Baden wine route actually starts in Franconia, for the lower Tauber valley with Tauberbischofsheim and Wertheim/Main belongs to Baden.

A flowery, almost aromatic Müller-Thurgau grows here, and as this is really Franconian land – it only came to Baden in 1803 – the wine is offered in typically Franconian Bocksbeutel.

It is not known whether Bonifatius, who owned Tauberbischofsheim in 730, already cultivated wine there. Today viticulture flourishes in a dozen or more villages and communities up and down the River Tauber from Beckstein to Wertheim.

In the Middle Ages the Tauber valley was one of the rallying points for the peasants uprising in 1525, and, in Lauda, a wayside plaque still commemorates the executions that took place there on the personal orders of the Bishop of Würzburg.

Today, it is hard to believe that so gentle and charming a countryside should have witnessed such terrible scenes – a countryside in which so many statues of the Madonna abound that it has been given the name of "Madonnenländchen" (land of Madonnas).

Badische Bergstrasse Kraichgau

From Tauberbischofsheim via Walldürn, a place of pilgrimage to the "Heilig-Blut-Altar" (altar of the Sacred Blood) visitors

can drive to the Neckar and then along its banks to Heidelberg where the giant cask of 1751, which can hold 200,000 litres of wine, can be seen in Heidelberg Schloss. Along the Badische Bergstrasse from Heidelberg in a northerly direction provides the opportunity to sample the wines of Lützelsachsen and Leutershausen.

That part of the region has fewer historical attractions due to the ravages

Sign post on the Baden wine route

of many wars. The Swedes and the German emperor's troops fought there during The 30 Years' War, and in the campaigns of Louis XIV not only the Heidelberger Schloss, but many castles, palaces and towns were destroyed.

After Wiesloch and to the south of Heidelberg, the Kraichgau begins, where fruity Ruländer and a remarkable Riesling wine grows. The wine route is no longer the B3 here, and branches off into side roads leading eastward to Eichelberg, Tiefenbach and Odenheim. Further on, at Sulzfeld, there is the Ravensburg castle with its castle precinct 30 metres high and a magnificent Renaissance palace.

Through the medieval town of Bretten, which houses the largest library from the time of the Reformation in its Melanchtonhaus, the route continues in the direction of Bruchsal to the Pfinzgau, where a visit can be made to the palace of the Bruchsaler Prince Bishops with its Balthasar Neumann staircase.

Ruländer

Main types of vine in Baden:

Müller-Thurgau	34.5%
Blauer Spätburgunder	18.6%
Ruländer	12.5%
Gutedel	9.9%
Riesling	7.4%
Silvaner	4.6%

Visitors' Gazetteer

Baden-Baden: *Kurhaus; Trinkhalle (spa water drinking hall); new palace; Roumanian chapel; ruins of castle Eberstein.*
Breisach: *High altar at St. Stephans-Münster.*
Bruchsal: *Palace of sovereign bishops with Balthasar Neumann staircase and palace gardens.*
Emmendingen: *Town hall; margraves' palace; castle ruins of Landeck and Hochburg.*

Ettlingen: *Palace; town hall; jesters' fountain.*
Freiburg: *Münster; medieval shop; Schwabentor (town gate); Martinstor (town gate); town hall; museums.*
Heidelberg: *Old university; Heiliggeist-kirche (church); Haus zum Riesen with geological collection; Haus zum Ritter (Renaissance façade); town hall; Karls-tor (town gate); palace.*
Karlsruhe: *Palace with regional museum; federal exhibition hall; pyramid; palace square; views from the Turmberg.*

Offenburg: *Heiligkreuzkirche (church); town hall; Vinzentiusgarten (gardens).*
Ortenberg: *Palace.*
Weinheim: *Towers of the old town fortifications; market square fountain; Löwen Apotheke (old pharmacy); palace of the Counts of Berckheim; castle ruin Windeck; Wachenburg castle.*
Wertheim: *Marienkapelle (chapel); town hall; ruins of castle.*

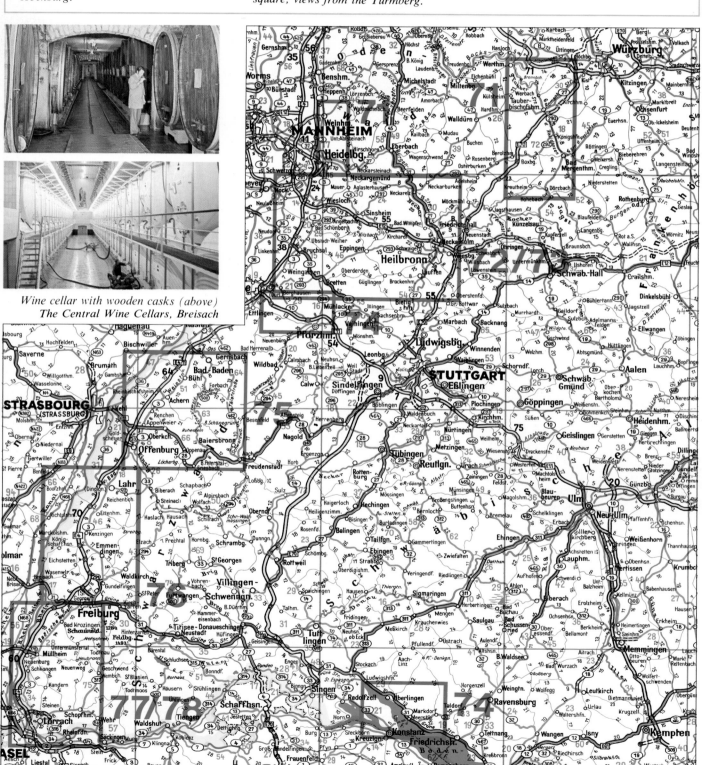

Wine cellar with wooden casks (above)
The Central Wine Cellars, Breisach

Ortenau is "soft and warm..."

Thus Goethe thought, and he was right about this fertile little piece of land that nestles at the edge of the Black Forest. Ortenau is the land of Simplicius Simplizissimus, where people drink a strong, wholesome red wine called Affentaler, bottled in its unusual "Affen" (monkey) bottle.

At the entrance to the Rench valley lies Oberkirch, with the ruins of the Schauenburg castle towering above. Sheltered by the mountains of the Black Forest, a splendid wine grows in its vineyards. Ten km further south there is Durbach and the Ritterburg (knight's castle) of Staufenberg, where Riesling wine is called Klingelberger, and Traminer Clevner.

Breisgau

The Breisgau extends from Offenburg to Freiburg, and it is here that the historically most interesting section of the wine route starts. Freiburg alone offers a wide variety of attractions.

Kaiserstuhl-Tuniberg – the essence of Baden wine

The mighty volcanic rock of the Kaiserstuhl stands guard and gives shelter to the vine. The Tuniberg mountain towers on its southern side. Viticulture started in this region as long ago as the 7th century.

Strong, fiery wine grows around the Kaiserstuhl, such as fruity Ruländer. Even

Loess-soil terraces on the slopes of Tuniberg

the mild Silvaner has a subdued fire in this region. The bouquet of Traminer and Gewürztraminer opens up like the scent of a flower. Full-flavoured Spätburgunder ripens predominantly in the southern half and is much appreciated as a red wine or a vigorous Weissherbst.

The wall paintings by Martin Schongauer in the Münster of Breisach (west wing) and the main altar, which is a masterpiece of German wood-carving, are particularly fascinating.

The Markgräflerland

Travelling south from Freiburg leads to the ancestral land of the Margrave of Baden.

St. Urban, Patron Saint of wine

His wine, the Markgräfler, was valued beyond Baden's boundaries a hundred years ago. The Gutedelrebe is a vine that grows particularly well in this domain, producing light, lively wine.

As a borderland, the Markgräflerland inevitably suffered in times of war; but the beauty of the landscape has finally proved to be indestructable. Peter Hebel named it "Paradiesgärtlein" ("little paradisegarden"), and René Schickele called it the "the most beautiful place of exile".

The Lake Constance wines

The Badische Weinstrasse ends at Weil, but travelling on along the Rhine to Erzingen, the wines start to take on the vigorous aroma of the Lake Constance wines.

The ancient fortified refuge, fortress and castle of Hohentwiel is almost at the lake. During The 30 Years' War it withstood five sieges and became the stronghold of the Protestants. Later, when Napoleon's army besieged it, its commandant capitulated without a fight, hoping that he could thereby save the castle. But Napoleon ordered its destruction.

Around Lake Constance, the important wine-growing communities of Meersburg and Hagnau are near Constance and Überlingen which are also respected wine producers. The sun, reflected from the surface of the lake, still helps to ripen the lively, elegant Müller-Thurgau and the fruity Spätburgunder Weissherbst today. Hagnau, where the Baden wine route ends, has lovely late Gothic and Baroque houses.

For more information about Baden, its towns and its vintage festivals, enquiries should be made to:
Weinwerbezentrale
Badische Winzergenossenschaften
Ettlinger Strasse 12
7500 Karlsruhe
Western Germany

Data and facts

Geographical notes: *The wine-growing region stretches for approximately 400 km from Lake Constance in the south to the Badische Bergstrasse and the Tauber river in the north.*

Climate: *Sunny and warm, thanks to sheltered positions at the extremities of the Black Forest and the Odenwald, and good climatic conditions in the lowlands of the upper Rhine region.*

Soil: *From heat-retaining moraine gravel in the Lake Constance region – via tertiary limestone, clay and marl, with loess deposits distributed throughout the volcanic stone-soil structure, to shell-lime and keuper in the Kraichgau and Taubergrund; the soil is rich and fertile throughout.*

Cultivated area: *12,599 ha, composed of 7 Districts, 15 General Sites, and 306 Individual Sites.*

Types of vine: *Variations in altitude and differing soil conditions produce a remarkable number of species. Müller-Thurgau (4,345 ha), almost unknown in this region two decades ago, is now the most widely cultivated vine; near the Kaiserstuhl it is mainly Ruländer (1,814 ha) and in the Markgräfler area Gutedel (1,247 ha); Riesling (930 ha) can be found predominantly in the Ortenau area, while Silvaner, Weisser (white) Burgunder and Traminer grow throughout the district.*

Yield: *On average 1975–1977: 1.4m hl, 14.8% of the German must harvest.*

Production structure: *Well-organized by wine-growers' co-operatives; also a fair number of vintagers and wine-estates which market their own produce. At present, 120 vintners' co-operatives with 23,000 members produce 80% of Baden's wine. The Zentralkellerei badischer Winzergenossenschaften (central winery of Baden wine-growers' co-operatives) in Breisach ranks as the largest and most modern cellar in Europe.*

Birnau Monastery, Bodensee

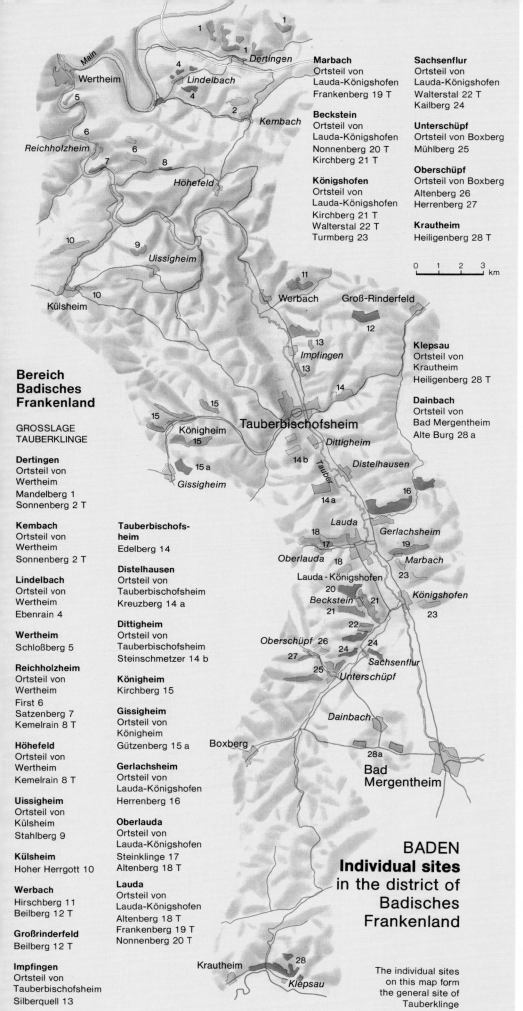

Bereich Badisches Frankenland

GROSSLAGE TAUBERKLINGE

Dertingen
Ortsteil von Wertheim
Mandelberg 1
Sonnenberg 2 T

Kembach
Ortsteil von Wertheim
Sonnenberg 2 T

Lindelbach
Ortsteil von Wertheim
Ebenrain 4

Wertheim
Schloßberg 5

Reichholzheim
Ortsteil von Wertheim
First 6
Satzenberg 7
Kemelrain 8 T

Höhefeld
Ortsteil von Wertheim
Kemelrain 8 T

Uissigheim
Ortsteil von Külsheim
Stahlberg 9

Külsheim
Hoher Herrgott 10

Werbach
Hirschberg 11
Beilberg 12 T

Großrinderfeld
Beilberg 12 T

Impfingen
Ortsteil von Tauberbischofsheim
Silberquell 13

Tauberbischofsheim
Edelberg 14

Distelhausen
Ortsteil von Tauberbischofsheim
Kreuzberg 14 a

Dittigheim
Ortsteil von Tauberbischofsheim
Steinschmetzer 14 b

Königheim
Kirchberg 15

Gissigheim
Ortsteil von Königheim
Gützenberg 15 a

Gerlachsheim
Ortsteil von Lauda-Königshofen
Herrenberg 16

Oberlauda
Ortsteil von Lauda-Königshofen
Steinklinge 17
Altenberg 18 T

Lauda
Ortsteil von Lauda-Königshofen
Altenberg 18 T
Frankenberg 19 T
Nonnenberg 20 T

Marbach
Ortsteil von Lauda-Königshofen
Frankenberg 19 T

Beckstein
Ortsteil von Lauda-Königshofen
Nonnenberg 20 T
Kirchberg 21 T

Königshofen
Ortsteil von Lauda-Königshofen
Kirchberg 21 T
Walterstal 22 T
Turmberg 23

Sachsenflur
Ortsteil von Lauda-Königshofen
Walterstal 22 T
Kailberg 24

Unterschüpf
Ortsteil von Boxberg
Mühlberg 25

Oberschüpf
Ortsteil von Boxberg
Altenberg 26
Herrenberg 27

Krautheim
Heiligenberg 28 T

Klepsau
Ortsteil von Krautheim
Heiligenberg 28 T

Dainbach
Ortsteil von Bad Mergentheim
Alte Burg 28 a

0 1 2 3 km

BADEN Individual sites in the district of Badisches Frankenland

The individual sites on this map form the general site of Tauberklinge

---

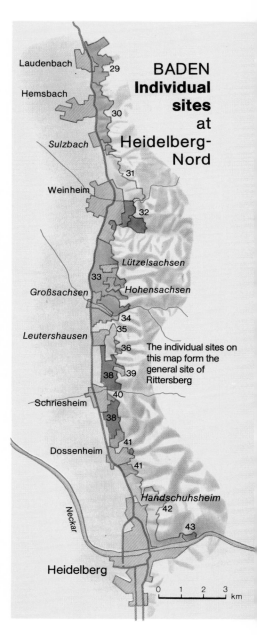

Bereich Badische Bergstraße/ Kraichgau

GROSSLAGE RITTERSBERG

Laudenbach
Sonnberg 29

Hemsbach
Herrnwingert 30 T

Sulzbach
Ortsteil von Weinheim
Herrnwingert 30 T

Weinheim
Hubberg 31
Wüstberg 32

Lützelsachsen
Ortsteil von Weinheim
Stephansberg 33 T

Hohensachsen
Ortsteil von Weinheim
Stephansberg 33 T

Großsachsen
Ortsteil von Hirschberg
Sandrocken 34

Leutershausen
Ortsteil von Hirschberg
Kahlberg 35
Staudenberg 36 T

Schriesheim
Staudenberg 36 T
Kuhberg 38
Madonnenberg 39
Schloßberg 40

Dossenheim
Ölberg 41

Heidelberg
Heiligenberg 42
Sonnenseite ob der Bruck 43

BADEN Individual sites at Heidelberg-Nord

The individual sites on this map form the general site of Rittersberg

0 1 2 3 km

Heidelberg

GROSSLAGE
MANNABERG

Heidelberg
Burg 44
Dachsbuckel 45
Herrenberg 46 T

Leimen
Herrenberg 46 T
Kreuzweg 47

Nußloch
Wilhelmsberg 48

Wiesloch
Bergwäldle 49
Spitzenberg 50
Hägenich 51

Rauenberg
Burggraf 52

Dielheim
Teufelskopf 53
Rosenberg 54 T

Tairnbach
Ortsteil von
Mühlhausen
Rosenberg 54 T

Horrenberg
Ortsteil von
Dielheim
Osterberg 55

Rotenberg
Ortsteil von
Rauenberg
Schloßberg 56

Mühlhausen
Heiligenstein 57

Malschenberg
Ortsteil von
Rauenberg
Ölbaum 58 T

Rettigheim
Ortsteil von
Mühlhausen
Ölbaum 58 T

Malsch
Ölbaum 58 T
Rotsteig 59

Mingolsheim
und
Langenbrücken
Ortsteile von
Bad Schönborn
Goldberg 60

Östringen
Ulrichsberg 61
Hummelberg 62
Rosenkranzweg 63

Zeutern
Ortsteil von
Ubstadt-Weiher
Himmelreich 64 T

Stettfeld
Ortsteil von
Ubstadt-Weiher
Himmelreich 64 T

Ubstadt
Ortsteil von
Ubstadt-Weiher
Weinhecke 65 T

Oberöwisheim,
Unteröwisheim
Ortsteile von
Kraichtal
Kirchberg 66

Bruchsal
Weinhecke 65 T
Klosterberg 68

Obergrombach
Ortsteil von
Bruchsal
Burgwingert 69 T

GROSSLAGE
STIFTSBERG

Eberbach
Schollerbuckel*

Binau
Herzogsberg 73 T

Diedesheim
Ortsteil von
Mosbach
Herzogsberg 73 T

Neckarzimmern
Wallmauer 75
Götzhalde 76
Kirchweinberg 77 T

Herbolzheim
Berg 80 T

Neudenau
Berg 80 T

Eschelbach
Ortsteil von
Sinsheim
Sonnenberg 81 T

Eichtersheim
Ortsteil von
Angelbachtal
Sonnenberg 81 T

Michelfeld
Ortsteil von
Angelbachtal
Sonnenberg 81 T
Himmelberg 83

**BADEN
Individual sites
at Heidelberg – Bruchsal**

Untergrombach
Ortsteil von
Bruchsal
Michaelsberg 70

Heidelsheim
Ortsteil von
Bruchsal
Altenberg 71

Helmsheim
Ortsteil von
Bruchsal
Burgwingert 69 T

Haßmersheim
Kirchweinberg 77 T

Neckarmühlbach
Ortsteil von
Haßmersheim
Hohberg 78

Heinsheim
Ortsteil von Bad
Rappenau
Burg Ehrenberg 79

Steinsfurt
Ortsteil von
Sinsheim
Steinsberg 84 T

Weiler
Ortsteil von
Sinsheim
Steinsberg 84 T
Goldberg 86

Hilsbach
Ortsteil von
Sinsheim
Eichelberg 87

0 1 2 3
km

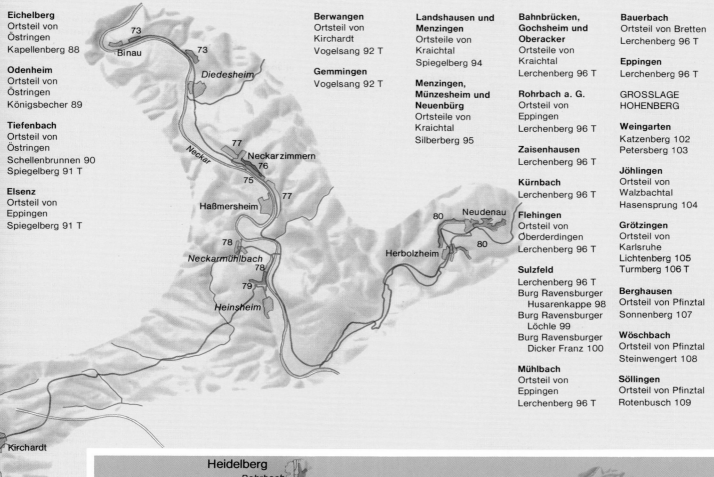

Eichelberg
Ortsteil von
Östringen
Kapellenberg 88

Odenheim
Ortsteil von
Östringen
Königsbecher 89

Tiefenbach
Ortsteil von
Östringen
Schellenbrunnen 90
Spiegelberg 91 T

Elsenz
Ortsteil von
Eppingen
Spiegelberg 91 T

Berwangen
Ortsteil von
Kirchardt
Vogelsang 92 T

Gemmingen
Vogelsang 92 T

**Landshausen und
Menzingen**
Ortsteile von
Kraichtal
Spiegelberg 94

**Menzingen,
Münzesheim und
Neuenbürg**
Ortsteile von
Kraichtal
Silberberg 95

**Bahnbrücken,
Gochsheim und
Oberacker**
Ortsteile von
Kraichtal
Lerchenberg 96 T

Rohrbach a. G.
Ortsteil von
Eppingen
Lerchenberg 96 T

Zaisenhausen
Lerchenberg 96 T

Kürnbach
Lerchenberg 96 T

Flehingen
Ortsteil von
Oberderdingen
Lerchenberg 96 T

Sulzfeld
Lerchenberg 96 T
Burg Ravensburger
   Husarenkappe 98
Burg Ravensburger
   Löchle 99
Burg Ravensburger
   Dicker Franz 100

Mühlbach
Ortsteil von
Eppingen
Lerchenberg 96 T

Bauerbach
Ortsteil von Bretten
Lerchenberg 96 T

Eppingen
Lerchenberg 96 T

GROSSLAGE
HOHENBERG

Weingarten
Katzenberg 102
Petersberg 103

Jöhlingen
Ortsteil von
Walzbachtal
Hasensprung 104

Grötzingen
Ortsteil von
Karlsruhe
Lichtenberg 105
Turmberg 106 T

Berghausen
Ortsteil von Pfinztal
Sonnenberg 107

Wöschbach
Ortsteil von Pfinztal
Steinwengert 108

Söllingen
Ortsteil von Pfinztal
Rotenbusch 109

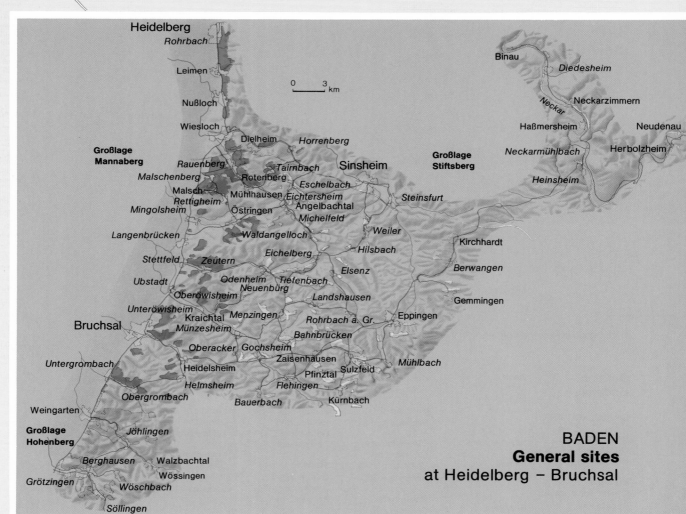

BADEN
General sites
at Heidelberg – Bruchsal

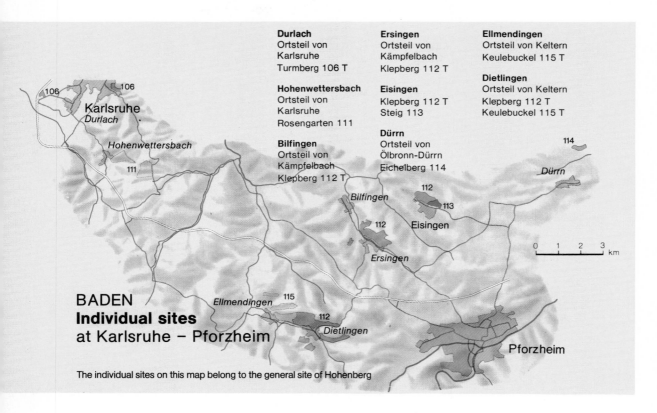

Durlach
Ortsteil von
Karlsruhe
Turmberg 106 T

Hohenwettersbach
Ortsteil von
Karlsruhe
Rosengarten 111

Bilfingen
Ortsteil von
Kämpfelbach
Klepberg 112 T

Ersingen
Ortsteil von
Kämpfelbach
Klepberg 112 T

Eisingen
Klepberg 112 T
Steig 113

Dürrn
Ortsteil von
Ölbronn-Dürrn
Eichelberg 114

Ellmendingen
Ortsteil von Keltern
Keulebuckel 115 T

Dietlingen
Ortsteil von Keltern
Klepberg 112 T
Keulebuckel 115 T

BADEN
Individual sites
at Karlsruhe – Pforzheim

The individual sites on this map belong to the general site of Hohenberg

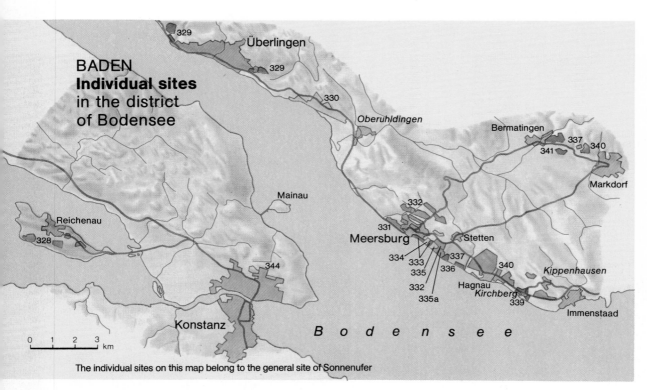

BADEN
Individual sites
in the district
of Bodensee

The individual sites on this map belong to the general site of Sonnenufer

Bereich
Bodensee

GROSSLAGENFREI

Rechberg
Ortsteil von Klettgau
Kapellenberg*

Erzingen
Ortsteil von Klettgau
Kapellenberg*

Nack
Ortsteil von
Lottstetten
Steinler*

GROSSLAGE
SONNENUFER

Singen
Elisabethenberg*
Olgaberg*

Hilzingen
Elisabethenberg*

Reichenau
Hochwart 328

Überlingen
Felsengarten 329

Oberuhldingen
Ortsteil von
Uhldingen-Mühlhof
Kirchhalde 330

Meersburg
Chorherrenhalde
331

Fohrenberg 332 T
Riesschen 333
Jungfernstieg 334
Bengel 335
Haltnau 335 a
Lerchenberg 336 T
Sängerhalde 337 T

Stetten
Fohrenberg 332 T
Lerchenberg 336 T
Sängerhalde 337 T

Hagnau
Burgstall 340 T

Kirchberg
Ortsteil von Salem
Schloßberg 339

Kippenhausen
Ortsteil von
Immenstaad
Burgstall 340 T

Immenstaad
Burgstall 340 T

Bermatingen
Leopoldsberg 341

Markdorf
Sängerhalde 337 T
Burgstall 340 T

Konstanz
Sonnenhalde 344

Bereich
Ortenau

GROSSLAGE
SCHLOSS RODECK

Baden-Baden
Eckberg 116
Sätzler 117 T

Sinzheim
Sätzler 117 T
Frühmeßler 118
Sonnenberg 119 T
Klostergut
  Fremersberger
  Feigenwäldchen
  131

Varnhalt
Ortsteil von
Baden-Baden
Sonnenberg 119 T
Klosterberg-
  felsen120
Steingrübler 121

Steinbach
Ortsteil von
Baden-Baden
Stich den Buben
  122
Yburgberg 123

Neuweier
Ortsteil von
Baden-Baden
Altenberg 124
Schloßberg 125
Mauerberg 126
Gänsberg 127
Heiligenstein 128

Eisental
Ortsteil von Bühl
Sommerhalde 129
Betschgräber 130

Altschweier
Ortsteil von Bühl
Sternenberg 132 T

Bühlertal
Engelsfelsen 133
Klotzberg 134

Neusatz
Ortsteil von Bühl
Sternenberg 132 T
Wolfhag 135 T
Burg Windeck
  Kastanienhalde
  136

Ottersweier
Wolfhag 135 T
Althof 137

Lauf
Schloß
  Neu-Windeck 138
Gut Alsenhof 139
Alter Gott 140

Niederschopfhei

74

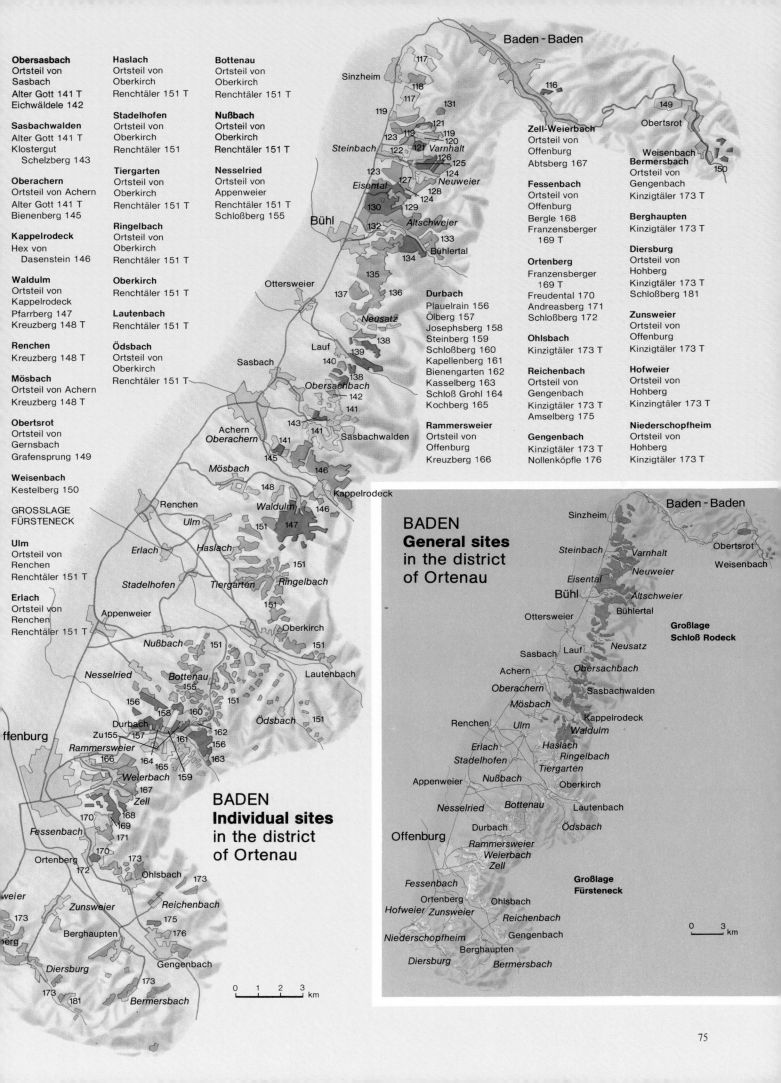

Obersasbach
Ortsteil von
Sasbach
Alter Gott 141 T
Eichwäldele 142

Sasbachwalden
Alter Gott 141 T
Klostergut
  Schelzberg 143

Oberachern
Ortsteil von Achern
Alter Gott 141 T
Bienenberg 145

Kappelrodeck
Hex von
  Dasenstein 146

Waldulm
Ortsteil von
Kappelrodeck
Pfarrberg 147
Kreuzberg 148 T

Renchen
Kreuzberg 148 T

Mösbach
Ortsteil von Achern
Kreuzberg 148 T

Obertsrot
Ortsteil von
Gernsbach
Grafensprung 149

Weisenbach
Kestelberg 150

GROSSLAGE
FÜRSTENECK

Ulm
Ortsteil von
Renchen
Renchtäler 151 T

Erlach
Ortsteil von
Renchen
Renchtäler 151 T

Haslach
Ortsteil von
Oberkirch
Renchtäler 151 T

Stadelhofen
Ortsteil von
Oberkirch
Renchtäler 151

Tiergarten
Ortsteil von
Oberkirch
Renchtäler 151 T

Ringelbach
Ortsteil von
Oberkirch
Renchtäler 151 T

Oberkirch
Renchtäler 151 T

Lautenbach
Renchtäler 151 T

Ödsbach
Ortsteil von
Oberkirch
Renchtäler 151 T

Bottenau
Ortsteil von
Oberkirch
Renchtäler 151 T

Nußbach
Ortsteil von
Oberkirch
Renchtäler 151 T

Nesselried
Ortsteil von
Appenweier
Renchtäler 151 T
Schloßberg 155

Durbach
Plauelrain 156
Ölberg 157
Josephsberg 158
Steinberg 159
Schloßberg 160
Kapellenberg 161
Bienengarten 162
Kasselberg 163
Schloß Grohl 164
Kochberg 165

Rammersweier
Ortsteil von
Offenburg
Kreuzberg 166

Zell-Weierbach
Ortsteil von
Offenburg
Abtsberg 167

Fessenbach
Ortsteil von
Offenburg
Bergle 168
Franzensberger
  169 T

Ortenberg
Franzensberger
  169 T
Freudental 170
Andreasberg 171
Schloßberg 172

Ohlsbach
Kinzigtäler 173 T

Reichenbach
Ortsteil von
Gengenbach
Kinzigtäler 173 T
Amselberg 175

Gengenbach
Kinzigtäler 173 T
Nollenköpfle 176

Weisenbach
Bermersbach
Ortsteil von
Gengenbach
Kinzigtäler 173 T

Berghaupten
Kinzigtäler 173 T

Diersburg
Ortsteil von
Hohberg
Kinzigtäler 173 T
Schloßberg 181

Zunsweier
Ortsteil von
Offenburg
Kinzigtäler 173 T

Hofweier
Ortsteil von
Hohberg
Kinzigtäler 173 T

Niederschopfheim
Ortsteil von
Hohberg
Kinzigtäler 173 T

BADEN
Individual sites
in the district
of Ortenau

BADEN
General sites
in the district
of Ortenau

Großlage
Schloß Rodeck

Großlage
Fürsteneck

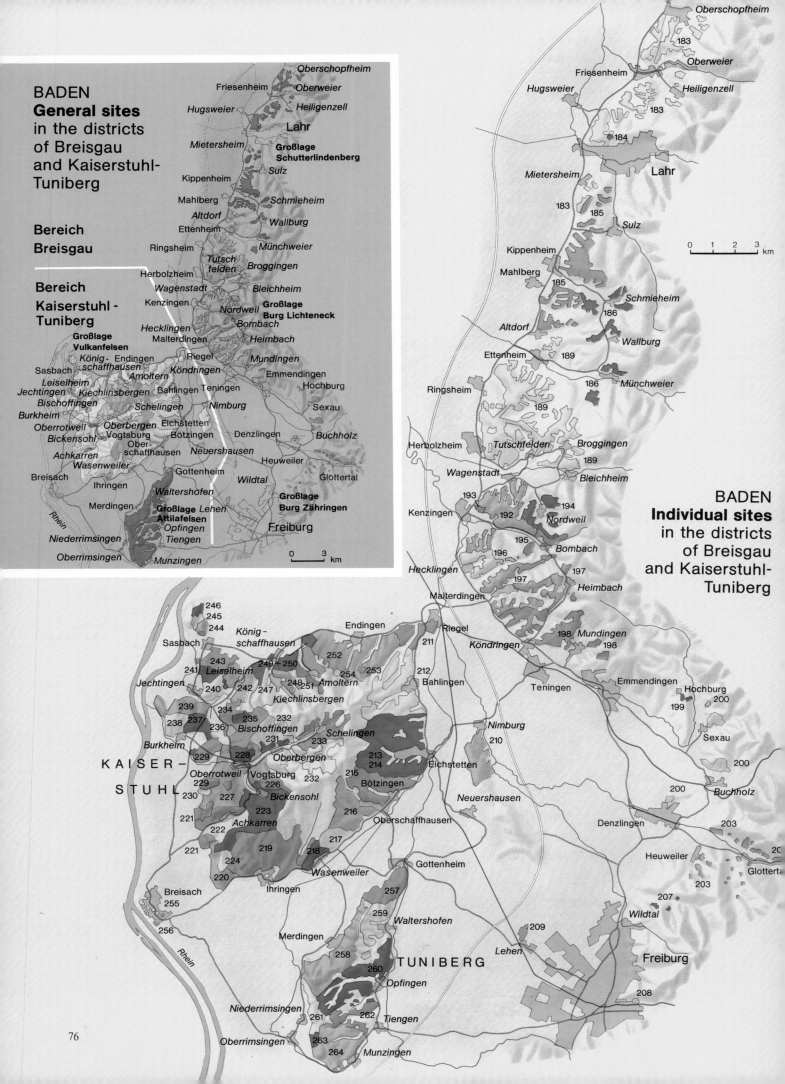

BADEN
General sites
in the districts
of Breisgau
and Kaiserstuhl-
Tuniberg

Bereich
Breisgau

Bereich
Kaiserstuhl-
Tuniberg

Oberschopfheim
Friesenheim
Oberweier
Hugsweier
Heiligenzell
Lahr
Mietersheim
Großlage
Schutterlindenberg
Kippenheim
Sulz
Mahlberg
Schmieheim
Altdorf
Wallburg
Ettenheim
Münchweier
Ringsheim
Tutsch
felden
Broggingen
Herbolzheim
Wagenstadt
Bleichheim
Kenzingen
Nordweil
Großlage
Großlage
Burg Lichteneck
Vulkanfelsen
Hecklingen
Bombach
König-
Endingen
Malterdingen
Heimbach
schaffhausen
Riegel
Sasbach
Amoltern
Köndringen
Mundingen
Leiselheim
Kiechlinsbergen
Bahlingen
Teningen
Emmendingen
Jechtingen
Hochburg
Bischoffingen
Schelingen
Nimburg
Burkheim
Sexau
Oberrotweil
Oberbergen
Eichstetten
Bickensohl
Vogtsburg
Bötzingen
Denzlingen
Buchholz
Achkarren
Ober-
schaffhausen
Neuershausen
Wasenweiler
Heuweiler
Breisach
Gottenheim
Wildtal
Glottertal
Ihringen
Großlage
Waltershofen
Großlage
Burg Zähringen
Großlage
Lehen
Merdingen
Attilafelsen
Opfingen
Niederrimsingen
Tiengen
Freiburg
Oberrimsingen
Rhein
Munzingen

0   3
km

BADEN
Individual sites
in the districts
of Breisgau
and Kaiserstuhl-
Tuniberg

Oberschopfheim
183
Oberweier
Friesenheim
Heiligenzell
Hugsweier
183
184
Mietersheim
Lahr
183
185
Sulz
Kippenheim
Mahlberg
185
Schmieheim
186
Altdorf
189
Wallburg
Ettenheim
186
Münchweier
Ringsheim
189
Herbolzheim
Tutschfelden
Broggingen
189
Wagenstadt
Bleichheim
193
194
Kenzingen
192
Nordweil
195
Bombach
196
Hecklingen
197
197
Malterdingen
Heimbach
Riegel
198
Mundingen
211
198
Köndringen
Emmendingen
Hochburg
200
Bahlingen
199
212
Teningen
Nimburg
Sexau
210
200
Eichstetten
Bötzingen
200
Neuershausen
Denzlingen
203
Oberschaffhausen
Heuweiler
Gottenheim
203
Glottertal
207
Wildtal
209
208
Lehen
Freiburg

0 1 2 3
km

246
245
244
König-
schaffhausen
Endingen
Sasbach
252
243
249+250
Leiselheim
254
253
241
248
251
Amoltern
212
240
242
247
Kiechlinsbergen
Bahlingen
239
234
235
232
238
237
236
Bischoffingen
Schelingen
213
231
233
214
Burkheim
229
228
Oberbergen
215
229
232
Bötzingen
230
Oberrotweil
Vogtsburg
226
216
227
Bickensohl
221
223
Oberschaffhausen
222
Achkarren
217
221
219
218
224
Wasenweiler
Gottenheim
220
Breisach
Ihringen
257
255
259
256
Waltershofen
258
260
Merdingen
Opfingen
TUNIBERG
261
262
Tiengen
Niederrimsingen
263
Oberrimsingen
264
Munzingen
Rhein

KAISER-
STUHL

76

Bereich Breisgau

GROSSLAGE SCHUTTER-LINDENBERG

Oberschopfheim
Ortsteil von Friesenheim
Kronenbühl 183 T

Oberweier
Ortsteil von Friesenheim
Kronenbühl 183 T

Friesenheim
Kronenbühl 183 T

Heiligenzell
Ortsteil von Friesenheim
Kronenbühl 183 T

Hugsweier
Ortsteil von Lahr
Kronenbühl 183 T

Lahr
Kronenbühl 183 T
Herrentisch 184

Mietersheim
Ortsteil von Lahr
Kronenbühl 183 T

Sulz
Ortsteil von Lahr
Haselstaude 185 T

Kippenheim
Haselstaude 185 T

Mahlberg
Haselstaude 185 T

Schmieheim
Ortsteil von Kippenheim
Kirchberg 186 T

Wallburg
Ortsteil von Ettenheim
Kirchberg 186 T

Münchweier
Ortsteil von Ettenheim
Kirchberg 186 T

GROSSLAGE BURG LICHTENECK

Altdorf
Ortsteil von Ettenheim
Kaiserberg 189 T

Ettenheim
Kaiserberg 189 T

Ringsheim
Kaiserberg 189 T

Herbolzheim
Kaiserberg 189 T

Tutschfelden
Ortsteil von Herbolzheim
Kaiserberg 189 T

Broggingen
Ortsteil von Herbolzheim
Kaiserberg 189 T

Bleichheim
Ortsteil von Herbolzheim
Kaiserberg 189 T

Wagenstadt
Ortsteil von Herbolzheim
Hummelberg 192 T

Kenzingen
Hummelberg 192 T
Roter Berg 193

Nordweil
Ortsteil von Kenzingen
Herrenberg 194

Bombach
Ortsteil von Kenzingen
Sommerhalde 195

Hecklingen
Ortsteil von Kenzingen
Schloßberg 196

Malterdingen
Bienenberg 197 T

Heimbach
Ortsteil von Teningen
Bienenberg 197 T

Köndringen
Ortsteil von Teningen
Alte Burg 198 T

Mundingen
Ortsteil von Emmendingen
Alte Burg 198 T

GROSSLAGE BURG ZÄHRINGEN

Hochburg
Halde 199

Sexau
Sonnhalde 200 T

Buchholz
Ortsteil von Waldkirch
Sonnhalde 200 T

Denzlingen
Sonnhalde 200 T
Eichberg 203 T

Glottertal
Eichberg 203 T
Roter Bur 205

Heuweiler
Eichberg 203 T

Wildtal
Ortsteil von Gundelfingen
Sonnenberg 207

Freiburg
Schloßberg 208

Lehen
Ortsteil von Freiburg
Bergle 209

Bereich Kaiserstuhl-Tuniberg

GROSSLAGE VULKANFELSEN

Nimburg
Ortsteil von Teningen
Steingrube 210 T

Neuershausen
Ortsteil von March
Steingrube 210 T

Riegel
St. Michaelsberg 211

Bahlingen
Silberberg 212

Eichstetten
Herrenbuck 213
Lerchenberg 214
The sites 213 and 214 cannot be drawn accurately, as their borders overlap

Bötzingen
Lasenberg 215
Eckberg 216

Wasenweiler
Ortsteil von Ihringen
Lotberg 217
Kreuzhalde 218 T

Ihringen
Kreuzhalde 218 T
Fohrenberg 219
Winklerberg 220
Schloßberg 221 T
Castellberg 222 T
Steinfelsen 223 T
Doktorgarten 224

Achkarren
Ortsteil von Vogtsburg im Kaiserstuhl
Schloßberg 221 T
Castellberg 222 T

Bickensohl
Ortsteil von Vogtsburg im Kaiserstuhl
Steinfelsen 223 T
Herrenstück 226

Oberrotweil
Ortsteil von Vogtsburg im Kaiserstuhl
Schloßberg 221 T
Käsleberg 227
Eichberg 228
Henkenberg 229
Kirchberg 230

Oberbergen
Ortsteil von Vogtsburg im Kaiserstuhl
Pulverbuck 231
Baßgeige 232

Schelingen
Ortsteil von Vogtsburg im Kaiserstuhl
Kirchberg 233

Bischoffingen
Ortsteil von Vogtsburg im Kaiserstuhl
Enselberg 234 T
Rosenkranz 235
Steinbuck 236

Burkheim
Ortsteil von Vogtsburg im Kaiserstuhl
Feuerberg 237
Schloßgarten 238

Jechtingen
Ortsteil von Sasbach
Enselberg 234 T
Steingrube 239
Hochberg 240
Eichert 241
Gestühl 242 T

Sasbach
Scheibenbuck 243
Lützelberg 244
Rote Halde 245
Limburg 246

Leiselheim
Ortsteil von Sasbach
Gestühl 242 T

Kiechlinsbergen
Ortsteil von Endingen
Teufelsburg 247
Ölberg 248

Königschaffhausen
Ortsteil von Endingen
Hasenberg 249
Steingrüble 250

Amoltern
Ortsteil von Endingen
Steinhalde 251

Endingen
Engelsberg 252
Steingrube 253
Tannacker 254

Breisach
Augustinerberg 255
Eckartsberg 256

GROSSLAGE ATTILAFELSEN

Gottenheim
Kirchberg 257

Merdingen
Bühl 258

Waltershofen
Ortsteil von Freiburg
Steinmauer 259

Opfingen
Ortsteil von Freiburg
Sonnenberg 260

Niederrimsingen
Ortsteil von Breisach
Rotgrund 261

Tiengen
Ortsteil von Freiburg
Rebtal 262

BADEN
General sites in the district of Markgräfler-land

Oberrimsingen
Ortsteil von Breisach
Franziskaner 263

Munzingen
Ortsteil von Freiburg
Kapellenberg 264

Bereich Markgräflerland

GROSSLAGE LORETTOBERG

Freiburg
Steinler 265
Jesuitenschloß 266 T

Merzhausen
Jesuitenschloß 266 T

Wittnau
Kapuzinerbuck 267

Mengen
Ortsteil von Schallstadt-Wolfenweiler
Alemannenbuck 268

Biengen
Ortsteil von Bad Krozingen
Maltesergarten 269 T

Schlatt
Ortsteil von Bad Krozingen
Maltesergarten 269 T
Steingrüble 271 T

Bad Krozingen
Steingrüble 271 T

Tunsel
Ortsteil von Bad Krozingen
Maltesergarten 269 T

Wolfenweiler
Ortsteil von Schallstadt-Wolfenweiler
Batzenberg 273 T
Dürrenberg 274

Ebringen
Sommerberg 275

Scherzingen
Ortsteil von Ehrenkirchen
Batzenberg 273 T

Norsingen
Ortsteil von Ehrenkirchen
Batzenberg 273 T

Pfaffenweiler
Batzenberg 273 T
Oberdürrenberg 276

Kirchhofen
Ortsteil von Ehrenkirchen
Batzenberg 273 T
Höllhagen 277
Kirchberg 278

Ehrenstetten
Ortsteil von Ehrenkirchen
Oelberg 279
Rosenberg 280

Bollschweil
Steinberg 281

Staufen im Breisgau
Schloßberg 282 T

Wettelbrunn
Ortsteil von Staufen im Breisgau
Maltesergarten 269 T

Grunern
Ortsteil von Staufen im Breisgau
Schloßberg 282 T
Altenberg 284

Eschbach
Maltesergarten 269 T

Heitersheim
Maltesergarten 269 T
Sonnhole 286

Seefelden
Ortsteil von
Buggingen
Maltesergarten
269 T

Buggingen
Maltesergarten
269 T
Höllberg 288

**GROSSLAGE
BURG NEUENFELS**

**Ballrechten-
Dottingen**
Castellberg 289
Altenberg 290 T

Sulzburg
Altenberg 290 T

Laufen
Ortsteil von
Sulzburg
Altenberg 290 T

Britzingen
Ortsteil von
Müllheim
Altenberg 290 T
Sonnhohle 293 T
Rosenberg 294 T

Dattingen
Ortsteil von
Müllheim
Altenberg 290 T
Sonnhohle 293 T
Rosenberg 294 T

Zunzingen
Ortsteil von
Müllheim
Rosenberg 294 T

Hügelheim
Ortsteil von
Müllheim
Höllberg 295
Gottesacker 296
Schloßgarten 297

Müllheim
Sonnhalde 298
Reggenhag 299
Pfaffenstück 300

Niederweiler
Ortsteil von
Müllheim
Römerberg 301 T

Badenweiler
Römerberg 301 T

Lipburg
Ortsteil von
Badenweiler
Kirchberg 303

Feldberg
Ortsteil von
Müllheim
Paradies 304

Auggen
Letten 305
Schäf 306 T

Mauchen
Ortsteil von
Schliengen
Frauenberg 307
Sonnenstück 308 T

Schliengen
Sonnenstück 308 T

Steinenstadt
Ortsteil von Neuen-
burg am Rhein
Schäf 306 T
Sonnenstück 308 T

Niedereggenen
Ortsteil von
Schliengen
Sonnenstück 308 T
Röthen 310 T

Obereggenen
Ortsteil von
Schliengen
Röthen 310 T

Liel
Ortsteil von
Schliengen
Sonnenstück 308 T

Bad Bellingen
Sonnenstück 308 T

**BADEN
Individual sites
in the district of
Markgräflerland**

Winterswiler
Ortsteil von
Efringen-Kirchen
Steingässle 311 T

Efringen-Kirchen
Steingässle 311 T
Kirchberg 319 T
Oelberg 321
Sonnenhohle 322 T

Egringen
Ortsteil von
Efringen-Kirchen
Sonnenhohle 322 T

Schallbach
Sonnenhohle 322 T

Fischingen
Sonnenhohle 322 T

Rümmingen
Sonnenhohle 322 T

Eimeldingen
Sonnenhohle 322 T

Binzen
Sonnenhohle 322 T

Ötlingen
Ortsteil von
Weil am Rhein
Sonnenhohle 322 T
Stiege 324 T

Haltingen
Ortsteil von
Weil am Rhein
Stiege 324 T

Weil am Rhein
Stiege 324 T
Schlipf 325

Lörrach
Sonnenbrunnen 320

Grenzach
Ortsteil von Whylen
Hornfelsen 326

Herten
Ortsteil von
Rheinfelden
Steinacker 327

Wollbach
Ortsteil von
Kandern
Steingässle 311 T

Bamlach
Ortsteil von
Bad Bellingen
Kapellenberg 316 T

Rheinweiler
Ortsteil von
Bad Bellingen
Kapellenberg 316 T

**GROSSLAGE
VOGTEI RÖTTELN**

Feuerbach
Ortsteil von
Kandern
Steingässle 311 T

Hertingen
Ortsteil von
Bad Bellingen
Sonnenhohle 322 T

Tannenkirch
Ortsteil von
Kandern
Steingässle 311 T

Riedlingen
Ortsteil von
Kandern
Steingässle 311 T

Holzen
Ortsteil von
Kandern
Steingässle 311 T

Blansingen
Ortsteil von
Efringen-Kirchen
Wolfer 317 T

Kleinkems
Ortsteil von
Efringen-Kirchen
Wolfer 317 T

Welmlingen
Ortsteil von
Efringen-Kirchen
Steingässle 311 T

Huttingen
Ortsteil von
Efringen-Kirchen
Kirchberg 319 T

Istein
Ortsteil von
Efringen-Kirchen
Kirchberg 319 T

Map labels:

Freiburg · 265 · 266 · Merzha · 268 · Schallstadt-Wolfenweiler · Ebringen · 266 · Mengen · 275 · Wittnau · Scherzingen · 274 · 276 · Pfaffenweiler · 267 · Biengen · 273 · 269 · Norsingen · 278 · Schlatt · Ehrenkirchen · Kirchhofen · 281 · 269 · 271 · 277 · 279 · Bollschweil · Tunsel · Ehrenstetten · Bad Krozingen · 280 · Eschbach · 269 · Staufen · 282 · Heitersheim · Wettelbrunn · 286 · 269 · 269 · Grunern · Seefelden · Dottingen · 284 · Ballrechten · Buggingen · 269 · 289 · Laufen · 290 · 288 · 290 · Sulzburg · Hügelheim · Dattingen · 296 · 295 · 293 · 297 · 294 · Müllheim · 298 · Britzingen · 299 · Zunzingen · 301 · Oberweiler · 300 · Niederweiler · Auggen · 298 · Badenweiler · 303 · 305 · 306 · Lipburg · Steinenstadt · 307 · 304 · Feldberg · Schliengen · Mauchen · 310 · Obereggenen · 308 · 308 · Niedereggenen · Bad Bellingen · 311 · Liel · Hertingen · Feuerbach · 316 · 322 · Riedlingen · Bamlach · 311 · Rheinweiler · 311 · Tannenkirch · 311 · 316 · Blansingen · 317 · Welmlingen · Holzen · Kleinkems · 311 · 311 · Huttingen · 319 · Winterswiler · Istein · 311 · Egringen · 321 · Wollbach · 322 · Rhein · Fischingen · 322 · Binzen · Rümmingen · Efringen-Kirchen · Eimeldingen · Ötlingen · 322 · Haltingen · 324 · 325 · 320 · Weil · Lörrach · Basel · 326 · Grenzach · Herten · 327

0 1 2 3 km

Register

Daubhaus (Groß-lage) *Rhg* 29
Dausenau *Mrh* 24
Dautenheim (Ortsteil von Alzey) *Rhh* 41
Degerloch (Ortsteil von Stuttgart) *W* 66
Deidesheim *Rhpf* 47
Dellhofen (Ortsteil von Oberwesel) *Mrh* 24
Denzlingen *B* 77
Dernau *A* 12
Dertingen (Ortsteil von Wertheim) *B* 71
Desloch *N* 34
Dettelbach *F* 54
Detzem *MSR* 19
Deutelsberg (Groß-lage) *Rhg* 29
Deutsche Weinstraße siehe Mittelhaardt/ Deutsche Wein-straße
Dexheim *Rhh* 40
Dhron (Ortsteil von Neumagen-Dhron) *MSR* 19
Dieblich *MSR* 16
Diedesfeld (Ortsteil von Neustadt a. d. Weinstraße) *Rhpf* 47
Diedesheim (Orts-teil von Mosbach) *B* 72
Diefenbach (Ortsteil von Steinenfels) *W* 65
Dielheim *B* 72
Dienheim *Rhh* 40
Dierbach *Rhpf* 49
Diersburg (Ortsteil von Hohberg) *B* 75
Dietersheim (Orts-teil von Bingen) *Rhh* 38
Dietlingen (Ortsteil von Keltern) *B* 74
Dietzenbach *HB* 50
Dimbach (Ortsteil von Bretzfeld) *W* 63
Dingolshausen *F* 56
Dirmstein *Rhhf* 46
Distelhausen (Orts-teil von Tauber-bischofsheim) *B* 71
Dittelsheim-Heß-loch *Rhh* 41
Dittigheim (Ortsteil von Tauber-bischofsheim) *B* 71
Dörrenbach *Rhpf* 49
Dörscheid *Mrh* 24
Dörzbach *W* 61
Dolgesheim *Rhh* 40
Domblick (Groß-lage) *Rhh* 41
Domherr (Großlage) *Rhh* 40
Donnersdorf *F* 56
Dorfprozelten *F* 52
Dorn-Dürkheim *Rhh* 41
Dorsheim *N* 32
Dossenheim *B* 71
Dottingen siehe Ballrechten-Dot-tingen
Dotzheim (Ortsteil von Wiesbaden) *Rhg* 29
Dreis *MSR* 18
Dromersheim (Orts-teil von Bingen) *Rhh* 38
Druswiler siehe Kapellen-Drus-weiler
Duchroth *N* 34

Dürkheim, Bad siehe Bad Dürk-heim
Dürrenzimmern (Ortsteil von Brackenheim) *W* 64
Dürrn (Ortsteil von Ölbronn-Dürrn) *B* 74
Durbach *B* 75
Durlach (Ortsteil von Karlsruhe) *B* 74
Duttenberg (Ortsteil von Bad Fried-richshall) *W* 62
Duttweiler (Ortsteil von Neustadt a. d. Weinstraße) *Rhpf* 47

E

Eberbach *B* 72
Ebernach (Ortsteil von Cochem) *MSR* 16
Ebernburg (Ortsteil von Bad Mün-ster-Ebernburg) *N* 34
Ebersheim (Ortsteil von Mainz) *Rhh* 40
Eberstadt *W* 62
Ebringen *B* 77
Eckelsheim *Rhh* 40
Eckenroth *N* 32
Edenkoben *Rhpf* 48
Edesheim *Rhpf* 48
Ediger (Ortsteil von Ediger-Eller) *MSR* 17
Ediger-Eller *MSR* 17
Edingen *MSR* 21
Efringen-Kirchen *B* 78
Egringen (Ortsteil von Efringen-Kirchen) *B* 78
Ehrenbreitstein (Ortsteil von Koblenz) *Mrh* 24
Ehrenkirchen *B* 77
Ehrenstetten (Orts-teil von Ehren-kirchen) *B* 77
Ehrental (Ortsteil von St. Goars-hausen) *Mrh* 24
Eibelstadt *F* 54
Eibensbach (Ortsteil von Güglingen) *W* 64
Eich *Rhh* 40
Eichelberg (Ortsteil von Obersulm) *W* 63
Eichelberg (Ortsteil von Östringen) *B* 73
Eichstetten *B* 77
Eichtersheim (Orts-teil von Angel-bachtal) *B* 72
Eimeldingen *B* 78
Eimsheim *Rhh* 41
Einersheim, Markt siehe Markt Einersheim
Einselthum *Rhhf* 46
Eisental (Ortsteil von Bühl) *B* 74
Eisingen *B* 74
Eitelsbach (Ortsteil von Trier) *MSR* 20
Ellenz-Poltersdorf *MSR* 17
Eller (Ortsteil von Ediger-Eller) *MSR* 17
Ellerstadt *Rhpf* 47
Ellhofen *W* 62, 63

Ellmendingen (Ortsteil von Kel-tern) *B* 74
Elpersheim (Ortsteil von Weikers-heim) *W* 61
Elsenfeld *F* 52
Elsenz (Ortsteil von Eppingen) *B* 73
Elsenz siehe Stadecken-Els-heim
Eltmann *F* 56
Eltville *Rhg* 29
Emmendingen *B* 77
Ems siehe Bad Ems
Endersbach (Ortsteil von Weinstadt) *W* 66
Endingen *B* 77
Engehöll (Ortsteil von Oberwesel) *Mrh* 24
Engelsberg (Ortsteil von Großheu-bach) *F* 52
Engelstadt *Rhh* 40
Enkirch *MSR* 18
Ensch *MSR* 19
Ensheim *Rhh* 40
Ensingen (Ortsteil von Vaihingen) *W* 65
Enzweihingen (Ortsteil von Vai-hingen) *W* 64
Eppelsheim *Rhh* 41
Eppingen *B* 73
Erbach (Ortsteil von Eltville) *Rhg* 29
Erbach (Ortsteil von Heppenheim) *HB* 50
Erbersheim (Ortsteil von Mainz) *Rhh* 40
Erbes-Büdesheim *Rhh* 40
Erden *MSR* 18
Erdmannhausen *W* 65
Ergersheim *F* 55
Erlabrunn *F* 54
Erlach (Ortsteil von Renchen) *B* 75
Erlenbach *W* 62
Erlenbach am Main *F* 32
Erlenbach bei Marktheidenfeld *F* 52
Erligheim *W* 65
Ernsbach (Ortsteil von Forchten-berg) *W* 61
Ernst *MSR* 16
Erntebringer (Groß-lage) *Rhg* 29
Erpolzheim *Rhpf* 46
Ersingen (Ortsteil von Kämpfel-bach) *B* 74
Erzingen (Ortsteil von Klettgau) *B* 74
Eschbach *Rhpf* 48
Eschbach *B* 77
Eschelbach (Ortsteil von Kesselfeld) *W* 63
Eschelbach (Ortsteil von Sinsheim) *B* 72
Eschenau (Ortsteil von Obersulm) *W* 63
Escherndorf (Orts-teil von Volkach) *F* 54
Esingen siehe Hel-fant-Esingen
Esselborn *Rhh* 41
Essenheim *Rhh* 40
Essingen *Rhpf* 48
Eßlingen *W* 66
Ettenheim *B* 77
Eußenheim *F* 54
Ewig Leben (Groß-lage) *F* 54

F

Fachbach *Mrh* 24
Fahr *F* 54
Falkenstein (Ortsteil von Konz) *MSR* 20
Fankel siehe Brut-tig-Fankel
Fastrau siehe Fell
Feldberg (Ortsteil von Müllheim) *B* 78
Feilbingert *N* 34
Fell (mit Fastrau) *MSR* 19
Fellbach *W* 66
Fellerich (Ortsteil von Tawern) *MSR* 21
Fessenbach (Ortsteil von Offenburg) *B* 75
Feuerbach (Ortsteil von Kandern) *B* 78
Feuerberg (Groß-lage) *Rhpf* 47
Feuerthal (Ortsteil von Hammel-burg) *F* 53
Filsen *Mrh* 24
Filzen (Mittelmosel) siehe Brauneberg
Filzen (Ortsteil von Konz) *MSR* 20
Finthen (Ortsteil von Mainz) *Rhh* 40
Fisch (Ortsteil von Trier) *MSR* 20
Fischingen *B* 78
Flein *W* 64
Flehingen (Ortsteil von Oberderdin-gen) *B* 73
Flemlingen *Rhpf* 48
Flörsheim *Rhg* 29
Flörsheim-Dalsheim *Rhh* 41
Flomborn *Rhh* 41
Flonheim *Rhh* 40
Flußbach *MSR* 18
Forchtenberg *W* 61
Forst a. d. Wein-straße *Rhpf* 47
Framersheim *Rhh* 41
Franken (Anbauge-biet) 51
Frankenwinheim *F* 54
Frankfurt *Rhg* 29
Frankweiler *Rhpf* 48
Franzenheim *MSR* 20
Frauenstein (Orts-teil von Wies-baden) *Rhg* 29
Frauenzimmern (Ortsteil von Güglingen) *W* 64
Freckenfeld *Rhpf* 49
Freiberg/Neckar *W* 65
Freiburg *B* 77
Frei-Laubersheim *Rhh* 40
Freimersheim *Rhh* 41
Freimersheim *Rhpf* 48
Freinsheim *Rhpf* 46
Frettenheim *Rhh* 41
Freudenstein (Orts-teil von Knittlin-gen) *W* 64
Freudental *W* 65
Frickenhausen *F* 54
Frickenhausen *W* 67
Friedelsheim *Rhpf* 47
Friedrichshall, Bad siehe Bad Fried-richshall

Friesenheim *Rhh* 40
Friesenheim *B* 77
Fürfeld *Rhh* 40
Fürsteneck (Groß-lage) *B* 75

G

Gabsheim *Rhh* 40
Gaibach *F* 54
Gaisburg (Ortsteil von Stuttgart) *W* 66
Gambach (Ortsteil von Karlstadt) *F* 54
Gau-Algesheim *Rhh* 40
Gau-Bickelheim *Rhh* 40
Gau-Bischofsheim *Rhh* 39
Gauersheim *Rhpf* 46
Gaugrehweiler *N* 34
Gau-Heppenheim *Rhh* 41
Gaulsheim (Ortsteil von Bingen) *Rhh* 38
Gau-Odernheim *Rhh* 40, 41
Gau-Weinheim *Rhh* 40
Geddelsbach (Orts-teil von Bretzfeld) *W* 63
Gedeonseck (Groß-lage) *Mrh* 24
Geinsheim (Ortsteil von Neustadt/ Weinstraße) *Rhpf* 47
Geisenheim *Rhg* 29
Gellmersbach (Orts-teil von Weins-berg) *W* 62
Gemmingen *B* 73
Gemmrigheim *W* 65
Gengenbach *B* 75
Genheim (Ortsteil von Waldalges-heim) *N* 32
Gensingen *Rhh* 38
Geradstetten (Orts-teil von Remshal-den) *W* 66
Gerlachsheim (Orts-teil von Lauda-Königshofen) *B* 71
Gerlingen *W* 66
Gernsbach *B* 75
Gerolsheim *Rhpf* 46
Gerolzhofen *F* 56
Gimbsheim *Rhh* 40
Gimmeldingen (Ortsteil von Neustadt a. d. Weinstraße) *Rhpf* 47
Gipfel (Großlage) *MSR* 21
Gissigheim (Ortsteil von Königsheim) *B* 71
Gleishorbach siehe Gleiszellen-Gleis-horbach
Gleisweiler *Rhpf* 48
Gleiszellen-Gleis-horbach *Rhpf* 48
Glottertal *B* 77
Gochsheim (Ortsteil von Kraichtal) *B* 73
Godendorf *MSR* 21
Godramstein (Orts-teil von Landau) *Rhpf* 48
Göcklingen *Rhpf* 48
Gönnheim *Rhpf* 47
Gössenheim *F* 54

Goldbäumchen (Großlage) *MSR* 16
Gommersheim *Rhpf* 48
Gondorf siehe Kobern-Gondorf
Gottenheim *B* 77
Gotteshilfe (Groß-lage) *Rhh* 41
Gottesthal (Groß-lage) *Rhg* 29
Graach *MSR* 19
Gräfenhausen *Rhpf* 48
Grafenstück (Groß-lage) *Rhpf* 46
Grafschaft (Groß-lage) *MSR* 17
Grantschen (Ortsteil von Weinsberg) *W* 63
Grenzach (Ortsteil von Wyhlen) *B* 78
Greuth *F* 54
Grewenich *MSR* 21
Grötzingen (Ortsteil von Karlsruhe) *B* 73
Grolsheim *Rhh* 38
Gronau (Ortsteil von Oberstenfeld) *W* 63
Gronau siehe Rö-dersheim-Gronau
Großbottwar *W* 63
Großfischlingen siehe Groß- und Kleinfischlingen
Großheppach (Orts-teil von Wein-stadt) *W* 66
Großherbach, Orts-teil Engelsberg siehe Engelsberg
Großheubach *F* 52
Großingersheim (Ortsteil von Ingersheim) *W* 65
Großkarlbach *Rhpf* 46
Großlangheim *F* 54
Großniedesheim *Rhpf* 46
Großostheim *F* 52
Großrinderfeld *B* 71
Großsachsen (Orts-teil von Hirsch-berg) *B* 71
Groß-Umstadt *HB* 50
Groß- und Klein-fischlingen *Rhpf* 48
Großwallstadt *F* 52
Groß-Winternheim siehe Ingelheim
Grünstadt *Rhpf* 46
Grunbach (Ortsteil von Remshalden) *W* 66
Grunern (Ortsteil von Staufen) *B* 77
Güglingen *W* 64
Güldenmorgen (Großlage) *Rhh* 39
Güls (Ortsteil von Koblenz) *MSR* 16
Gündelbach (Orts-teil von Vaihin-gen) *W* 64
Güntersleben *F* 54
Guldental *N* 32
Gumbsheim *Rhh* 40
Gundelfingen *B* 77
Gundelsheim *W* 62
Gundersheim *Rhh* 41
Gundheim *Rhh* 41
Guntersblum *Rhh* 40, 41
Gutenberg *N* 33
Gutes Domtal (Großlage) *Rhh* 40

Guttenberg (Groß-lage) *Rhpf* 49

H

Haagen (Ortsteil von Weikers-heim) *W* 61
Haardt (Ortsteil von Neustadt a. d. Weinstraße) *Rhpf* 47
Haberschlacht (Orts-teil von Bracken-heim) *W* 64
Hackenheim *Rhh* 40
Häfnerhaslach (Ortsteil von Sachsenheim) *W* 65
Hagnau *B* 74
Hahnheim *Rhh* 40
Hainfeld *Rhpf* 48
Hallburg (Ortsteil von Volkach) *F* 54
Hallgarten (Ortsteil von Oestrich-Winkel) *Rhg* 29
Haltingen (Ortsteil von Weil) *B* 78
Hambach (Ortsteil von Neustadt a. d. Weinstraße) *Rhpf* 47
Hambach (Ortsteil von Heppen-heim) *HB* 50
Hamm (Ortsteil von Konz) *MSR* 20
Hammelburg *F* 53
Hammerstein *Mrh* 23
Hammerstein, Burg siehe Burg Ham-merstein
Handthal *F* 56
Hangen-Weisheim *Rhh* 41
Hanweiler (Ortsteil von Winnenden) *W* 66
Hargesheim *N* 34
Harsberg (Ortsteil von Pfedelbach) *W* 63
Harxheim *Rhh* 40
Harxheim (Ortsteil von Zellertal) *Rhpf* 46
Haslach (Ortsteil von Oberkirch) *B* 75
Haßmersheim *B* 72
Hattenheim (Orts-teil von Eltville) *Rhg* 29
Hatzenport (Ortsteil von Löf) *MSR* 16
Hausen (Ortsteil von Bracken-heim) *W* 64
Hebsack (Ortsteil von Remshalden) *W* 66
Hechtsheim (Orts-teil von Mainz) *Rhh* 40
Hecklingen (Ortsteil von Kenzingen) *B* 77
Heddesheim (Orts-teil von Gulden-tal) *N* 32
Hedelfingen (Orts-teil von Stuttgart) *W* 66
Heidelberg *B* 71, 72
Heidelsheim (Orts-teil von Bruchsal) *B* 72
Heidesheim *Rhh* 40
Heidesheim siehe Obrigheim

Heilbronn *W* 63, 64
Heiligenstock (Großlage) *Rhg* 29
Heiligenthal (Großlage) *F* 52
Heiligenzell (Ortsteil von Friesenheim) *B* 77
Heimbach (Ortsteil von Teningen) *B* 77
Heimersheim (Ortsteil von Bad Neuenahr-Ahrweiler) *A* 12
Heimersheim (Ortsteil von Alzey) *Rhh* 41
Heinsheim (Ortsteil von Bad Rappenau) *B* 72
Heitersheim *B* 77
Helfant-Esingen (Ortsteil von Palzem) *MSR* 21
Helmsheim (Ortsteil von Bruchsal) *B* 72
Hemsbach *B* 71
Heppenheim, Ortsteil von Worms *Rhh* 41
Heppenheim *HB* 50
Heppingen (Ortsteil von Bad Neuenahr-Ahrweiler) *A* 12
Herbolzheim (Ortsteil von Neudenau) *B* 72
Herbolzhim *B* 77
Hergenfeld *N* 32
Hergersweiler *Rhpf* 48
Herrenberg (Großlage) *Mrh* 24
Herrenberg (Großlage) *F* 54
Herrlich (Großlage) *Rhpf* 48
Herrnsheim (Ortsteil von Worms) *Rhh* 41
Herten (Ortsteil von Rheinfelden) *B* 78
Hertingen (Ortsteil von Bad Bellingen) *B* 78
Hertmannsweiler (Ortsteil von Winnenden) *W* 66
Herxheim am Berg *Rhpf* 46
Herxheim bei Landau i. d. Pfalz *Rhpf* 48
Herxheimweyher *Rhpf* 48
Heßheim *Rhpf* 46
Hessigheim *W* 65
Hessische Bergstraße (Anbaugebiet) 50
Heßloch siehe Dittelsheim-Heßloch
Hetzerath *MSR* 19
Heuchelberg (Großlage) *W* 64
Heuchelheim bei Frankenthal (Ortsteil von Grünstadt Land) *Rhpf* 46
Heuchelheim-Klingen *Rhpf* 48
Heuholz (Ortsteil von Pfedelbach) *W* 63
Heuweiler *B* 77
Hilsbach (Ortsteil von Sinsheim) *B* 72
Hillesheim *Rhh* 40
Hilzingen *B* 74
Himmelstadt *F* 54

Hirschau (Ortsteil von Tübingen) *W* 67
Hirschberg *B* 71
Hirzenach *Mrh* 24
Hochburg (Ortsteil von Emmendingen) *B* 77
Hochdorf-Assenheim *Rhpf* 47
Hochheim *Rhg* 29
Hochmess (Großlage) *Rhpf* 47
Hochstadt *Rhpf* 48
Hochstätten *N* 34
Hockweiler *MSR* 20
Höhefeld (Ortsteil von Wertheim) *B* 71
Höllenpfad (Großlage) *Rhpf* 46
Hönningen siehe Bad Hönningen
Höpfigheim (Ortsteil von Steinheim) *W* 65
Hörstein (Ortsteil von Alzenau i. Ufr.) *F* 52
Hößlinsülz (Ortsteil von Löwenstein) *W* 63
Hof (Ortsteil von Großbottwar) *W* 64
Hofen (Ortsteil von Bönnigheim) *W* 65
Hofrat (Großlage) *F* 54
Hofstück (Großlage) *Rhpf* 47
Hofweier (Ortsteil von Hohberg) *B* 75
Hohberg *B* 75
Hoheim (Ortsteil von Kitzingen) *F* 54
Hohenberg (Großlage) *B* 73
Hoheneck (Ortsteil von Ludwigsburg) *W* 64, 65
Hohenhaslach (Ortsteil von Sachsenheim) *W* 65
Hohenneuffen (Großlage) *W* 67
Hohensachsen (Ortsteil von Weinheim) *B* 71
Hohenstein (Ortsteil von Bönnigheim) *W* 65
Hohen-Sülzen *Rhh* 41
Hohenwettersbach (Ortsteil von Karlsruhe) *B* 74
Holzen (Ortsteil von Kandern) *B* 78
Homburg a. Main *F* 52
Honigberg (Großlage) *Rhg* 29
Honigberg (Großlage) *F* 54
Honigsäckel (Großlage) *Rhpf* 47
Honnef, Bad siehe Bad Honnef
Horchheim (Ortsteil von Worms) *Rhh* 41
Horkheim (Ortsteil von Heilbronn) *W* 63
Horrenberg (Ortsteil von Dielheim) *B* 72
Horrheim (Ortsteil von Vaihingen) *W* 65
Horrweiler *Rhh* 38
Hüffelsheim *N* 34

Hügelheim (Ortsteil von Müllheim) *B* 78
Hüttenheim *F* 55
Hugsweier (Ortsteil von Lahr) *B* 77
Hupperath *MSR* 18
Huttingen (Ortsteil von Efringen-Kirchen) *B* 78

I

Igel *MSR* 20
Ihringen *B* 77
Ibesheim *Rhpf* 48
Illingen *W* 65
Ilsfeld *W* 63, 64
Immenstaad *B* 74
Immesheim *Rhpf* 46
Impfingen (Ortsteil von Tauberbischofsheim) *B* 71
Impflingen *Rhpf* 48
Ingelfingen *W* 61
Ingelheim *Rhh* 40
Ingenheim siehe Billigheim-Ingenheim
Ingersheim *W* 65
Insheim *Rhpf* 48
Iphofen *F* 54
Ippesheim (Ortsteil von Bad Kreuznach) *N* 34
Ippesheim (Franken) *F* 55
Irsch (Ortsteil von Trier) *MSR* 20
Istein (Ortsteil von Efringen-Kirchen) *B* 78

J

Jagst siehe Kocher-Jagst-Tauber
Jechtingen (Ortsteil von Sasbach) *B* 77
Jöhlingen (Ortsteil von Walzbachtal) *B* 73
Johannisberg (Bereich) *Rhg* 29
Johannisberg (Ortsteil von Geisenheim) *Rhg* 29
Jugenheim *Rhh* 40

K

Kämpfelbach *B* 74
Kaimt (Ortsteil von Zell/Mosel) *MSR* 17
Kaiserpfalz (Großlage) *Rhh* 40
Kaiserstuhl-Tuniberg (Bereich) *B* 77
Kalkofen *N* 34
Kallstadt *Rhpf* 46, 47
Kammerforst (Ortsteil von Breitbach) *F* 56
Kamp-Bornhofen *Mrh* 24
Kandel *Rhpf* 49
Kandern *B* 78
Kanzem *MSR* 20
Kapellenberg (Großlage) *F* 56
Kapellen-Drusweiler *Rhpf* 49
Kappelrodeck *B* 75
Kappishäusern (Ortsteil von Neuffen) *W* 67

Kapsweyer *Rhpf* 49
Karden (Ortsteil von Treis-Karden) *MSR* 16
Karlburg (Ortsteil von Karlstadt) *F* 54
Karlruhe *B* 73, 74
Karlstadt *F* 54
Kasbach *Mrh* 23
Kasel *MSR* 20
Kastel-Staadt *MSR* 20
Kattenes (Ortsteil von Löf) *MSR* 16
Kaub *Mrh* 24
Keltern *B* 74
Kembach (Ortsteil von Wertheim) *B* 71
Kempten (Ortsteil von Bingen) *Rhh* 38
Kenn *MSR* 19
Kenzingen *B* 77
Kernen *W* 66
Kesselfeld (Ortsteil von Neuenstein) *W* 63
Kernscheid siehe Trier
Kerzenheim *Rhpf* 46
Kesten *MSR* 19
Kestert *Mrh* 24
Kettenheim siehe Alzey
Kiechlingsbergen (Stadtteil von Endingen) *B* 77
Kiedrich *Rhg* 29
Kindenheim *Rhpf* 46
Kinheim *MSR* 18
Kippenhausen (Ortsteil von Immenstaad) *B* 74
Kippenheim *B* 77
Kirchardt *B* 73
Kirchberg (Großlage) *F* 54
Kirchberg *W* 65
Kirchberg (Ortsteil von Salem) *B* 74
Kirchen siehe Efringen-Kirchen
Kirchenweinberg (Großlage) *W* 64
Kirchheim a. d. Weinstraße *Rhpf* 46
Kirchheim *W* 65
Kirchheimbolanden *Rhpf* 46
Kirchhofen (Ortsteil von Ehrenkirchen) *B* 77
Kirf *MSR* 21
Kirrweiler *Rhpf* 48
Kirschroth *N* 34
Kitzingen *F* 54
Kleinaspach (Ortsteil von Aspach) *W* 65
Kleinbottwar (Ortsteil von Steinheim) *W* 64
Kleinfischlingen siehe Groß- und Kleinfischlingen
Kleingartach (Ortsteil von Eppingen) *W* 64
Kleinheppach (Ortsteil von Korb) *W* 66
Kleiningersheim (Ortsteil von Ingersheim) *W* 65
Kleinkarlbach *Rhpf* 46
Kleinkems (Ortsteil von Efringen-Kirchen) *B* 78
Kleinlangheim *F* 54
Kleinniedesheim *Rhpf* 46

Kleinochsenfurt (Ortsteil von Ochsenfurt) *F* 54
Kleinsachsenheim (Ortsteil von Sachsenheim) *W* 65
Klein-Umstadt (Ortsteil von Groß-Umstadt) *HB* 50
Klein-Winternheim *Rhh* 40
Klepsau (Ortsteil von Krautheim) *B* 71
Klettgau *B* 74
Klingen siehe Heuchelheim-Klingen
Klingenberg a. Main *F* 52
Klingenberg (Ortsteil von Heilbronn) *W* 64
Klingenmünster *Rhpf* 48
Klosterberg (Großlage) *A* 12
Kloster Liebfrauenberg (Großlage) *Rhpf* 48
Klotten *MSR* 16
Klüsserath *MSR* 19
Knetzgau *F* 56
Knittelsheim *Rhpf* 48
Knittlingen *W* 64
Knörigen *Rhpf* 48
Kobern-Gondorf *MSR* 16
Koblenz *MSR* 16, *Mrh* 24
Kobnert (Großlage) *Rhpf* 46
Kocherberg (Großlage) *W* 61
Kocher-Jagst-Tauber (Bereich) *W* 61
Köhler (Ortsteil von Volkach) *F* 54
Köllig (Ortsteil von Nittel) *MSR* 21
Köndringen (Ortsteil von Teningen) *B* 77
Könen (Ortsteil von Konz) *MSR* 20
Köngernheim (Ortsteil von Gau-Odernheim) *Rhh* 40
Königheim *B* 71
Königsbach (Orsteil von Neustadt a. d. Weinstraße *Rhpf* 47
Königsberg (Großlage) *MSR* 20
Königschaffhausen (Stadtteil von Endingen) *B* 77
Königsgarten (Großlage) *Rhpf* 48
Königshofen (Ortsteil von Lauda-Königshofen) *B* 71
Königswinter *Mrh* 23
Köwerich *MSR* 19
Kohlberg *W* 67
Konstanz *B* 74
Konz *MSR* 20
Kopf (Großlage) *W* 66
Korb *W* 66
Korlingen (Ortsteil von Trier) *MSR* 20
Kostheim (Ortsteil von Mainz) *Rhg* 29
Kraichgau siehe Badische Bergstraße/Kraichgau
Kraichtal *B* 72
Krautheim *F* 54

Krautheim *B* 71
Kreßbronn/Bodensee *W* 67
Kreuznach (Bereich) *N* 32
Kreuznach *N* 33, 34
Kreuzweiler (Ortsteil von Palzem) *MSR* 21
Kreuzwertheim *F* 52
Kriegsheim siehe Monsheim
Krötenbrunnen (Großlage) *Rhh* 40
Kröv *MSR* 19
Kronenberg (Großlage) *N* 33
Krozingen, Bad siehe Bad Krozingen
Külsheim *B* 71
Künzelsau *W* 61
Kürenz (Ortsteil von Trier) *MSR* 20
Kürnbach *B* 73
Kues (Ortsteil von Bernkastel-Kues) *MSR* 19
Kurfürstenstück (Großlage) *Rhh* 39
Kurfürstlay (Großlage) *MSR* 19

L

Lachen-Speyerdorf (Ortsteil von Neustadt a. d. Weinstraße) *Rhpf* 47
Lahnstein *Mrh* 24
Lahntal (Großlage) *Mrh* 24
Lahr *B* 77
Lambsheim *Rhpf* 46
Landau i. d. Pfalz *Rhpf* 48
Landshausen (Ortsteil von Kraichtal) *B* 73
Langenbeutingen (Ortsteil von Langenbrettach) *W* 63
Langenbrettach *W* 62, 63
Langenbrücken (Ortsteil von Bad Schönborn) *B* 72
Langenlonsheim *N* 32
Langscheid (Ortsteil von Oberwesel) *Mrh* 24
Langsur *MSR* 20, 21
Laubenheim *N* 32
Laubenheim (Ortsteil von Mainz) *Rhh* 40
Lauda (Ortsteil von Lauda-Königshofen) *B* 71
Lauda-Königshofen *B* 71
Laudenbach *F* 54
Laudenbach (Ortsteil von Weikersheim) *W* 61
Laudenbach *B* 71
Lauf *B* 74
Laufen (Ortsteil von Sulzburg) *B* 78
Lauffen *W* 64
Laumersheim *Rhpf* 46
Lauschied *N* 34
Lautenbach *B* 75
Lay (Ortsteil von Koblenz) *MSR* 16

Lehen (Ortsteil von Freiburg) *B* 77
Lehmen *MSR* 16
Lehrensteinsfeld *W* 63
Leimen *B* 72
Leingarten *W* 64
Leinsweiler *Rhpf* 48
Leiselheim (Ortsteil von Worms) *Rhh* 41
Leiselheim (Ortsteil von Sasbach) *B* 77
Leistadt (Ortsteil von Bad Dürkheim) *Rhpf* 46
Leiwen *MSR* 19
Lembach (Ortsteil von Großbottwar) *W* 64
Lengfurt *F* 52
Leonbronn (Ortsteil von Burgbronn) *W* 64
Lettweiler *N* 34
Leubsdorf *Mrh* 23
Leutershausen (Ortsteil von Hirschberg) *B* 71
Leutesdorf *Mrh* 23
Lichteneck, Burg siehe Burg Lichteneck (Großlage)
Liebfrauenberg, Kloster siehe Kloster Liebfrauenberg
Liebfrauenmorgen (Großlage) *Rhh* 41
Liel (Ortsteil von Schliengen) *B* 78
Lienzingen (Ortsteil von Mühlacker) *W* 64
Liersberg (Ortsteil von Igel) *MSR* 21
Lieser *MSR* 19
Lindau *W* 66
Lindauer Seegarten (Großlage) *W* 66
Lindelbach (Ortsteil von Wertheim) *B* 71
Lindelberg (Großlage) *W* 63
Linsenhofen (Ortsteil von Frickenhausen) *W* 67
Linz *Mrh* 23
Lipurg (Ortsteil von Badenweiler) *B* 78
Löchgau *W* 65
Löf *MSR* 16
Lörrach *B* 78
Lörsch (Ortsteil von Mehring) *MSR* 19
Lörzweiler *Rhh* 40
Lösnich *MSR* 18
Löwenstein *W* 63
Longen *MSR* 19
Longuich *MSR* 19
Lonsheim *Rhh* 40
Lorch *Rhg* 29
Lorchhausen (Ortsteil von Lorch) *Rhg* 29
Loreleyfelsen (Großlage) *Mrh* 24
Lorettoberg (Großlage) *B* 77
Ludwigsburg *W* 64, 65
Ludwigshöhe *Rhh* 40, 41
Ludwigshöhe, Schloß siehe Schloß Ludwigshöhe
Lützelsachsen (Ortsteil von Weinheim) *B* 71
Lustadt *Rhpf* 48

M

Mahlberg *B* 77
Maienfels (Ortsteil von Wüstenrot) *W* 63
Maikammer *Rhpf* 48
Mainberg (Ortsteil von Schonungen) *F* 54
Mainbernheim *F* 54
Maindreieck (Bereich) *F* 52
Mainstockheim *F* 54
Mainviereck (Bereich) *F* 52
Mainz *Rhg* 29, *Rhh* 40
Malsch *B* 72
Malschenberg (Ortsteil von Rauenberg) *B* 72
Malterdingen *B* 77
Mandel *N* 34
Mandelhöhe (Großlage) *Rhpf* 48
Mannaberg (Großlage) *B* 72
Mannweiler-Cölln *N* 34
Manubach *Mrh* 25
Marbach (Ortsteil von Lauda-Königshofen) *B* 71
Marbach/Neckar *W* 65
March *B* 77
Mariengarten (Großlage) *Rhpf* 47
Marienthal (Ortsteil von Bad Neuenahr-Ahrweiler) *A* 12
Maring-Noviand *MSR* 19
Markdorf *B* 74
Markelsheim (Ortsteil von Bad Mergentheim) *W* 60
Markgräflerland (Bereich) *B* 77
Markgröningen *W* 65
Marksburg (Großlage) *Mrh* 24
Marktbreit *F* 54
Markt Einersheim *F* 54
Marktheidenfeld *F* 52
Marnheim *Rhpf* 46
Martinsheim *F* 56
Martinstein *N* 34
Martinsthal (Ortsteil von Eltville) *Rhg* 29
Massenbachhausen *W* 64
Mauchen (Ortsteil von Schliengen) *B* 78
Mauchenheim *Rhh* 41
Maulbronn *W* 64
Maximin Grünhaus (Ortsteil von Mertesdorf) *MSR* 20
Mayschoß *A* 12
Meckenheim *Rhpf* 47
Meddersheim *N* 34
Meersburg *B* 74
Meerspinne (Großlage) *Rhpf* 47
Mehrhölzchen (Großlage) *Rhg* 29
Mehring *MSR* 19
Meimsheim (Ortsteil von Brackenheim) *W* 64
Meisenheim *N* 34

Mengen (Ortsteil von Schallstadt-Wolfenweiler) *B* 77
Mennig siehe Niedermennig und Obermennig
Menzingen (Ortsteil von Kraichtal) *B* 73
Merdingen *B* 77
Mergentheim, Bad siehe Bad Mergentheim
Merl (Ortsteil von Zell/Mosel) *MSR* 18
Mertesdorf *MSR* 20
Mertesheim *Rhpf* 46
Merxheim *N* 34
Merzhausen *A* 77
Mesenich *MSR* 17
Mesenich (Ortsteil von Langsur) *MSR* 20
Mettenheim *Rhh* 40
Metzdorf *MSR* 19
Metzingen *W* 67
Meurich *MSR* 21
Michelau *F* 56
Michelbach (Ortsteil von Alzenau i. Ufr.) *F* 52
Michelbach am Wald (Ortsteil von Öhringen) *W* 63
Michelfeld (Ortsteil von Angelbachtal) *B* 72
Michelsberg (Großlage) *MSR* 19
Mietersheim (Ortsteil von Lahr) *B* 77
Miltenberg *F* 52
Minfeld *Rhpf* 49
Mingolsheim (Ortsteil von Bad Schönborn) *B* 72
Minheim *MSR* 19
Mittelhaardt/Deutsche Weinstraße (Bereich) *Rhpf* 46
Mittelheim (Ortsteil von Oestrich-Winkel) *Rhg* 29
Mittelrhein (Anbaugebiet) 22
Möckmühl *W* 61
Mölsheim *Rhh* 41
Mörstadt *Rhh* 41
Mörzheim (Ortsteil von Landau) *Rhpf* 48
Mösbach (Ortsteil von Achern) *B* 75
Mommenheim *Rhh* 40
Monsheim *Rhh* 41
Monzel siehe Osann-Monzel
Monzernheim *Rhh* 40
Monzingen *N* 34
Morscheid *MSR* 20
Morschheim *Rhpf* 46
Mosbach *B* 72
Moselkern *MSR* 16
Mosel Saar Ruwer (Anbaugebiet) 13
Moselsürsch *MSR* 16
Moseltor (Bereich) *MSR* 21
Moselweiß (Ortsteil von Koblenz) *MSR* 16
Müden *MSR* 16
Mühlacker *W* 64
Mühlbach *F* 54
Mühlbach (Ortsteil von Eppingen) *B* 73
Mühlhausen (Ortsteil von Mühlacker) *W* 64

Mühlhausen (Ortsteil von Stuttgart) *W* 66
Mühlhausen *B* 72
Mühlheim *Rhpf* 46
Mühlhofen *Rhpf* 49
Mülheim (Mosel) *MSR* 19
Müllheim *B* 78
Münchweier (Ortsteil von Ettenheim) *B* 77
Münster (Ortsteil von Bad Münster-Ebernburg) *N* 34
Münster (Ortsteil von Stuttgart) *W* 66
Münsterappel *N* 34
Münster-Sarmsheim *N* 32
Münzesheim (Ortsteil von Kraichtal) *B* 73
Münzlay (Großlage) *MSR* 19
Mundelsheim *W* 65
Mundingen (Ortsteil von Emmendingen) *B* 77
Munzingen (Ortsteil von Freiburg) *B* 77
Murr *W* 65
Mußbach (Ortsteil von Neustadt a. d. Weinstraße) *Rhpf* 47

N

Nack *Rhh* 40
Nack (Ortsteil von Klettgau) *B* 74
Nackenheim *Rhh* 40
Nacktarsch (Großlage) *MSR* 19
Nahe (Anbaugebiet) 30
Nassau *Mrh* 24
Neckarmühlbach (Ortsteil von Haßmersheim) *B* 72
Neckarsulm *W* 62
Neckarweihingen (Ortsteil von Ludwigsburg) *W* 65
Neckarwestheim *W* 64
Neckarzimmern *B* 72
Neef *MSR* 17
Nehren *MSR* 17
Neipperg (Ortsteil von Brackenheim) *W* 64
Nennig (Ortsteil von Perl) *MSR* 21
Nesselried (Ortsteil von Appenweier) *B* 75
Neu-Bamberg *Rhh* 40
Neudenau *W* 61, *B* 72
Neuenahr (Ortsteil von Bad Neuenahr-Ahrweiler) *A* 12
Neuenbürg (Ortsteil von Kraichtal) *B* 73
Neuenburg am Rhein *B* 78
Neuenfels, Burg siehe Burg Neuenfels
Neuenstadt am Kocher *W* 62
Neuenstein *W* 63

Neuershausen (Ortsteil von March) *B* 77
Neuffen *W* 67
Neuhausen (Ortsteil von Metzingen) *W* 67
Neuleiningen *Rhpf* 46
Neumagen (Ortsteil von Neumagen-Dhron) *MSR* 19
Neumagen-Dhron *MSR* 19
Neusatz (Ortsteil von Bühl) *B* 74
Neuses am Berg *F* 54
Neusetz *F* 54
Neustadt a. d. Weinstraße *Rhpf* 47
Neustadt (Ortsteil von Waiblingen) *W* 66
Neuweier (Ortsteil von Baden-Baden) *B* 74
Niederburg *Mrh* 24
Niederdollendorf (Ortsteil von Königswinter) *Mrh* 23
Niedereggenen (Ortsteil von Schliengen) *B* 78
Niederemmel siehe Piesport
Niederfell *MSR* 16
Nieder-Flörsheim siehe Flörsheim-Dalsheim
Niederhausen *N* 34
Niederrheinbach *Mrh* 25
Nieder-Hilbersheim *Rhh* 38
Niederhofen (Ortsteil von Schwaigern) *W* 64
Niederhorbach *Rhpf* 49
Niederkirchen *Rhpf* 47
Niedermennig (Ortsteil von Konz) *MSR* 20
Niedermoschel *N* 34
Niedernhall *W* 61
Nieder-Olm *Rhh* 40
Niederotterbach *Rhpf* 49
Niederrimsingen (Ortsteil von Breisach) *B* 77
Niederschopfheim (Ortsteil von Hohberg) *B* 75
Niederstetten *W* 61
Niederwalluf (Ortsteil von Walluf) *Rhg* 29
Niederweiler (Ortsteil von Müllheim) *B* 78
Nieder-Wiesen *Rhh* 40
Niefernheim (Ortsteil von Zellertal) *Rhpf* 46
Nierstein *Rhh* 40
Nierstein (Bereich) *Rhh* 40
Nimburg (Ortsteil von Teningen) *B* 77
Nittel *MSR* 21
Nochern *Mrh* 25
Nonnenhorn *W* 66
Nordhausen (Ortsteil von Nordheim) *W* 64
Nordheim *F* 54
Nordheim *W* 64
Nordweil (Ortsteil von Kenzingen) *B* 77

Norheim *N* 34
Norsingen (Ortsteil von Ehrenkirchen) *B* 77
Noviand siehe Maring-Noviand
Nußbach (Ortsteil von Oberkirch) *B* 75
Nußbaum *N* 34
Nußdorf (Ortsteil von Landau) *Rhpf* 48
Nußloch *B* 72

O

Oberachern (Ortsteil von Achern) *B* 75
Oberacker (Ortsteil von Kraichtal) *B* 73
Oberbergen (Ortsteil von Vogtsburg im Kaiserstuhl) *B* 77
Oberbillig *MSR* 21
Oberderdingen *W* 64
Oberderdingen *B* 73
Oberdiebach *Mrh* 25
Oberdollendorf (Ortsteil von Königswinter) *Mrh* 23
Obereggenen (Ortsteil von Schliengen) *B* 78
Obereisenheim *F* 54
Oberemmel (Ortsteil von Konz) *MSR* 20
Oberfell *MSR* 16
Ober-Flörsheim *Rhh* 41
Obergrombach (Ortsteil von Bruchsal) *B* 72
Oberhausen *N* 34
Oberhausen *Rhpf* 48
Oberheimbach *Mrh* 25
Ober-Hilbersheim *Rhh* 38
Oberhof *Mrh* 24
Oberhofen siehe Pleisweiler-Oberhofen
Oberkirch *B* 75
Oberlauda (Ortsteil von Lauda-Königshofen) *B* 71
Oberleinach *F* 54
Obermennig (Ortsteil von Konz) *MSR* 20
Obermosel (Bereich) *MSR* 20
Obernau *F* 52
Oberndorf *N* 34
Obernhof *Mrh* 24
Oberöwisheim (Ortsteil von Kraichtal) *B* 72
Oberohrn (Ortsteil von Pfedelbach) *W* 63
Ober-Olm *Rhh* 40
Oberotterbach *Rhpf* 49
Oberperl (Ortsteil von Perl) *MSR* 21
Oberrimsingen (Stadtteil von Breisach) *B* 77
Oberrotweil (Ortsteil von Vogtsburg im Kaiserstuhl) *B* 77
Obersasbach (Ortsteil von Sasbach) *B* 75

Oberschopfheim (Ortsteil von Friesenheim) *B* 77
Oberschüpf (Ortsteil von Boxberg) *B* 71
Oberschwappach (Ortsteil von Knetzgau) *F* 56
Oberschwarzach *F* 56
Obersöllbach (Ortsteil von Kesselfeld) *W* 63
Oberstenfeld *W* 63
Oberstetten (Ortsteil von Niederstetten) *W* 61
Oberstreit *N* 34
Obersülzen *Rhpf* 46
Obersulm *W* 63
Obertsrot (Stadtteil von Gernsbach) *B* 75
Obertürkheim (Ortsteil von Stuttgart) *W* 66
Oberuhldingen (Ortsteil von Uhldingen-Mühlhof) *B* 74
Obervolkach *F* 54
Oberwalluf (Ortsteil von Walluf) *Rhg* 29
Oberweier (Ortsteil von Friesenheim) *B* 77
Oberwesel (mit Ortsteil Weiler-boppard) *Mrh* 24
Obrigheim (Ortsteil von Mühlheim) *Rhpf* 46
Ochsenbach (Ortsteil von Sachsenheim) *W* 65
Ochsenburg (Ortsteil von Burgbronn) *W* 64
Ochsenfurt *F* 54
Ockenheim *Rhh* 38
Ockfen *MSR* 20
Odenheim (Ortsteil von Östringen) *B* 73
Odernheim am Glau *N* 34
Oedheim *W* 62
Ödsbach (Stadtteil von Oberkirch) *B* 75
Öhringen *W* 63
Ölbronn-Dürrn *B* 74
Ölspiel (Großlage) *F* 54
Oestrich (Ortsteil von Oestrich-Winkel) *Rhg* 29
Oestrich-Winkel *Rhg* 29
Östringen *B* 72, 73
Ötisheim *W* 64
Ötlingen (Ortsteil von Weil) *B* 78
Offenau (Ortsteil von Bad Friedrichshall) *W* 62
Offenbach *Rhpf* 48
Offenburg *B* 75
Offenheim *Rhh* 41
Offstein *Rhh* 41
Ohlsbach *B* 75
Olewig (Ortsteil von Trier) *MSR* 20
Onsdorf *MSR* 21
Opfingen (Ortsteil von Freiburg) *B* 77
Oppenheim *Rhh* 40
Ordensgut (Großlage) *Rhpf* 48
Ortenau (Bereich) *B* 74
Ortenberg *B* 75

Osann-Monzel *MSR* 19
Osterspai *Mrh* 24
Osthofen *Rhh* 41
Ottersheim bei Germersheim *Rhpf* 48
Ottersheim/Zellertal *Rhpf* 46
Ottersweier *B* 74

P

Palzem *MSR* 21
Paradiesgarten (Großlage) *N* 34
Partenheim *Rhh* 38
Patersberg *Mrh* 24
Pellingen *MSR* 20
Perl *MSR* 21
Perscheid *Mrh* 24
Petersberg (Großlage) *Mrh* 23
Petersberg (Großlage) *Rhh* 39
Pfaffengrund (Großlage) *Rhpf* 47
Pfaffenhofen *W* 64
Pfaffen-Schwabenheim *Rhh* 38
Pfaffenweiler *B* 77
Pfarrgarten (Großlage) *N* 32
Pfeddersheim (Ortsteil von Worms) *Rhh* 41
Pfedelbach *W* 63
Pfinztal *B* 73
Piesport (mit Niederemmel) *MSR* 19
Pilgerpfad (Großlage) *Rhh* 41
Planig (Ortsteil von Bad Kreuznach) *N* 34
Platten *MSR* 18
Pleisweiler-Oberhofen *Rhpf* 49
Pleitersheim *Rhh* 39
Pölich *MSR* 19
Poltersdorf siehe Ellenz-Poltersdorf
Pommern *MSR* 16
Poppenweiler (Ortsteil von Ludwigsburg) *W* 65
Portz *MSR* 21
Prichsenstadt *F* 56
Probstberg (Großlage) *MSR* 19
Pünderich *MSR* 18

R

Ralingen *MSR* 21
Rammersweier (Ortsteil von Offenburg) *B* 75
Ramsthal *F* 53
Randersacker *F* 54
Ranschbach *Rhpf* 48
Rappenau, Bad siehe Bad Rappenau
Rauenberg *B* 72
Rauenthal (Ortsteil von Eltville) *Rhg* 29
Raumbach *N* 34
Ravensburg (Großlage) *F* 54
Ravensburg *W* 67
Rebstöckel (Großlage) *Rhpf* 47
Rech *A* 12
Rechberg (Ortsteil von Klettgau) *B* 74
Rechtenbach siehe Schweigen-Rechtenbach
Rehbach (Großlage) *Rhh* 39

Rehborn *N* 34
Rehlingen (Ortsteil
von Nittel)
MSR 21
Reichenau *B* 74
Reichenbach (Stadt-
teil von Gengen-
bach) *B* 75
Reichenstein,
Schloß siehe
Schloß Reichen-
stein
Reicholzheim (Orts-
teil von Wert-
heim) *B* 71
Reil *MSR* 18
Remshalden *W* 66
Remstal-Stuttgart
(Bereich) *W* 66
Renchen *B* 75
Repperndorf *F* 54
Rettigheim (Ortsteil
von Mühlhausen)
B 72
Retzbach (Ortsteil
von Zellingen)
F 54
Retzstadt *F* 54
Reuschberg (Groß-
lage) *F* 52
Rheinblick (Groß-
lage) *Rhh* 39
Rheinbrohl *Mrh* 23
Rheinburgengau
(Bereich) *Mrh* 23
Rheinfelden *B* 78
Rheingau (Anbau-
gebiet) 26
Rheingrafenstein
(Großlage)
Rhh 39
Rheinhessen
(Anbaugebiet) 35
Rheinpfalz (Anbau-
gebiet) 42
Rheinweiler (Orts-
teil von Bad Bel-
lingen) *B* 78
Rhens *Mrh* 24
Rhodt unter Riet-
burg *Rhpf* 48
Rhöndorf (Ortsteil
von Bad Honnef)
Mrh 23
Riedlingen (Stadtteil
von Kandern)
B 78
Riegel *B* 77
Rielingshausen
(Ortsteil von
Marbach/Neckar)
W 65
Riet (Ortsteil von
Vaihingen) *W* 65
Rietenau (Ortsteil
von Aspach)
W 65
Rimbach *F* 54
Rimpar *F* 54
Ringelbach (Orts-
teil von Ober-
kirch) *B* 75
Ringsheim *B* 77
Riol *MSR* 19
Rittersheim *Rhpf* 46
Rivenich *MSR* 19
Riveris *MSR* 20
Rittersberg (Groß-
lage) *B* 71
Rodeck, Schloß
siehe Schloß
Rodeck
Rodenstein, Burg
siehe Burg
Rodenstein
Rödelsee *F* 54
Rödersheim-Gronau
Rhpf 47
Römerberg (bei
Speyer) *Rhpf* 48
Römerlay (Groß-
lage) *MSR* 20
Röttingen *F* 54
Rohracker (Ortsteil
von Stuttgart)
W 66
Rohrbach a. G.
(Ortsteil von
Eppingen) *B* 73

Rohrbach *Rhpf* 48
Rommelshausen
(Ortsteil von Ker-
nen) *W* 66
Rommersheim
siehe Wörrstadt
Roschbach *Rhpf* 48
Rosenbühl (Groß-
lage) *Rhpf* 46
Rosengarten (Groß-
lage) *N* 34
Rosenhang (Groß-
lage) *MSR* 16
Roßdorf *HB* 50
Roßtal (Großlage)
F 54
Roßwag (Ortsteil
von Vaihingen)
W 64
Rotenberg (Ortsteil
von Stuttgart)
W 66
Rotenberg (Ortsteil
von Rauenberg)
B 72
Rott (Großlage)
HB 50
Rottenberg *F* 52
Rottenburg *W* 67
Roxheim *N* 34
Rück (Ortsteil von
Elsenfeld) *F* 52
Rüdesheim *Rhg* 29,
N 34
Rümmelsheim *N* 32
Rümmingen *B* 78
Rüssingen *Rhpf* 46
Ruppertsberg
Rhpf 47
Ruwer (Ortsteil von
Trier) *MSR* 20
Ruwer, siehe
Mosel-Saar-Ru-
wer

S

Saaleck (Ortsteil
von Hammel-
burg) *F* 53
Saar siehe Mosel-
Saar-Ruwer
Saarburg *MSR* 20
Saar-Ruwer
(Bereich) *MSR* 20
Sachsenflur (Ortsteil
von Lauda-
Königshofen)
B 71
Sachsenheim *W* 65
Salem *B* 74
Salzberg (Großlage)
W 63
Sankt Alban (Groß-
lage) *Rhh* 40
Sankt Aldegund
MSR 17
Sankt Goarshausen
Mrh 24
Sankt Goar *Mrh* 24
Sankt Johann
Rhh 38
Sankt Johann siehe
Alsweiler
Sankt Katharinen
N 34
Sankt Martin
Rhpf 48
Sankt Michael
(Großlage)
MSR 19
Sankt Rochus-
kapelle (Groß-
lage) *Rhh* 38
Sarmsheim siehe
Münster-Sarms-
heim
Sasbach *B* 75, 77
Sasbachwalden *B* 75
Saulheim *Rhh* 40
Saumagen (Groß-
lage) *Rhpf* 47
Sausenheim (Orts-
teil von Grün-
stadt) *Rhpf* 46
Schäftersheim (Orts-
teil von Weikers-
heim) *W* 61

Schalkstein (Groß-
lage) *W* 65
Schallbach *B* 78
Schallstadt-Wolfen-
weiler *B* 77
Scharzberg (Groß-
lage) *MSR* 20
Scharzhofberg (Orts-
teil von Wiltin-
gen) *MSR* 20
Schellingen (Ortsteil
von Vogtsburg
im Kaiserstuhl)
B 77
Schenkenböhl
(Großlage)
Rhpf 47
Scherzingen (Orts-
teil von Ehren-
kirchen) *B* 77
Schierstein (Ortsteil
von Wiesbaden)
Rhg 29
Schild (Großlage)
F 54
Schirmsheim siehe
Armsheim
Schlatt (Ortsteil von
Bad Krozingen)
B 77
Schleich *MSR* 19
Schliengen *B* 78
Schloßberg (Groß-
lage) *HB* 50
Schloßberg (Groß-
lage) *F* 54
Schloßböckelheim
N 34
Schloß Böckelheim
(Bereich) *N* 34
Schloßkapelle
(Großlage) *N* 32
Schloß Ludwigs-
höhe (Großlage)
Rhpf 48
Schloß Reichenstein
(Großlage)
Mrh 25
Schloß Rodeck
(Großlage) *B* 74
Schloß Schönburg
(Großlage)
Mrh 25
Schloß Stahleck
(Großlage)
Mrh 24
Schloßstück (Groß-
lage) *F* 55
Schmachtenberg
(Ortsteil von Zeil
a. Main) *F* 56
Schmieheim (Orts-
teil von Kippen-
heim) *B* 77
Schnait (Ortsteil
von Weinstadt)
W 66
Schnepfenflug an
der Weinstraße
(Großlage)
Rhpf 47
Schnepfenflug vom
Zellertal (Groß-
lage) *Rhpf* 46
Schoden *MSR* 20
Schönberg (Ortsteil
von Bensheim)
siehe Bensheim-
Schönberg
Schönburg (Groß-
lage) *Mrh* 24
Schöneberg *N* 32
Schöntal *W* 61
Schonungen *F* 54
Schorndorf *W* 66
Schornsheim
Rhh 40
Schozach (Ortsteil
von Ilsfeld) *W* 64
Schozachtal (Groß-
lage) *W* 63
Schriesheim *B* 71
Schützingen (Orts-
teil von Illingen)
W 65
Schutterlindenberg
(Großlage) *B* 77

Schwabbach (Orts-
teil von Bretzfeld)
W 63
Schwabenheim
Rhh 40
Schwabsburg siehe
Nierstein
Schwaigern *W* 64
Schwarze Katz
(Großlage)
MSR 18
Schwarzerde (Groß-
lage) *Rhpf* 46
Schwarzlay (Groß-
lage) *MSR* 18
Schwegenheim
Rhpf 48
Schweich *MSR* 19
Schweigen-Rech-
tenbach *Rhpf* 49
Schweighofen
Rhpf 49
Schweinfurt *F* 54
Schweppenhausen
N 32
Seefelden (Ortsteil
von Buggingen)
B 78
Seeheim *HB* 50
Segnitz *F* 54
Sehl (Ortsteil von
Cochem) *MSR* 16
Sehlem *MSR* 19
Sehndorf (Ortsteil
von Perl)
MSR 21
Seinsheim *F* 55
Selzen *Rhh* 40
Senhals (Ortsteil
von Senheim)
MSR 16
Senheim *MSR* 17
Serrig *MSR* 20
Sexau *B* 77
Sickershausen (Orts-
teil von Kitzin-
gen) *F* 54
Siebeneich (Ortsteil
von Bretzfeld)
W 63
Siebengebirge
(Bereich) *Mrh* 23
Siebeldingen
Rhpf 48
Siefersheim *Rhh* 40
Siglingen (Ortsteil
von Neudenau)
W 61
Singen *B* 74
Sinsheim *B* 72, 73,
74
Sobernheim *N* 34
Söllingen (Ortsteil
von Pfinztal)
B 73
Sörgenloch *Rhh* 40
Soest *MSR* 21
Sommerach *F* 54
Sommerau *MSR* 20
Sommerhausen
F 54
Sommerloch *N* 33
Sonnenborn (Groß-
lage) *W* 66
Sonnenufer (Groß-
lage) *B* 74
Spabrücken *N* 32
Spay *Mrh* 24
Speyerdorf siehe
Lachen-Speyer-
dorf
Spiegelberg (Groß-
lage) *Rhh* 40
Spielberg (Ortsteil
von Sachsen-
heim) *W* 65
Spiesheim *Rhh* 41
Sponheim *N* 34
Sponsheim (Ortsteil
von Bingen)
Rhh 38
Sprendlingen
Rhh 38
Staadt siehe Kastel-
Staadt
Stadecken-Elsheim
Rhh 40

Stadelhofen (Orts-
teil von Ober-
kirch) *B* 75
Stahleck, Schloß
siehe Schloß
Stahleck
Stammheim *F* 54
Starkenburg
(Bereich) *HB* 50
Starkenburg
(Großlage)
MSR 20
Staudernheim *N* 34
Staufen *B* 77
Staufenberg (Groß-
lage) *W* 62
Steckweiler siehe
Bayerfeld-Steck-
weiler
Steeg (Ortsteil von
Bacharach)
Mrh 24
Stegen siehe Esch-
bach
Steigerwald
(Bereich) *F* 54
Steil (Großlage)
Rhg 29
Steinbach *F* 56
Steinbach (Stadtteil
von Baden-
Baden) *B* 74
Stein-Bockenheim
Rhh 40
Steinfeld *Rhpf* 49
Steinhard (Ortsteil
von Sobernheim)
N 34
Steinheim *W* 64, 65
Steinmächer (Groß-
lage) *Rhg* 29
Steinsfurt (Ortsteil
von Sinsheim)
B 72
Steinweiler *Rhpf* 48
Sternenfels *W* 64,
65
Stetten *Rhpf* 46
Stetten *F* 54
Stetten (Ortsteil von
Schwaigern) *W* 64
Stetten (Ortsteil von
Kernen) *W* 66
Stetten *B* 74
Stettfeld (Ortsteil
von Ubstadt-
Weiher) *B* 72
Stiftsberg (Großlage)
B 72
Stockheim (Ortsteil
von Bracken-
heim) *W* 64
Stromberg (Groß-
lage) *W* 64
Strümpfelbach
(Ortsteil von
Weinstadt) *W* 66
Stuttgart *W* 66
Südliche Wein-
straße (Bereich)
Rhpf 48
Sülzbach (Ortsteil
von Obersulm)
W 63
Sulz (Ortsteil von
Lahr) *B* 77
Sulzbach (Ortsteil
von Weinheim)
B 71
Sulzburg *B* 78
Sulzfeld *F* 54
Sulzfeld *B* 73
Sulzheim *Rhh* 40
Sybillenstein (Groß-
lage) *Rhh* 41

T

Tairnbach (Ortsteil
von Mühlhausen)
B 72
Talheim *W* 63, 64

Tannenkirch (Stadt-
teil von Kandern)
B 78
Tarforst (Ortsteil
von Trier)
MSR 20
Tauber siehe Ko-
cher-Jagst-Tauber
Tauberberg (Groß-
lage) *W* 61
Tauberbischofsheim
B 71
Tauberklinge
(Großlage) *B* 71
Tauberrettersheim
F 54
Tawern *MSR* 20, 21
Temmels *MSR* 21
Teningen *B* 77
Tettingen *MSR* 21
Teufelstor (Groß-
lage) *F* 54
Thörnich *MSR* 19
Thüngersheim *F* 54
Tiefenbach (Ortsteil
von Östringen)
B 73
Tiefenstockheim
F 56
Tiefenthal *Rhh* 40
Tiengen (Ortsteil
von Freiburg)
B 77
Tiergarten (Ortsteil
von Oberkirch)
B 75
Traben (Ortsteil von
Traben-Trarbach)
MSR 18
Traben-Trarbach
MSR 18
Traisen *N* 34
Trappenberg (Groß-
lage) *Rhpf* 48
Trarbach (Ortsteil
von Traben-Trar-
bach) *MSR* 18
Trechtingshausen
Mrh 25
Treis (Ortsteil von
Treis-Karden)
MSR 16
Treis-Karden
MSR 16
Trier *MSR* 20
Trittenheim
MSR 19
Tübingen *W* 67
Tuniberg siehe Kai-
serstuhl-Tuniberg
Tunsel (Ortsteil von
Bad Krozingen)
B 77
Tutschfelden (Stadt-
teil von Herbolz-
heim) *B* 77

U

Ubstadt (Ortsteil
von Ubstadt-
Weiher) *B* 72
Udenheim *Rhh* 40
Überlingen *B* 74
Uelversheim
Rhh 40, 41
Ürzig *MSR* 18
Uffhofen siehe
Flonheim
Uhlbach (Ortsteil
von Stuttgart)
W 66
Uissigheim (Ortsteil
von Külsheim)
B 71
Ulm (Stadtteil von
Renchen) *B* 75
Umstadt (Bereich)
HB 50
Undenheim *Rhh* 40
Ungstein (Ortsteil
von Bad Dürk-
heim) *Rhpf* 46, 47
Unkel *Mrh* 23

Unkenbach *N* 34
Untereisenheim
F 54
Untereisesheim
W 62
Untergrombach
(Ortsteil von
Bruchsal) *B* 72
Untergruppenbach
W 63, 64
Unterheimbach
(Ortsteil von
Bretzfeld) *W* 63
Unterheinrit (Orts-
teil von Unter-
gruppenbach)
W 63
Unterjesingen (Orts-
teil von Tübin-
gen) *W* 67
Unteröwisheim
(Ortsteil von
Kraichtal) *B* 72
Unterschüpf (Orts-
teil von Boxberg)
B 71
Untersteinbach
(Ortsteil von
Pfedelbach) *W* 63
Untertürkheim
(Ortsteil von
Stuttgart) *W* 66
Urbar *Mrh* 24
Urbar (Ortsteil von
Oberwesel)
Mrh 25

V

Vaihingen/Enz
W 64, 65
Vallendar *Mrh* 24
Valwig *MSR* 16
Varnhalt (Stadtteil
von Baden-
Baden) *B* 74
Veitshöchheim *F* 54
Veldenz *MSR* 19
Vendersheim
Rhh 40
Venningen *Rhpf* 48
Verrenberg (Ortsteil
von Öhringen)
W 63
Vogelsburg (Ortsteil
von Volbach)
F 54
Vogelsgärten (Groß-
lage) *Rhh* 41
Vogtei Rötteln
(Großlage) *B* 78
Volkach *F* 54
Vollmersweiler
Rhpf 49
Volxheim *Rhh* 39
Vom Heißen Stein
(Großlage)
MSR 18
Vorbachzimmern
(Ortsteil von Nie-
derstetten) *W* 61
Vulkanfelsen
(Großlage) *B* 77

W

Wachenheim
Rhh 41
Wachenheim
Rhpf 47
Wackernheim
Rhh 40
Wagenstadt (Stadt-
teil von Herbolz-
heim) *B* 77
Wahlheim *Rhh* 41
Waiblingen *W* 66
Waldalgesheim
N 32
Waldangelloch
(Ortsteil von
Sinsheim) *B* 72

Z

Wine Law and Labelling

On September 1, 1977, "Community regulations ruling specification and presentation of wines and grape must" (EEC decree No. 2133/74 and No. 1608/76) became law.

Adjustment of the German wine law to the new EEC laws had been partly achieved on 15 July, 1977, by the third decree of alterations to the wine-regulations order. The Ministry of Youth, Family and Health envisages a new draft wording of the wine law for 1979.

What alterations in the specification laws can we expect to see on labels, starting with the vintage year of 1977?

Regulated Information
Regulated information includes, as before, the naming of the specified growing region (Anbaugebiet), quality range – with "Prädikat" if applicable – the official control number, name of bottling/dispatch agency and, as a new regulation, the nominal volume. All this information has to be given on the same, main label; to display some of it on additional labels is not allowed; other permitted, but not regulated, information may be shown on other presentation labels. In accordance with the packaging-regulations order, the nominal volume (bottle content) has to be shown, combined with the EEC packaging sign ("EUROPA"). Its minimum size is 3mm.

Size of Lettering
In future, the lettering used for a specified region is to be the main guide-line for size. Quality classes, whether "Quality Wine" ("Qualitätswein") or "Quality wine with Distinction", ("Qualitätswein mit Prädikat") and the "Prädikat" signs themselves, may not be shown in larger lettering than that used for the name of the growing region. The name of a bottling firm has no size limit, but the place-name (town or village) of the firm has: its lettering may be only half as large as that of the specified growing region.

Description of Taste
To describe the taste of a wine, the following adjectives may be used: dry (trocken), medium dry (halb trocken), pleasing (lieblich) and sweet (süss); "dry" wines must have no more than a maximum of 4g or 9g sugar-content per litre, with a total acid-content of no more than 2g maximum below the sugar-content (formula: acid + 2).

A medium wine is allowed a maximum of 18g per litre, but no more than the total acid content plus 10 (formula: acid + 10). The adjectives "pleasing" (lieblich) and "sweet" (süss) are also permitted and no value limits have been laid down for them. Judgement as to their use is left to the individual vintager.

Grape Variety/Vintage
A grape variety may be mentioned if the wine has been prepared from at least 85% of that variety and therefore determines its type. Two grape varieties may be mentioned where a wine has been produced entirely from the two varieties named; they should be mentioned in descending order to their percentage proportions. Blended vintages must also have a percentage proportion of 85 to 15.

Table Wine
"Table wine" must be specified as such; home-grown table wine is to be marked "German Table Wine" (Deutscher Tafelwein). If a table wine is a blend of produce from several EEC member states, it is to be marked "Wine from several member states of the EEC". This information must be repeated in the official language of the member state in which it is being offered, if the official language used on the label is that of a different EEC member state. Table wine not prepared in the same member state as that in which the grapes were harvested, must bear the marking "EEC" ("EWG").

The new EEC specification laws will probably mean the loss of some label designs known and cherished throughout decades and many wine-lovers will regret the changes affecting familiar graphic and artistic designs. On the other hand, the fear that the value of old-established designs – and with it a good deal of the history and "profile" of wine firms – will be lost through the "Europeanization" of wine labels, may be compensated for by the hope that it will end the confusion caused by varying regulations hitherto imposed by individual EEC member states.

Main types of grape varieties in German wine-growing regions

Soil, climate and type of vine are the factors which determine the character of all wine, but they are particularly important in the case of German wine.

Some experts say that the type of vine is the third factor when it comes to determining character, excellence of taste and aroma in German wine.

German viticultural research has scientifically examined several hundred descendants of the original European vine (*vitis vinifera*) during recent centuries in order to find the sites and conditions best suited to each variety.

In the last 50 years some remarkable new species have been developed: especially Müller-Thurgau, Scheurebe and Morio-Muskat.

The breakdown of vine species given here shows the main classical types as well as the more important newly-developed ones (their cultivation area is over 1,000 ha). New types – often of great regional importance – promise to add even more variety to the quality and taste of German wine.

Of the total German wine cultivation area of 89,398 ha, the greater part (87.9%) is covered by white species (78,588 ha) and 12.9% (= 10,810 ha) by red (source: Statistisches Bundesamt, Wiesbaden; 1974).

White Species

Müller-Thurgau

Area: 24,419 ha (27.3%)

A Geisenheimer cultivation, produced in 1862 by the respected Swiss cultivator, Prof. Müller, from the kanton of Thurgau. The Müller-Thurgau is thought to be a cross of Riesling and Silvaner. It ripens early and brings a good yield of mild, well-balanced, forthcoming wine with a delicate muscat bouquet and taste. This vine is found mainly in Franconia, Rheinhessen, Baden, the Nahe region and in the Rhenish Palatinate.

Riesling

Area: 18,327 ha (20.5%)

The noblest white wine grape in the world. Small, insignificant-looking berries, very late ripening; finds favourable growing conditions in all German regions, particularly in the Mosel-Saar-Ruwer region, Rheingau, Rhenish Palatinate, and the Nahe and Mittelrhein regions. Riesling wines are racy, of high quality, and delicately fragrant. They have laid the foundation of Germany's world-wide wine reputation. The true Riesling can never be confused with other vine species, which inaccurately carry Riesling as part of their names (as, for example, the so-called Welsch or Italian Riesling).

Silvaner

Area: 13,404 ha (15%)

Silvaner is grown predominantly in Rheinhessen, Rhenish Palatinate, the Nahe region and Franconia. The grapes are of middle size, very juicy, producing a pleasant, mild wine with a pleasing low acid content.

Ruländer

Area: 3,263 ha (3.6%)

Grapes of middle size; heavy and strong, the Ruländer is also called Grauer Burgunder (Pinot Gris); it likes a rich, deep soil; ripens fairly early to late. Favours growing conditions in Baden, Rhenish Palatinate, Rheinhessen and Hessische Bergstrasse. Its wine is fiery, full-bodied and of uniquely delicate bouquet. Its Spätlese and Auslese, belong to the range of German high quality wines.

Morio-Muskat

Area: 2,827 ha (3.1%)

A crossing of Silvaner and Weisser Burgunder (Pinot Blanc); ripens fairly early and gives a very good yield; grows particularly well in the Rhenish Palatinate and Rheinhessen. Its wine has a strong muscat bouquet, which can become extremely potent in very ripe wine.

Scheurebe

Area: 2,714 ha (3%)

A new breeding: cross between Silvaner and Riesling; ripens late; grows well in Rheinhessen, Rhenish Palatinate and Franconia. Produces full-bodied, flowery wines of Riesling character; its bouquet is strongly aromatic reminiscent of black-currants.

Kerner

Area: 2,708 ha (3%)

Newly developed, out of the Trollinger and the Riesling vine; grows in all soil conditions. Favoured regions: Württemberg, Rhenish Palatinate and Franconia. Its wine is lively, pleasing, Riesling-like, with a light muscat bouquet.

Weisser Gutedel

Area: 1,276 ha (1.4%)

This vine needs sites that are well-sheltered against winds, and a rich, deep humus soil, found most readily in Baden. Ripening period falls between that of the Müller-Thurgau and the Silvaner. The wine is light, pleasing, and agreeable. The soft, sweet Gutedel grape is also much appreciated as a dessert grape.

Red Species

Blauer (Blue) Portugieser

Area: 3,841 ha (4.3%)

Does not originate in Portugal, despite its name, but came to Germany around 1800 from the Danube region. Its grapes are deep blue. The vine is modest in its demands regarding site and soil, and grows mainly in the Ahr region, Rhenish Palatinate, Württemberg and Rheinhessen. Ripens early; gives a pleasant "little wine" (Carafe wine); light, agreeable, mild.

Blauer (Blue) Spätburgunder (Pinot Noir)

Area: 3,161 ha (3.5%)

Has been cultivated for over 500 years; small, blue grapes need deep, fertile soil; grows best in the Ahr region, Baden and Württemberg; ripens fairly early to late. Its deep red wine ranks as Germany's best red wine; velvety in taste, with a bouquet reminiscent of bitter almonds.

Blauer (Blue) Trollinger

Area: 1,891 ha (2.1%)

Large, sweet, reddish blue grapes. The vine needs very favourable sites, but grows also in poor, not too dry soil; almost exclusive to Württemberg; ripens late. Its wine tastes fresh, racy, fruity, and is usually of a light red colour.

Regional Wines – specified wine-growing regions form characteristic types of wine

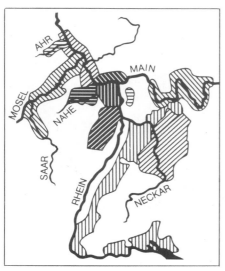

The traditional "birthplace" of Liebfraumilch

In a centuries-old evolution, the wine-growing lands developed their own culture and their own characteristic varieties of wine. The typical wine of a particular region is the result of traditions evolved through many generations, and of specific climatic and soil conditions. Time-honoured vintners' traditions, mirrored in equally traditional forms of trade – often reaching back centuries – have made typical wines, grown in certain geographic-

ally-defined areas, famous the world over for their characteristic and excellent quality. Therefore such typical wines can only be produced within the borders of their traditional home-countries, which are now exactly defined by legal regulations.

The wine whose "birthplace" and label has made it best-known in all wine-markets trading in German Rhine wine is Liebfrauenmilch (sometimes spelt Liebfraumilch). Documents of the 18th century already mention the name of "Der lieben Frauenmilch zu Worms". Historically the name goes back to the Wormser Lieb-frauenstift monastery, and the word "milch" (milk) is probably a distortion of the medieval word "minch" (Mönch = monk). In the 19th century German white wines of superior quality, mild in character and grown in the viticultural areas of the Rhine, were already called Liebfrauen-milch in the international wine-trade; and gradually that name became the best known mark of origin for a typical Rhine wine.

Former wine laws had also defined – through precedence quoted by law courts, and through customs of trading – certain typical wines according to their regions of origin. In the wine laws of 1971, article 10, paragraph 9, special provision was made for such wines, with rules governing the definition of wines according to geographical origin, quality and characteristics.

For the time being the following definitions of origin have been laid down in the 1971 wine law regulations:

1. **Liebfrauenmilch/Liebfraumilch,** must be according to article 4 of the first Landesverordnung Rheinland-Pfalz (decree for the Federal State of the Rhenish Palatinate) of 12/8/71 must be a white quality wine from the specified wine-growing regions of Rheinhessen, Nahe, Rhenish Palatinate and Rheingau, with a minimum gravity of must of 60 Oechsle, pressed from Riesling, Silvaner, or Müller-Thurgau grapes and being of "mild" taste, Liebfrauenmilch, as a Quality Wine, must be furnished with the usual official examination number after having passed the Qualitätsprü-fung (quality examination).

2. **Affentaler Spätburgunder,** (red wine) must be, according to a Baden-Württemberg decree of 3/8/1971 for

wines of quality or Prädikat, wine pressed from Blauer Spätburgunder grapes grown in special regions (Gemarkungen) of Baden, in the area Bühl/Baden-Baden.

3. **Ehrentrudis Spätburgunder Weiss-herbst,** must be, according to a Baden-Württemberg decree of the 4/7/1973 for Badener Rosé Wines of quality or Prädikat, a wine pressed from Blauer Spätburgunder grapes grown in the Bereich of Kaiserstuhl-Tuniberg.

4. **"Badisch Rotgold"** In accordance with paragraph 7 of the wine decree of June 4, 1977 (BGBl. 1S.1416), a quality wine may, instead of being specified as "Rotling", bear the name of "Badisch Rotgold", with the additional speci-fication "Grauburgunder und Spät-burgunder", if the products used in its preparation have been harvested ex-clusively in the designated growing regions of Baden.

These four typical definitions of origin, laid down by law, guarantee that a name given to such a wine actually relates to the particular wine, and that, in the interests of the consumer, geographical origin, quality and characteristics of taste are examined and then confirmed by an official stamp of approval (certificate number).

Rheinwein: "linguistic" excursion through the valley of the Rhine

Language and trade traditions develop through centuries, taking little notice of legislation: in everyday gastronomic par-lance Rheinwein means wine from lands along the river Rhine, namely from quality wine-growing regions of the Mittelrhein, Rheingau, Rheinhessen and Rhenish Palatinate – in short, the Table Wine region Rhein; but though Baden wine also grows in Rhine regions, the Baden Quality Wines are not classed among the Rhine wines and, to add to the complica-tion, ordinary Baden Table Wines are called Oberrhein Wein. Nobody calls the wines on the opposite bank of the Rhine – the French wines of Alsace – Rheinwein. English-speaking countries call all Ger-man wines from the Rhine, Rhine wine, or, particularly in England, hock – a centuries-old name, derived from the little wine-growing town of Hochheim.

Excerpt from German Wine Law

The official register of vineyards given in this new German Wine Atlas has been compiled according to the new regulations. The main section for legislation referring to the reorganization of geographical specification is article 10 of the Wine Law decree of July 14, 1971 (Bundesgesetzblatt 1, page 893 ff.).

Article 10 – Geographical Specification

(1) To specify the origin of a wine, or of the component parts used in its production, only the following markings may be used:

1. Names of Sites and Districts which appear in the official register of vineyards.
2. Names of communities and place names.
3. Names of Specified Regions for Quality Wines and Table Wines, Areas and Sub-Regions.
4. The word German.
5. Any specification approved by legislation (paragraph 9).

For Table Wine the names of Specified Regions and Sites are not required.

(2) A Site is a specified cultivated area (Einzellage), or the combination of several such areas into a larger unit (Grosslage), producing wines of similar quality and character, and belonging to a community or communities in the same Specified Region for Quality Wines. A name can only be entered as a Lage specification if it refers to a cultivated area commonly known under that name, or is entered under it in the official land registry, or is derived from such a name.

(3) A Site can only be entered in the official vineyards register if its size is no less than 5 hectares; a smaller area may be admitted if local cultivating conditions, or the special character of the wine growing from it, make the forming of a larger unit impossible.

(4) A District is formed by several Sites that produce wine with similar characteristics, and are situated within neighbouring communities belonging to the same Specified Region; a cultivated area which is not part of any Site may be included if all other pre-conditions have been met. The name of a District is formed by choosing one which can represent the vineyards within its area and setting the word District before it. If suitable traditional names for the definition of a District exist, such a name should be chosen.

(5) The Governments (Landesregierungen) of the wine-growing Federal States determine legislation for the following procedures, as long as they are not covered by a Federal Law (Landesgesetz).

1. The setting up and maintaining of the register of vineyards.
2. Details concerning registering and de-registering, including the determination of the names of Sites and Districts.
3. Admission of applications, form and content of applications.
4. Official entries and de-registrations.
5. Responsibility of authorities.

(6) The following bestimmte Anbaugebiete are Specified Regions for cultivation of quality wines:

1. Ahr.
2. Hessische Bergstrasse.
3. Mittelrhein.
4. Mosel-Saar-Ruwer.
5. Nahe.
6. Rheingau.
7. Rheinhessen.
8. Rhenish Palatinate.
9. Franconia.
10. Württemberg.
11. Baden.

(7) The following wine-growing regions and their sub-regions are specified Table Wine areas:

1. Rhine and Mosel
   a) Rhine
   b) Mosel.
2. Main.
3. Neckar.
4. Oberrhein
   a) Römertor
   b) Burgengau.

(8) The regions mentioned in paragraphs 6 and 7 form the German Wine-Growing Area; their specific areas are determined by legislation. Where regions extend into several federal states (Bundesländer), where laws governing unfermented sugar-retention (Restzuckerbegrenzungen, article 9, para. 2) differ, legislation ruling the permissible sugar-retention in each named region may be passed.

(9) Governments of wine-growing federal states may pass legislation for further specification, giving more detail of the origin of a typical wine from a certain area, in order to enhance its market value.

(10) Wine, and the component parts used in its production, must be marked with a geographical specification according to paragraph 1; this rule does not apply to partially fermented grape-must which is consumed immediately or in the near future and specified as such according to local custom.

(11) If a narrower geographical specification than the name of a Specified Region or Table Wine Area or Sub-Region is chosen, then the Specified Region where the grapes were harvested must be added in the case of Quality Wine, and the Wine-growing Area or Sub-Region in the case of Table Wine. A Site specification must also include the name of the community or village in which the Site is situated. If a Site extends over several communities only one of these need be mentioned. Where a community extends over several Wine-Growing Areas the State (Land) Government may pass legislation decreeing that in the case of wine from specified villages only the name of the village, or the village name combined with the name of the community may be used.

(12) A narrower specification than just the word Deutsch may be used when at least 75% of the grapes are harvested in the specified area and determine the character of the wine; and where other products of different origin are used are of the same quality and stem from the same Wine-Growing Area or Specified Region as the name-giving grapes. Beerenauslesen and Trockenbeerenauslesen produced from grapes of several Sites may carry the name of the Site from which more than 50% of the grapes are harvested.

(13) The specification Deutsch, or any narrower specification may only be chosen if (according to article 2, para. 5) no grapes harvested in other countries have been used.

(14) Table Wine grown within designated areas must be specified as Deutscher Tafelwein (German Table Wine).

Rules and regulations have been issued by all wine-growing federal states, partly based on the wine law of 1969, and primarily concerned with instituting and maintaining vineyard registers. It is quite possible that new EEC regulations may necessitate modification of some of the present rules.

IMPORTANT GERMAN WINE FESTIVALS

Ahr: Gebietsweinmarkt der Ahr, Ahrweiler, May; Winzerfest, Dernau, September.
Baden: Freiburger Weintage, Freiburg, June; Kurpfälzisches Winzerfest, Wiesloch, August/September; Kaiserstuhl-Tuniberg-Weinfest, Breisach, September.
Franken: Fränkisches Weinfest, Volkach, Middle of August; Winzerfest, Klingenberg, Middle of August; Fränkisches Weinfest, Sulzfeld, August; Winzerfest, Würzburg, September/October.
Hessische Bergstrasse: Bergsträsser Weinmarkt, Heppenheim, June; Bergsträsser Winzerfest, Bensheim, September.
Mittelrhein: Weinblütenfest, Bacharach, June; Weinlesefest, Bacharach, September; Weinwoche, St. Goarshausen, September; Weinfest, Boppard, September.
Mosel-Saar-Ruwer: Mosel-Wein-Woche, Cochem, June; Saarweinfest, Saarburg, September; Weinfest der Mittelmosel, Bernkastel, September.
Nahe: Fest rund um die Naheweinstrasse, in each of the greater communities of the Nahewein route. End of August.
Rheingau: Hilchenfest, Lorch, June; Hochheimer Weinfest, Hochheim, July; Lindenfest, Geisenheim, July; Weinfest, Rüdesheim, August; Weinfest, Hattenheim, August.
Rheinhessen: Winzerfest, Nierstein, August; Kellerwegfest, Guntersblum, August; Backfischfest, Worms, August; Mainzer Weinmarkt, Mainz, August/September; Rotweinfest, Ingelheim, September.
Rheinpfalz: Dürkheimer Wurstmarkt, Bad Dürkheim, September; Weinfest, der Südlichen Weinstrasse, Edenkoben, September; Deutsches Weinlesefest, Neustadt, October; Fest des Federweissen, Landau, October.
Württemberg: Heilbronner Herbst, Heilbronn, September; Fellbacher Herbst, Fellbach, October.

UNITED KINGDOM AND IRELAND
Wines From Germany Information Service
15 Thayer Street, London W.1
Tel: 01-935 8164

USA
German Wine Information Bureau
666 Fifth Avenue
New York, N.Y. 10019
Tel: 212/JU6-2600

CANADA
German Wine Information Service
20 Eglinton Avenue East, Toronto
Tel: 416/481-4438

GERMANY
Deutsches Weininstitut
Gutenbergplatz 3-5
65 Mainz, Western Germany
Tel: 06131-25818

German Wine Academy

Wine experts and interested wine-lovers can participate at five-day seminars of the German Wine Academy, based at Kloster Eberbach. The programme includes lectures by experts, visits to wine-growing regions, vineyards, cellars, and tastings. All lectures are in English. Each seminar ends with a festive wine tasting and dinner at Kloster Eberbach, and a presentation of certificates. Every year seminars are planned from May to September with an additional Postgraduate Course in October. For detailed programme and price please apply to Germany Wine Academy, 65 Mainz, Gutenbergplatz 3-5. PO Box 3860, Western Germany.